The Quest for Quality of Life
Edited by Elisabeth Hense, Christoph Hübenthal, and Willem Marie Speelman

The Quest for Quality of Life

Approaches, concepts and images with a special focus on The Netherlands

Edited by
Elisabeth Hense, Christoph Hübenthal and
Willem Marie Speelman

Aschendorff
Verlag

Einbandabbildung
manfredrichter / pixabay

Printed in Germany

Gedruckt auf säurefreiem, alterungsbeständigem Papier ∞

ISBN 978-3-402-13119-0

TABLE OF CONTENTS

INTRODUCTION

Elisabeth Hense, Christoph Hübenthal, and Willem Marie Speelman

During the last few decades, our society has been confronted increasingly with so called 'wicked problems' or 'social messes'.[1] We have passed through a mixture of social, economic, and environmental problems such as unemployment, poverty, the rise of inequality, water and food shortages, increased numbers of political and economic refugees, and the exhaustion of natural resources. The complexity of these problems is alarming to many contemporaries; they even judge it to be a threat to democracy and peace. But how can we get out of these difficulties? Many of us feel helpless because the solutions to these problems require a great number of people to change their behavior and mindset.

On the other hand, everyone has experienced (more or less) the potential of alternative ways of living and working. We have experienced certain activities or conditions that lead to a fuller, richer, deeper, more inspiring, more admirable, and more worthwhile way of living.[2] These activities and conditions relate to caring for people and our environment; respecting people independent of their race, gender, sexual orientation, and social class and doing justice to them; providing programs for education and development; appreciating sustainability; looking for other values besides economic growth; inventing a new kind of world community that can deal with diversity in a constructive manner, etc. These experiences may inspire our discernment and our choices; they contribute to the dynamics of societal renewal. However, in order to be fruitful, our intuitive decisions should not be conceived as absolute; any intuition remains subject to critical reflection and evaluation.

This book contributes to the critical reflection on, and evaluation of, what is currently referred to as 'a good life', 'quality of life' or 'fullness

1 J. Conklin, *Dialogue Mapping: Building Shared Understanding of Wicked Problems* (Chichester: Wiley & Sons Ltd., 2006); R. E. Horn & R. P. Weber, *New Tools for Resolving Wicked Problems: Mess Mapping and Resolution Mapping Processes* (MacroVU(r), Inc. and Strategy Kinetics L.L.C., 2007).

2 Ch. Taylor, *A Secular Age* (Cambridge: Belknap, Harvard University Press, 2007), 1–22; E. Hense, „Present-day spiritualities in confessional, popular, professional and aesthetic contexts: contrasts or overlap? Introduction", in *Present-Day Spiritualities: Contrasts and Overlaps* (eds. E. Hense, F. Jespers and P. Nissen; Leiden: Brill, 2014), 1–17.

of life'. We suffer from a current overestimation of one-sided materialistic control systems. We realize that we need to cross the boundaries of the status quo and reshape our evaluation systems following our spiritual and ethical desires. In order to make the right decisions, we need to re-think what is truly valuable to us. Those exposed to experiences of poverty, lack of power, unfulfilled need, indignation, inner conflicts, and emptiness are the focus of this book. How are they able to create more depth, fullness, and flourishing in their lives and the lives of others? This human striving is the worthwhile subject of what might be called the research into spiritual discernment and choice in the context of societal renewal. Central to our research are the following questions: (a) what is seen as quality of life, (b) in which human conditions and practices do we detect quality of life, (c) how can we enhance these conditions and practices?

When comparing different struggles for quality of life, we need to view the data through various disciplines e.g. theology, spirituality studies, management studies, economics, and medical science. These disciplines not only provide an insight into different human conditions and activities, but also relate them to various perspectives on life quality. Assuming that quality of life is a relative category that can be judged from different points of view and continually enhanced, these disciplines are integral to our search for a wide range of possible improvements.

This book will start with some disciplinary approaches regarding our question on quality of life; we will then look at aspects of life quality in concepts and images drawn from scientific or spiritual literature. Working in this way, we elucidate our findings with life quality cases in The Netherlands.

Disciplinary approaches

Christoph Hübenthal introduces public theology as a relevant approach for identifying quality of life and contributing to an improvement of life quality. Public theology serves a twofold apologetic purpose: On the one hand, it wants to initiate a public discourse on what is ultimately significant for every human being. On the other hand, it wants to exhibit Christian faith and the corresponding faith praxis as a credible candidate for what is of ultimate significance. Elisabeth Hense presents Christian spirituality studies as another relevant approach. In addition to the criteria of adequacy and appropriateness – which have already been widely agreed upon in Christian spirituality – she argues that there might be a need for the 'criteria of respondence' when quality of life is at stake. She illustrates her argument with some reflections on current initiatives of societal renewal concerning issues of food, care, and money in the Netherlands. Eric de Jongh uses a management approach and explores how discernment may help managers to expand their hermeneutical horizon. After an explanation of the hermeneutic mode of inquiry, an exploration of some high-profile examples of a limited hermeneutical horizon in management literature and a cross-textual reading of two recent examples of discernment in the discipline of management, de Jongh evaluates the standards which are deemed mandatory for the practice of discernment in managerial contexts. Aloys Wijngaards takes an economic approach and explores the question of the meaningfulness of banking. To this effect, he first discusses the economic activities of banks. Second, he elaborates on the concept of economic spirituality as a starting point for the relation between banking and spirituality. Third, he takes a pivotal step in connecting banking and spirituality by focusing on trust and societal responsibility. Fourth, financing a sustainable society is explored as a possible way for connecting banking and spirituality. In the concluding section, he reflects on the possible impact of connecting banking and spirituality. Willem Marie Speelman uses a spiritual-narrative approach while working on physiotherapeutic cases. He deals with the question of spiritual coping in the practice of care in recent years. Taking the case of Ms. Albert as an example, he shows how to dig deep into the nature of the spiritual dimension, and develop a way to describe her spirituality in non-traditional terms. Although she may not believe in God, pray or fast, she develops ways to relate to the same realm of transcendence that religious traditions have given names of divinity.

Concepts and images

Krijn Pansters deals with the ethical problems of personal property in today's world, the benefits of individual ethics of 'virtue ownership', and the concept of 'de-ownership' from corporate to individual ethics. From a perspective of Franciscan moral spirituality, he focuses on the virtues of poverty, self-renunciation, self-restraint, and temperance. He also looks at the cultivation of personal goodness; the art of living a respectful, responsible, and sustainable life; the characteristics of care for creation; and the choice of de-ownership as a spiritual strategy. Sharda Nandram discusses the concept of intuition as a powerful resource in the decision making process of entrepreneurs. She argues that intuition has been studied in the mystical and spiritual traditions, especially in the Eastern context where intuition is a means of obtaining penetrating knowledge and functions as a gateway to a wider and richer world. She focuses in particular on the teachings of Sri Aurobindo: the process of knowing, consciousness, and the role of spiritual based intuition as part of it. Jacobine Gelderloos explains how the concepts of quality of life or liveability have been developed into collective terms in

The Netherlands encompassing various areas of life. She explores the quality of life in rural Brabant and Groningen by analysing regional newspapers and church newsletters. In these sources, quality of life is conceptualized in various ways. Her study of these newspapers and church newsletters prove to be complementary to how personal and community well-being are related to each other. Margareta Gruber analyses the image of the new city of Jerusalem: God's heavenly garden of immense size, splendid, precious and flooded with light, with God's throne in the center from which a flow of life and salvation is emanating; and God's people living here comprising all peoples, excluding only idolaters and the cruel. Gruber depicts the dynamism of the eschatological vision concerning its specific and subversive power of forming current and future urban living environments.

We will conclude our collective research by offering a synthesis of our debate on life quality. We will identify the conditions and activities that are unsatisfactory and misguided in present times and those that are acceptable, making an improvement to life features. Working in this way, we hope to make visible some aspects of societal renewal that is favored by our fellow citizens, especially in The Netherlands.

DISCIPLINARY APPROACHES

QUEST FOR QUALITY OF LIFE: A PERSPECTIVE FROM PUBLIC THEOLOGY

Christoph Hübenthal

Abstract

In the first part of this paper, a concept of public theology will be developed which draws on a decisively theological agenda. Public theology, as will be argued, serves a twofold apologetic purpose. On the one hand, it has to initiate a public discourse on what is ultimately significant for every human being. On the other hand, it has to exhibit Christian faith and the corresponding faith praxis as a credible candidate for what is ultimate significance. This double apologetic task of public theology will be referred to as *discourse* and *witnessing*. – The advance of an *anthropological reductionism* then can be seen as a main obstacle to performing this double apologetic task. Therefore, in the second part, economization, naturalization, and depersonalization as obvious manifestations of anthropological reductionism will be outlined. Moreover, it will be explained that public theology first has to overcome these devaluating tendencies before it can start to perform its genuine tasks of discourse and witnessing. Accordingly, the struggle against anthropological reductionism is a subsidiary but nevertheless urgent task of public theology. – However, this struggle has hitherto been exclusively vindicated by theological reasons. So one might ask whether public theology is even permitted to transform the entire society in the light of its own particular purposes. The last part seeks to tackle this *justificatory problem.* Here, it will be shown that the capabilities approach, one of the most prominent theories of quality of life, suffers from a similar justificatory problem, which, however, has recently found a cogent solution. By invoking the action-reflective moral theory of Alan Gewirth, the capabilities approach can indeed be provided with a stable foundational basis. This solution, as will be argued, fits perfectly with the justificatory problem of public theology. So public theology eventually turns out to be justified in attacking anthropological reductionism and in modeling the public realm according to its own purposes. An additional advantage of employing the capabilities approach as well as Gewirth's account can be seen in the fact that the subsidiary task of public theology will gain a much sharper profile, for now it appears to be a struggle for social justice.

Introduction

Perhaps I should begin this chapter with a warning to the reader. In what follows, a rather *sober* and *formal account* will be given of what public theology is, how it defines quality of life, and how it suggests enhancing this quality. I will largely refrain from describing quality of life in amiable images, charming metaphors or mellow narratives. One reason for this reservation is that I simply do not have the literary skills to paint beautiful aesthetic scenarios. But this is not the main reason. The quite prosaic style I will employ here is primarily indebted to a currently dominant trend which will later be expounded under the label 'anthropological reductionism'. In brief, anthropological reductionism prevents us from appropriately recognizing the true *grandeur* and the true *misery* of human existence. Against this trend I wish to set some considerations which can, at least, make plausible that humans may still handle notions like 'truth', 'ultimate meaning' or 'moral goodness' reasonably and may thereby reach out beyond the confinements of a flattened existence. Moreover, I wish to show that the use of such notions is possible without invoking an outdated *philosophia perennis* and its corresponding ontological framework.[1] The language game to be played in order to make such reflections, however, requires an unaffected and dispassionate diction. The primary reason for the prosaic style of this chapter is thus the simple fact that this style is more appropriate for the chapter's content than a narrative portrayal. Sure, the price to be paid for these fairly sober considerations about constitutive aspects of the human existence is that some readers will not hesitate to indicate them as 'foundationalist'. Yet I can live with this qualification, not in the least because the foundations that I will present here – albeit densely and in some cases even insufficiently – are intrinsically connected to ideas like discourse and openness for revision. My apologies for the unattractive style of the following are therefore accompanied by a cordial invitation to enter into an open dialogue on the topics discussed. In my opinion, this should be a dialogue on issues that really matter.

Having said this, I will now spell out the concrete outline of this paper. In the first part, I wish to delineate some features of public theology. I will do this in a way that shows why public theology is a decisively *theological* enterprise. In fact, it will be presented as a twofold *apologetic* endeavor which seeks to embark on both a public debate on ultimate questions and the presentation of the Christian faith praxis as a credible answer to such questions. The twofold apologetic task can thus be called *discourse and witnessing*.

As has already been mentioned, anthropological reductionist tendencies turn out to be a major impediment for performing the double apol-

1 C. Hübenthal, *Moderne orthodoxie: Verdediging van een denkvorm voor de publieke theologie* (Nijmegen: Radboud Universiteit, 2015).

ogetic task. For that reason, some illuminating examples of *anthropological reductionism* will be given in the second part. Furthermore, I will show that public theology first has to meet this reductionist challenge before it can begin to deal with its genuine tasks, that is, discourse and witnessing. Hence the struggle against anthropological reductionism can be seen as an additional yet more urgent task of public theology. In the course of the second part, I also want to make clear why public theology determines the conditions of a qualitatively good life as a societal environment within which discourse and witnessing are possible.

Up to there, the line of argument will be purely theological. After all, the reductionist challenge is to be faced solely because anthropological reductionism turns out to be a central obstacle to performing the apologetic assignment. From there, one could ask whether public theology is at all justified in attempting to transform the shape of the entire society in order to make discourse and witnessing possible. The third part will tackle this *justificatory problem.* First, it will be shown that another approach defining the quality of life in its own terms suffers from a comparable problem. Yet this problem has already been resolved by employing a foundationalist ethical theory. I will make plausible that the same theory can also be used to overcome the justificatory problem of public theology. Furthermore, the struggle against anthropological reductionism will gain a sharper profile, for it now appears to be a fight for social justice.

1 Discourse and Witnessing – The Double Task of Public Theology

In the framework of his system-theoretical approach, Niklas Luhmann describes modern society as outcome of a functional differentiation. For him, society is divided into numerous subsystems, each of which fulfills a particular societal function. To do this successfully, subsystems employ a specific binary code that translates selected information from their environment into the subsystem's own communicative operations. In this way, subsystems reduce the complexity of the environment while increasing their internal complexity. As soon as they have reached a certain level of internal complexity, subsystems will develop reflexive instances which orientate their communicative operations and so warrant their permanent autopoietic reproduction, continually redefining the distinction between subsystem and environment.[2] Among other subsystems, Luhmann has thoroughly analyzed the religious

2 N. Luhmann, *Soziale Systeme: Grundriß einer allgemeinen Theorie* (Frankfurt: Suhrkamp, 1984).

subsystem several times.[3] For him, the binary code employed by the religious subsystem is the distinction between *immanence* and *transcendence*, and the reflexive instance orientating and reproducing the entire subsystem is *theology*.[4]

If Luhmann is right, a thing like 'public theology' seems hardly possible, for the workings of the reflexive instance are exclusively directed toward the interiority of the subsystem but not toward its environment. Though I think that a conception of public theology still can be developed within the confinements of the system-theoretical approach, I do not want to go into this here. I have mentioned Luhmann only because he points out that a public orientation of theology is far from being self-evident. If, therefore, many public theologians take it for granted that theology has to fulfill a task beyond the religious realm, they have to give good reasons for this assumption. The fact that public debates may benefit from theological contributions is, however, not sufficient as a reason. Though arguments like that are often heard,[5] they are nevertheless flawed. For if contributing to public debates were the only motive to engage in public theology, critics like Charles Mathewes were fairly right in lamenting that "[t]ypically 'public theologies' are self-destructively accommodationist: they let the 'larger' secular world's self-understanding set the terms, and then ask how religious faith contributes to the purposes of public life, so understood."[6] The cogency of this critique can hardly be denied. Hence the function of public theology must not be restricted to ornamenting social debates held anyway, because otherwise public theology wouldn't have any specific function at all – neither a public nor a theological one. So the *raison d'être* of public theology must somehow be linked to the reflexive task that theology fulfills within the religious system.

With regard to Christian theology, this reflexive task can be spelled out by taking a closer look at the normative base upon which the entire belief system or faith praxis rests. As a whole, the Christian faith praxis depends on the *constitutive belief* that the Christ event is of ultimate significance for every human being, so that each operation of the belief system can be conceived as an expression of this belief – albeit a mostly implicit one.[7]

3 N. Luhmann, *Funktion der Religion* (Frankfurt: Suhrkamp, 1977); N. Luhmann, *Die Religion der Gesellschaft* (Frankfurt: Suhrkamp, 2000).

4 Luhmann, *Funktion der Religion*, 59.

5 S. Kim, *Theology in the Public Square: Public Theology as a Catalyst for Open Debate* (London: SCM Press, 2011), 3; H. Breitenberg Jr., "What is Public Theology?," in *Public Theology for a Global Society. Essays in Honor of Max L. Stackhouse* (eds. D.K. Hainsworth and S. Paeth; Grand Rapids: Eerdmans, 2011), 3–17 (5).

6 C. Mathewes, *A Theology of Public Life* (Cambridge: Cambridge University Press, 2007), 1.

7 C. Hübenthal, "Eén taak met twee speerpunten: Over kerkelijke en publieke theologie," in *Verdeelde wijsheid: Tussen Kerk en academische theologie* (eds. F. Bosman and H. Goris; Nijmegen: Valkhof, 2014), 135–153.

Consequently, the Christian faith praxis is characterized by a universal addressedness which necessarily reaches out beyond the borders of the belief system and directs itself towards the public sphere. The operations of the Christian belief system, in other words, cannot be restricted to the interiority of the system, but also exhibit an external reference. If, therefore, theology is rightly characterized as the instance that reflexively orientates these operations, it is not only charged with the internal task of reproducing the faith system, but also has to fulfill a public function which, on its part, is not primarily defined by public demands but by the system's constitutive belief. Obviously, a rationale of this kind is more suitable as a foundation of public theology than the mere appeal for Christians to enter into ongoing public debates.

A couple of years ago, Max Stackhouse, one of the leading figures of the public theology movement, made the suggestion to identify public theology with apologetics.[8] Basically, this fits in with the rationale just given very well. However, the concept of apologetics needs further clarification if it wishes to provide a comprehensive account of public theology. In that light, Elaine Graham has recently argued that "an apologetic public theology is concerned less with words than actions, and that a defence of faith is to be found in its power to liberate and transform situations of injustice and human suffering."[9] Though this statement is certainly not mistaken, one can still wonder whether it doesn't fall prey to the aforementioned suspicion that public theology rather serves external interests than pursuing a clear theological agenda. So again, we are faced with the necessity to develop a conception of apologetics from within the Christian faith system and not from whatever public demands.

At this point, it should be clear that apologetic public theology is concerned with public communication of the constitutive belief that the Christ event is ultimately significant for every human being. A closer look can reveal that this constitutive belief can be analytically divided into two separate *claims*. On the one hand, it is claimed that there is something which is ultimately significant for every human being. Obviously, this claim is not specifically Christian, for it only contends that there is 'something' of which the ultimate significance can generally be demonstrated to every human being. And exactly this, then, is the reason why a second claim has to be made, namely the claim that this ominous 'something' can be found in the Christ event. Sure, at first glance, this distinction may seem quite mysterious. For wouldn't it be more appropriate to simply claim that the Christ event is of

8 Cf. M.L. Stackhouse, *Globalization and Grace: God and Globalization 4* (New York: Continuum, 2007), 107.

9 E. Graham, *Between a Rock and a Hard Place: Public Theology in a Post-Secular Age* (London: SCM Press, 2013), 212.

ultimate significance for every human being, as it is, after all, this single claim that lies at the bottom of the Christian faith praxis? We should nevertheless make this distinction, and I will shortly explain why. For now, let's take it for granted and take a look at the first claim.

My thesis is that an apologetic public theology has to defend a *universal truth claim* concerning the assertion that there is something which is of ultimate significance for every human being. I am well aware that making universal truth claims is an undertaking not valued highly in our postmodern times. Kevin Vanhoozer, for instance, asserted that, for postmodern theologians, 'truth' is nothing but a "compelling story told by persons in positions of power in order to perpetuate their way of seeing and organizing the natural and social world."[10] Likewise, John Thiel has argued that a "universal or foundationalist justification is a logical impossibility, [...] Christian claims are, and remain, particular."[11] Countless other quotations could be added here. Yet the decisive question is whether they are right. In a certain sense, they are apparently wrong, since any denial of truth claims must necessarily claim to be true, otherwise the speaker would not make a meaningful statement at all. If, therefore, a speaker necessarily claims truth for the assertion that there is no truth, the very making of this claim contradicts the propositional content of the assertion and the speaker eventually gets lost in a *performative contradiction*. On a logical level, therefore, the denial of truth cannot be maintained seriously.

But there is more to it than a simple logical error. Within the context of his transcendental-pragmatic approach, Karl-Otto Apel has convincingly shown that no rational subject can avoid making truth claims. Any denial of this unavoidability would, again, lead to a performative contradiction. Likewise, Apel has demonstrated that neither the classical correspondence theory of truth nor modern evidence or coherence theories can sufficiently explain how such truth claims are to be validated.[12] Only a *consensus theory* – which, on its part, integrates all the other theories – can serve for a satisfying explanation. According to this theory, a truth claim is valid only on the condition that all possible interlocutors consent to it. Since the community of possible interlocutors is virtually universal, each truth claim is universally addressed. From this follows, that definite truth – i. e. the final consensus of the universal interpretative community – is but a regulative idea which can never be accomplished in the real world. In spite of this inaccessibility

10 K. Vanhoozer, "Theology and the Condition of Postmodernity: A Report on Knowledge (of God)," in *The Cambridge Companion to Postmodern Theology* (ed. K. Vanhoozer; Cambridge: Cambridge University Press, 2003), 3–25 (11).

11 J.E. Thiel, *Nonfoundationalism* (Minneapolis: Fortress Press, 1994), 102.

12 Cf. K.-O. Apel, *Auseinandersetzungen: In Erprobung des transzendentalpragmatischen Ansatzes* (Frankfurt: Suhrkamp, 1998), 81–193.

of definite truth, however, the procedural requirements for the treatment of truth claims are quite clear. They have to be validated through an *intersubjective discourse* which aims at consensus.

How does this relate to the apologetic task of public theology? From Apel we can learn that making truth claims is an operation unavoidable for rational subjects. Secondly, Apel has shown that any truth claim is universally addressed. If thus the Christian faith praxis is based on the constitutive belief that something is ultimately significant for every human being, any factual utterance of this claim necessarily implies the making of a universally addressed truth claim. Thirdly, Apel has shown that the validation of such a truth claim is to be carried out by means of an intersubjective discourse. From this we can conclude that the Christian faith praxis unavoidably makes truth claims addressed to virtually everyone. If, therefore, apologetics is said to be charged with the public defense of the universal truth claim that something is ultimately significant for every human being, this may be at odds with the postmodern signature of our time, but certainly not with the logic of speaking nor with the very nature of theology.

Now the question arises as to which end public theology has to initiate and maintain such a societal discourse on ultimate human significance. Though the notion of a 'defense' might suggest that the primary purpose is to win a rhetoric competition, in fact, this is not the case. Apologetic public theology rather seeks to foster such a discourse in order to urge the participants to take an *existential decision* on what is of ultimate significance for them. For if public theology rightly claims truth for the proposition that there is something which is of ultimate significance for every human being, everyone faced with this claim has to take a stance towards it. Of course, for the time being, people can ignore such a claim – and in fact they do – but the more they are exposed to it, the less they can avoid forming an opinion. Hence the purpose of the public discourse is to invite people to decide whether there is something which is of ultimate significance for them and, if this question is answered affirmatively, what this 'something' in fact might be.

I'll come back to this, but first we have to answer the question why the constitutive belief underlying the Christian faith praxis is to be divided into two separate claims, only one of which can be conceived as a truth claim. The answer is that only this part of the constitutive belief of the Christian faith praxis can be validated discursively, whereas the other cannot. To understand why this is so, we should bear in mind that the Christian faith praxis is a *contingent* praxis. It owes its very existence to the non-necessary decision of the believers to take the Christ event as motivational basis for establishing and continuing the faith praxis. Hence the entire faith praxis draws upon a permanent execution of contingent faith acts. And it is exactly these faith acts the performance of which cannot be validated by means of an intersubjective discourse, because they belong to the *inner world* of the believers, to which other subjects do not have immediate access. An assertion the semantic referent of which is per definition not accessible to the universal interpretative community logically refuses any intersubjective examination. If, therefore, someone claims to believe in the ultimate significance of the Christ event, this statement cannot be validated by providing verifiable arguments. Yet the speaker still makes a claim which is universally addressed, since the corresponding statement insists on being valid for everyone who is capable of understanding it.

It was Jürgen Habermas who designated this type of claims as *sincerity claims*. He also stressed that sincerity claims – contrary to truth claims – can be validated only by means of consistent behavior. "That a speaker means what he says can be made credible only by the consequences of his behavior not by providing reasons. That's why addressees having accepted a sincerity claim can, to a certain extent, expect behavioral consistency [...]."[13] If thus the validation of sincerity claims requires acts in accordance with the semantic content of the utterance, the assertion to belief in the ultimate significance of the Christ event must be made believable by acts in accordance with the Christ event's significance. No matter how differently Christians may interpret this significance, their concordant behavior will appear as a form of *witnessing*. Hence Christians have to bear witness to their faith by acting in a way that corresponds to what they claim to believe. From this we may conclude that an apologetic public theology also has to care about a mode of witnessing that does justice to the content of Christian faith.

Public theology is thus not only charged with fostering a public discourse on ultimate human significance, but also has to display the Christian faith praxis in a way that, at least, makes credible that ultimate human significance can be found in the Christ event. As *discourse*, therefore, apologetics seeks to invite people to make an existential decision on what is of ultimate significance for them, and as *witnessing*, it seeks to invite people to recognize this significance in the Christ event. Now I am well aware that delineating the double task of public theology in this way must appear very formal. It does not say anything about the arguments that are to be employed within the public discourse, nor about the content Christians have to bear witness to, or the particular modes in which this is to be done. Yet the advantage of such formality can be seen in the fact that it is open to a wide range of interpretations and concretions. Moreover, even such a rather formal definition allows for a sufficiently detailed delineation of the conditions that public theology regards as relevant to assessing the quality of life.

13 J. Habermas, *Theorie des kommunikativen Handelns, Bd 1: Handlungsrationalität und gesellschaftliche Rationalisierung* (Frankfurt: Suhrkamp, 1981), 408 (my translation; C.H.).

2 Struggle against Anthropological Reductionism

So far we have seen that public theology turns out to be an apologetic endeavor, more particularly, it appears as discourse and witnessing. Now it could be further argued that both modes of apologetics have to exhibit an *ethical* design. With regard to witnessing this should be obvious, since it is primarily a praxis which has to show the credibility and attractiveness of the Christian faith.[14] However, the discursive mode, too, must display an ethical shape, for any discourse on ultimate significance can be seen as an extension of debates about what makes a human life worthwhile or meaningful, and such debates are primarily practical ones.

It would be rather challenging to unfold the idea of an *ethical apologetics*, but I will not go into that here. Rather, I would like to point a problem out which, to a certain extent, has to be resolved before the enterprise of an apologetic public theology can even be launched. This problem is directly related to the question of what public theology determines as quality of life. From what has been said so far, it should be clear that the business of public theology depends on societal conditions in which discourse and witnessing are possible. Hence the public sphere must be capable of discursively examining the truth claim that there is something which is of ultimate significance. Likewise, it must be able to understand the Christian faith praxis as bearing witness to the belief that the Christ event is of ultimate significance for every human being. *If the public sphere meets these requirements comprehensively, it fulfills,* from the perspective of public theology, *all the conditions that are necessary to live a qualitatively good life.* Put differently: *The degree to which the public sphere allows for both a discourse on ultimate significance and the witnessing of religious belief is also the degree to which it warrants quality of life.*

With these findings, our considerations on the quality of life as being defined by public theology could meaningfully stop. But, as has been said, there remains a problem which has to be resolved before public theology can even start with its genuine task of apologetic discourse and witnessing. The problem is that the public sphere as it currently appears hardly meets the requirements just mentioned. Of course, we should not sink into cultural pessimism too quickly, but there are, in fact, many indications that we are living in an age where it is extremely difficult to put issues of ultimate significance on the public agenda. As I said in the introduction, I tend to believe that the present culture is characterized by an *anthropological reductionism* which impedes any serious form of apologetics. To put it bluntly: If humans are permanently urged to think of themselves as *flat* and *mean*, they

14 Particularly, it was S. Hauerwas who always made a strong plea for an ethical shaping of the Christian faith praxis. S. Hauerwas, *A Community of Character: Toward a Constructive Christian Social Ethic* (Notre Dame: University of Notre Dame Press, 1991).

are incapable of developing an idea of the *grandeur* and *misery* of human existence and thus of *ultimate significance*. Unfortunately, I cannot provide a full-fledged analysis of anthropological reductionism here; instead I would like to provide three examples which will at least illustrate how threatening the current situation is.

Firstly, in one of his latest publications, Michael Sandel has masterly shown how economic market-principles are conquering all domains of human life.[15] In education, health care, administration, the military sector, ecology and even in the fields of morality and religion, an economic logic is successfully replacing all other forms of social coordination. As a consequence, people gradually get used to experiencing human relations in exclusively economic terms. Other authors, for instance Thomáš Sedlácek,[16] Wolfgang Streeck,[17] Peter Ulrich,[18] Robert and Edward Skidelsky[19] or Thomas Piketty,[20] from different perspectives, have pointed in the same direction. Though some of these scholars have made helpful suggestions of how to overcome purely market-based thinking, they all agree that we are currently faced with a growing *economization* of human affairs. Already more than three decades ago, Jürgen Habermas predicted a 'colonization of the human lifeworld' by systemic imperatives, among which economic imperatives are the most dominant.[21] It seems that this 'hostile takeover' is almost completed by now. Habermas has also shown that a serious disruption of the lifeworld's communicative reproduction necessarily leads to social pathologies which, on the cultural level, manifest themselves as a 'loss of meaning'.[22] It is this loss which makes an intersubjective examination of truth claims concerning ultimate significance almost impossible and so reflects the advance of anthropological reductionism.

15 M.J. Sandel, *What Money Can't Buy: The Moral Limits of the Markets* (New York: Farrar, Strauss and Giroux, 2012).

16 T. Sedlácek, *Economics of Good and Evil: The Quest for Economic Meaning from Gilgamesh to Wall Street* (New York: Oxford University Press, 2011).

17 W. Streeck, *Gekaufte Zeit: Die vertagte Krise des demokratischen Kapitalismus* (Berlin: Suhrkamp, 2013).

18 P. Ulrich, *Integrative Economic Ethics: Foundations of a Civilized Market Economy* (Cambridge: Cambridge University Press, 2006).

19 R. and E. Skidelsky, *How Much is Enough? The Love of Money, and the Case for the Good Life* (London: Allen Lane, 2012).

20 T. Picketty, *Capital in the Twenty-First Century* (transl. A. Goldhammer; Cambridge: The Belknap Press of Harvard University Press, 2014).

21 J. Habermas, *Theorie des kommunikativen Handelns, Bd. 2: Zur Kritik der funktionalistischen Vernunft* (Frankfurt: Suhrkamp, 1981), 229–293.

22 Habermas, *Theorie des kommunikativen Handelns 2*, 215.

A second phenomenon to be mentioned here is the *naturalization* of the human being. Again, it was Jürgen Habermas,[23] but also thinkers as Thomas Nagel[24] and others, who persuasively demonstrated that any attempt to understand the human nature in purely scientific terms is necessarily doomed to fail. As we have already seen, a speech act asserting its own causation exhibits a performative contradiction. Likewise, no naturalistic theory can explain its own genesis, for if it could, it would cease to be a theory at all. In spite of that simple logic, however, neuroscientists,[25] physiologists[26] or biologists[27] try to convince us that we are nothing but scientifically describable entities. If this were true, it wouldn't make sense to initiate a public discourse which aims at bringing people to a point where they can make an existential decision, because free decisions do not occur at all in the framework of a merely explanatory paradigm. Moreover, any attempt to speak about ultimate human significance is condemned to be a nonsense debate, since teleological terms as 'significance', 'meaning', 'destiny' and the like don't have a place in the scientific language game. Nevertheless, scientific naturalism seems to be highly plausible to most of our contemporaries, which again shows the advance of anthropological reductionism.

A third observation pertains to the growing *depersonalization* in the internet and especially on social media.[28] Here, two alarming trends unite into an unholy alliance. On the one hand, we recognize an increasing *exhibitionist inclination*, particularly among younger people. Of course, this inclination is by no means proof of moral degeneration; it rather shows how quickly the mindset of a whole generation can be changed. On the other hand, there is also a growing interest in all kinds of personal data, not only on the part of intelligence services, but also – and perhaps primarily – on the part of industrial or commercial enterprises and the advertising industry. Both the *exhibitionist inclination* and the corresponding *desire for data* eventually lead to a situation where the personality of an individual is completely transparent and deprived of its secrets. Against this backdrop,

23 J. Habermas, *Zwischen Naturalismus und Religion: Philosophische Aufsätze* (Frankfurt: Suhrkamp, 2005).

24 T. Nagel, *Mind and Cosmos: Why the Materialist Neo-Darwinian Conception of Nature is Almost Certainly False* (Oxford: Oxford University Press, 2012).

25 G. Roth, *Fühlen, Denken, Handeln: Wie das Gehirn unser Verhalten steuert* (Frankfurt: Suhrkamp, 2001).

26 W. Singer, *Ein neues Menschenbild? Gespräche über Hirnforschung* (Frankfurt: Suhrkamp, 2003).

27 R. Dawkins, *The Selfish Gene* (Oxford: Oxford University Press, 2006).

28 R.S. Laura et al., *The New Social Disease: From High Tech Depersonalization to Survival of Soul* (Lanham: University Press of America, 2008); Frank Schirrmacher, *Payback: Warum wir im Informationszeitalter gezwungen sind zu tun, was wir nicht tun wollen, und wie wir die Kontrolle über unser Denken zurückgewinnen* (München: Karl Blessing Verlag, 2009).

any discourse on ultimate human significance threatens to draw only on data that can be linked with other data and be further processed by subtle algorithms. The human being, then, is reduced to a point of intersection within a large informational network.[29]

Economization, naturalization and depersonalization, as has been said, can be seen as manifestations of an anthropological reductionism which widely characterizes our present situation. Now it would be a huge challenge to develop an exhaustive *theory of anthropological reductionism* which systematically connects the phenomena mentioned as well as other phenomena in order to gain a comprehensive picture of the difficulties one encounters when one attempts to initiate a public discourse on ultimate significance. Such a theory, however, would also have to take into consideration converse observations. In his epoch-making work *The Practice of Everyday Life*, for instance, Michel de Certeau has shown that every 'strategy' of what has here been called anthropological reductionism almost necessarily will be undermined by 'tactics' of everyday life. Whereas *strategies* are used by those in positions of power, seeking to determine the world according to their own standards, *tactics* are used by the powerless and can thus only work within territories defined by strategies.[30] Nevertheless, tactics efficiently counteract the logic of strategies and so ensure permanent disturbances. Applied to our field of inquiry, this would imply that, in spite of overwhelming evidence of the advance of a reductionist anthropology, an appropriate theory of such reductionism would also have to reckon with dissident mindsets and with permanent attempts to establish alternative forms of behavior.[31]

Unfortunately, such a theory cannot be developed here. Yet it should be clear that public theology has to deal with these issues before it can seriously consider launching its apologetic endeavor. As long as the general communication conditions are not suited for discourse and witnessing, the wider public does not allow an acceptable quality of life. For that reason, public theology will have to make tremendous efforts to model the public sphere in a way that it meets the required conditions. Though, strictly speaking, this task appears to be a task *subsidiary* to the *genuine* business of discourse and witnessing, it nevertheless seems to be of much greater urgency.[32] Accordingly, what public theology has to do now is to develop an

29 Y. Hofstetter, *Sie wissen alles: Wie intelligente Maschinen in unser Leben eindringen und warum wir für unsere Freiheit kämpfen müssen* (München: Bertelsmann, 2014).

30 M. de Certeau, *The Practice of Everyday Life* (transl. S.F. Rendall; Berkeley: University of California Press, 1988).

31 See the contribution of E. Hense in this volume.

32 In that sense, F. Höhne rightly states: "Öffentliche Theologie ist ein wirklichkeits- und traditionshermeneutisches Unterfangen, das auf Veränderung von Denken, Fühlen, Handeln und Strukturen zielt und dabei am gesellschaftlichen Leben nicht nur teilnehmen,

efficient approach to modeling the general communication conditions according to its own standards. To do this, it must first develop an explanatory theory of anthropological reductionism and then, in the light of this theory, look for effective instruments to gradually alter the situation. It needs no mentioning that public theology cannot achieve this by exclusively building on its own resources. Therefore it is reliant on allies found in the tactics of everyday life, in dissident mindsets and deviant practices.

3 The Justificatory Problem

Before I can give a preliminary account of how public theology might tackle this subsidiary, but tremendously urgent, task of modifying the current communication conditions, I first have to point out a justificatory problem. After all, we might ask ourselves whether it is readily allowed first to define the standards of a qualitatively good life in exclusively theological terms and then to seek to model the entire public realm according to this religious blueprint. Of course, the purpose of such an undertaking is not to establish a theocracy, let alone to execute fundamentalist religious terror. As has been shown sufficiently, public theology rather aims at inviting people to make a free decision and at providing a credible proposal to decide upon. But still it is a markedly theological project. After all, in the first section much emphasis has been put on the idea that public theology in general and apologetics in particular must not take whatever public needs as its point of departure but instead has to draw on a decisively theological agenda. Moreover, attributing negative connotations to the current communication conditions may be right from a particular theological point of view, but perhaps not from other perspectives. So what legitimizes the will to change these conditions in the light of a theological vision, apart from the apologetic rationale?

To resolve this justificatory problem, we should briefly recognize a prominent debate on the quality of life conducted outside the confinements of theology and Christian faith. For looking further than our noses may help us to recognize that other approaches, too, suffer from the problem of how to legitimize social transformation in the light of what they hold to be the quality of life. Furthermore, if a cogent solution to their justificatory problem can be found, this solution might also be applicable to the problem public theology is struggling with. After all, the more public attention a particular debate on the quality of life has gained hitherto, the more likely it is that its theoretical shortcomings have also been detected and even that suitable solutions have been developed. An additional advantage of broad-

sondern auch die Bedingungen dafür mitgestalten will." F. Höhne, *Öffentliche Theologie: Begriffsgeschichte und Grundfragen* (Leipzig: Evangelische Verlagsanstalt, 2015), 40.

ening the scope could be the fact that non-theological approaches may already have worked out appropriate schemes of how to transform the societal conditions. Provided that the envisaged objectives of these approaches exhibit far-reaching similarities with the aims of public theology, the latter could find a powerful ally in them and benefit from their findings.

The approach I would like to invoke now is the *capabilities approach*. This should not come as a surprise, since the capabilities approach is often referred to in discussions on the quality of life. Originally it was set up to measure the quality of life within the context of development economics;[33] shortly after, however, it also received philosophical attention. It was Martha Nussbaum, building on Aristotelian essentialism, who worked out a set of specific functionings which define a genuinely human life.[34] On the basis of these functionings, a list of ten capabilities serving as prerequisites of any form of human flourishing has been drawn up. Strikingly, some of the list items can easily be interpreted as conditions that must be met before truth claims can be publicly examined. The fourth item, for instance, mentions the capability "to use one's senses, to imagine, think, and reason – and to do these things in a 'truly human' way, a way informed and cultivated by an adequate education [...]. Being able to use one's mind in ways protected by guarantees of freedom of expression [...]." In the same manner, the seventh item speaks of the capability "to live with and toward others, to recognize and show concern for other human beings, to engage in various forms of social interaction [...]." And the tenth item makes a strong plea for the capability "to participate effectively in political choices that govern one's own life; having the right of political participation, protections of free speech and association." It leaves no doubt that humans having these capabilities are adequately equipped to discursively investigate the validity of truth claims. The sixth item unquestionably relates to the issue of ultimate significance and to the capacity to make existentially relevant decisions. It reads: "Being able to form a conception of the good and to engage in critical reflection about the planning of one's life. (This entails protection for the liberty of conscience and religious observance.)" Finally, some items on the list can be understood as endorsing an openness to others, which would include that their ways of life and their existential decisions have a non-coercive impact on us. The fifth item, for instance, mentions the capability "to have attachments to things and people outside ourselves," and the seventh item, as has been said, touches on the capability "to live with and toward others, to recognize and show concern for other human be-

33 M. Nussbaum and A. Sen (eds.), *The Quality of Life* (Oxford: Clarendon Press 1993).

34 M. Nussbaum, "Aristotle on Human Nature and the Foundation of Ethics," in *Mind and Ethics: Essays on the Ethical Philosophy of Bernard Williams* (eds. J.E.G. Altham and R. Harrison; Cambridge: Cambridge University Press, 1995), 86–131.

ings [...]."[35] Taken together, these capabilities are in striking concordance with what ensures the quality of life from the perspective of public theology. In other words, if all – or at least the majority of – human beings were in the possession of these capabilities, the subsidiary task of public theology would have been accomplished and it could start with carrying out its genuine apologetic task.

At this point it is important to notice that Nussbaum decisively rejects any religious foundation of the capabilities approach. Referring to John Rawls, she calls her account a 'freestanding conception' "without any grounding in metaphysical ideas of the sort that divide people along lines of culture and religion."[36] Hence the striking coincidence between the objectives of public theology and the capabilities approach by no means emerges from a shared religious doctrine. But there is more to it. Nussbaum, as has been said, mentions a total of ten capabilities which form a *coherent whole.* "[T]he capabilities," she argues, "are understood as both mutually supportive and all of central relevance to social justice. Thus a society that neglects one of them to promote the others has short-changed its citizens, and there is a failure of justice in the short-changing."[37] So it is the whole of these capabilities that has to be fostered.

If we take these findings seriously, and I think we should, two things become clear. Firstly, public theology is not the only actor attempting to improve societal communication conditions. The capabilities approach, too, pursues to empower human beings to participate competently in truth-seeking discourses, to take existential decisions, and to be sensitive to other forms of attributing meaning to human life. Secondly, the specific capabilities that, from the perspective of public theology, constitute the required communication conditions exhibit an intrinsic connection to all other capabilities on the list. Consequently, public theology cannot confine its activities to warranting only a selected set of capabilities, but has to promote the whole list. However, as Nussbaum argues, promoting the whole list is promoting social justice. If this proves to be correct, the subsidiary task of public theology might be delineated as a *struggle for social justice.*

Unfortunately, however, we cannot leave it at that, for the capabilities approach, as has been said, suffers from a serious justificatory problem. The last quotation already indicates that Nussbaum is firmly convinced that each society has to make sure that each of its members possesses the entire set of capabilities. Furthermore, she is convinced that achievement of this

35 All quotations taken from: M. Nussbaum, *Women and Human Development: The Capabilities Approach* (Cambridge: Cambridge University Press, 2000), 78–80.

36 M. Nussbaum, *Frontiers of Justice: Disability, Nationality, Species Membership* (Cambridge, London: The Belknap Press of Harvard University Press, 2006), 79.

37 Nussbaum, *Frontiers of Justice*, 75.

goal can be equated with the implementation of social justice. More particularly, Nussbaum holds that capabilities constitute *political entitlements,* so that a government is morally obligated to create social conditions within which each citizen has these capabilities at his or her disposal.[38] But this conclusion is far from evident. From the very fact that humans are in need of capabilities follows by no means automatically that they are entitled to them. As David Hume already pointed out, from a simple 'is' no 'ought' can be deduced.[39] So Nussbaum's assumption that a societal state of affairs in which every human possesses the whole set of capabilities can readily be identified with social justice, is, to say the least, insufficiently justified.

Recently, Rutger Claassen and Marcus Düwell have put their finger on this weak point of the capabilities approach.[40] Though they acknowledge that Nussbaum basically recognizes the problem, they rightly hold that she eventually fails to provide a satisfactory solution. Yet Claassen and Düwell do not only reveal an essential problem of the approach, they also make a promising suggestion of how to overcome it. For this purpose, they refer to Alan Gewirth's ethical account, which intends to demonstrate that every human being has undeniable moral rights to the whole set of capabilities or, as Gewirth puts it, to the 'preconditions of human action'. So if Gewirth indeed has succeeded in demonstrating this and if he, moreover, actually defines the content of 'preconditions of human action' in a way that resembles the content of Nussbaum's capabilities, the justificatory problem has in fact been resolved. Hence the question is: How does Gewirth undertake to demonstrate that every human being has undeniable moral rights to the preconditions of action?

In a nutshell, Gewirth's argument can be spelled out as follows.[41] His point of departure is a minimalistic concept of human action which he defines as voluntary and purposive behavior. The method to be employed is called the 'dialectically necessary method', because it seeks to unfold the propositions that each agent necessarily has to accept due to the simple fact that he or she is an agent, or a prospective purposive agent.[42] In a first step, Gewirth then shows that an agent, by pain of self-contradiction, has to affirm that he or she is in *necessary need of all the freedoms and goods* required

38 Nussbaum, *Frontiers of Justice*, 182: "[...] that these capabilities can be agreed by reasonable citizens to be important prerequisites of reasonable conceptions of human flourishing, in connection with the political conception of the person as a political animal, both needy and dignified; and thus these are good bases for an idea of basic political entitlements in a just society."

39 D. Hume, *A Treatise of Human Nature* (Mineola: Dover Publications, 2003), 334.

40 R. Claassen and M. Düwell, "The Foundations of the Capability Theory: Comparing Nussbaum and Gewirth," *Ethical Theory and Moral Practice* 16 (2013): 493–510.

41 A. Gewirth, *Reason and Morality* (Chicago: Chicago University Press, 1978).

42 Gewirth, *Reason and Morality*, 42–47.

to act and to act successfully. If an agent were to deny this, he or she would also deny being an agent, because denying is already an action and thus confirms him or her to be an agent. In the following step, Gewirth demonstrates why every agent necessarily has to claim *rights* to the preconditions of action for himself or herself. For if the agent refused to claim such rights for himself or herself, he or she would admit that others are at least permitted to interfere with his or her preconditions of action. Such a concession, however, contradicts the outcome of the first step, namely that he or she necessarily needs these freedoms and goods. In the last step a logical *universalization* is applied. If every agent necessarily has to claim rights for himself or herself simply because he or she is an agent, he or she is logically committed to grant these rights to every other agent, too. Consequently, Gewirth's argumentation ends up in a supreme moral principle which says: '*Act in accord with the generic rights of your recipients as well as of yourself.*'[43]

Of course, the subtleties of this moral theory, the objections to it as well as the corresponding responses cannot be spelled out here in detail.[44] Nevertheless, it should be clear that Gewirth makes a serious attempt to overcome the justificatory problem of, among other things, the capabilities approach. A closer look at Gewirth's later publication also reveals a striking resemblance between his approach and the capabilities approach with regard to content. In *The Community of Rights*, for instance, he unfolds the different steps of an 'economic biography' that departs from a state of absolute poverty and leads to a situation in which all members of a society can participate in its political and economic life unrestrictedly.[45] In his last book, he explicitly states that 'capacity-fulfillment' – next to 'aspiration fulfillment' – must be seen as a necessary aspect of a good life.[46] From all this we may conclude that Gewirth does not resolve an arbitrary justificatory problem but the exact justificatory problem the capabilities approach is suffering from. We have also observed a considerable overlap between the objectives of the capabilities approach and the objectives that public theology seeks to achieve before it can launch its apologetic endeavor. Therefore, Gewirth's moral theory can indeed be taken as the justificatory basis of the public theological attempt to transform the public communication conditions in such a way as to enable every human being to discursively examine truth claims pertaining to issues of ultimate significance, to take an auton-

43 Gewirth, *Reason and Morality*, 135.

44 D. Beyleveld, *The Dialectical Necessity of Morality: An Analysis and Defense of Alan Gewirth's Argument to the Principle of Generic Consistency* (Chicago: University of Chicago Press, 1991); Klaus Steigleder, *Grundlegung der normativen Ethik: Der Ansatz von Alan Gewirth* (München: Alber, 1999); P. Bauhn (ed.), *Gewirthian Perspectives* (London: Routledge, 2016).

45 A. Gewirth, *The Community of Rights* (Chicago: Chicago University Press, 1996).

46 A. Gewirth, *Self-Fulfillment* (Princeton: Princeton University Press, 1998), 107–158.

omous decision, and to assess the plausibility of a faith praxis emerging from a specific existential decision on what is ultimately significant. Since the capabilities approach has also shown – and Gewirth absolutely confirms this – that such an objective cannot be pursued without simultaneous striving for social justice, the subsidiary task of public theology can indeed be defined as promoting social justice.

At the end of this paper we thus may summarize that (1) from the perspective of public theology, *the quality of life* is determined by the degree to which it is possible for everyone (a) to publicly examine universal truth claims concerning ultimate significance; (b) to take an unforced existential decision about what is ultimately significant; and (c) to be sensitive to a faith praxis that bears witness to such an existential decision. The degree to which these prerequisites are met defines the degree to which public theology can perform its genuine tasks of apologetic discourse and witnessing. (2) Since these prerequisites can be equated with a thick notion of social justice, public theology regards *socially just conditions* as essential for the quality of life. (3) In this light, public theology eventually *suggests to enhance the quality of life* through fighting any form of anthropological reductionism and to struggle for social justice. It has been shown that public theology is completely justified in employing this definition, in applying these standards, and in making these suggestions. Likewise, it has been shown that public theology is not the only actor pursuing the goal of social justice.

Bibliography

Apel, K.-O., *Auseinandersetzungen: In Erprobung des transzendentalpragmatischen Ansatzes*. Frankfurt: Suhrkamp, 1998.

Bauhn, P. (ed.), *Gewirthian Perspectives*. London: Routledge, 2016.

Beyleveld, D., *The Dialectical Necessity of Morality: An Analysis and Defense of Alan Gewirth's Argument to the Principle of Generic Consistency*. Chicago: University of Chicago Press, 1991.

Breitenberg Jr., H., "What is Public Theology?" In *Public Theology for a Global Society: Essays in Honor of Max L. Stackhouse*, edited by D.K. Hainsworth and S. Paeth, 3–17. Grand Rapids: Eerdmans, 2011.

Certeau, M. de, *The Practice of Everyday Life*. Translated by S.F. Rendall. Berkeley: University of California Press, 1988.

Claassen, R. and M. Düwell, "The Foundations of the Capability Theory: Comparing Nussbaum and Gewirth." In *Ethical Theory and Moral Practice* 16 (2013): 493–510.

Dawkins, R., *The Selfish Gene*. Oxford: Oxford University Press, 2006.

Gewirth, A., *Reason and Morality*. Chicago: Chicago University Press, 1978.

—, *Self-Fulfillment*. Princeton: Princeton University Press, 1998.

—, *The Community of Rights*. Chicago: Chicago University Press, 1996.

Graham, E., *Between a Rock and a Hard Place: Public Theology in a Post-Secular Age*. London: SCM Press, 2013.

Habermas, J., *Theorie des kommunikativen Handelns, Bd 1: Handlungsrationalität und gesellschaftliche Rationalisierung and Bd. 2: Zur Kritik der funktionalistischen Vernunft*. Frankfurt: Suhrkamp, 1981.

—, *Zwischen Naturalismus und Religion: Philosophische Aufsätze*. Frankfurt: Suhrkamp, 2005.

Hauerwas, S., *A Community of Character: Toward a Constructive Christian Social Ethic*. Notre Dame: University of Notre Dame Press, 1991.

Hofstetter, Y., *Sie wissen alles: Wie intelligente Maschinen in unser Leben eindringen und warum wir für unsere Freiheit kämpfen müssen*. München: Bertelsmann, 2014.

Höhne, F., *Öffentliche Theologie: Begriffsgeschichte und Grundfragen*. Leipzig: Evangelische Verlagsanstalt, 2015.

Hübenthal, C., "Eén taak met twee speerpunten: Over kerkelijke en publieke theologie." In *Verdeelde wijsheid: Tussen Kerk en academische theologie*, edited by F. Bosman and H. Goris, 135–153. Nijmegen: Valkhof, 2014.

—, *Moderne orthodoxie: Verdediging van een denkvorm voor de publieke theologie* (Nijmegen: Radboud Universiteit, 2015).

Hume, D., *A Treatise of Human Nature*. Mineola: Dover Publications, 2003.

Kim, S., *Theology in the Public Square: Public Theology as a Catalyst for Open Debate*. London: SCM Press, 2011.

Laura, Ronald S., et al., *The New Social Disease: From High Tech Depersonalization to Survival of Soul*. Lanham: University Press of America, 2008.

Luhmann, N., *Die Religion der Gesellschaft*. Frankfurt: Suhrkamp, 2000.

—, *Funktion der Religion*. Frankfurt: Suhrkamp, 1977.

—, *Soziale Systeme: Grundriß einer allgemeinen Theorie*. Frankfurt: Suhrkamp, 1984.

Mathewes, C., *A Theology of Public Life*. Cambridge: Cambridge University Press, 2007.

Nagel, T., *Mind and Cosmos: Why the Materialist Neo-Darwinian Conception of Nature is Almost Certainly False*. Oxford: Oxford University Press, 2012.

Nussbaum, M., "Aristotle on Human Nature and the Foundation of Ethics." In *Mind and Ethics: Essays on the Ethical Philosophy of Bernard Williams*, edited by J.E.G. Altham and R. Harrison, 86–131. Cambridge: Cambridge University Press, 1995.

—, *Frontiers of Justice: Disability, Nationality, Species Membership*. Cambridge, London: The Belknap Press of Harvard University Press, 2006.

—, *Women and Human Development: The Capabilities Approach*. Cambridge: Cambridge University Press, 2000.

— and A. Sen (eds.), *The Quality of Life*. Oxford: Clarendon Press 1993.

Picketty, T., *Capital in the Twenty-First Century*. Translated by Arthur Goldhammer. Cambridge: The Belknap Press of Harvard University Press, 2014.

Roth, G., *Fühlen, Denken, Handeln: Wie das Gehirn unser Verhalten steuert*. Frankfurt: Suhrkamp, 2001.

Sandel, M.J., *What Money Can't Buy: The Moral Limits of the Markets*. New York: Farrar, Strauss and Giroux, 2012.

Schirrmacher, F., *Payback: Warum wir im Informationszeitalter gezwungen sind zu tun, was wir nicht tun wollen, und wie wir die Kontrolle über unser Denken zurückgewinnen*. München: Karl Blessing Verlag, 2009.

Sedlácek, T., *Economics of Good and Evil: The Quest for Economic Meaning from Gilgamesh to Wall Street*. New York: Oxford University Press, 2011.

Singer, W., *Ein neues Menschenbild? Gespräche über Hirnforschung*. Frankfurt: Suhrkamp, 2003.

Skidelsky, E. and R., *How Much is Enough? The Love of Money, and the Case for the Good Life*. London: Allen Lane, 2012.

Stackhouse, M.L. *Globalization and Grace: God and Globalization 4*. New York: Continuum, 2007.

Steigleder, K., *Grundlegung der normativen Ethik: Der Ansatz von Alan Gewirth*. München: Alber, 1999.

Streeck, W., *Gekaufte Zeit: Die vertagte Krise des demokratischen Kapitalismus*. Berlin: Suhrkamp, 2013.

Thiel, J.E., *Nonfoundationalism*. Minneapolis: Fortress Press, 1994.

Ulrich, P., *Integrative Economic Ethics: Foundations of a Civilized Market Economy*. Cambridge: Cambridge University Press, 2006.

Vanhoozer, K., "Theology and the Condition of Postmodernity: A Report on Knowledge (of God)." In *The Cambridge Companion to Postmodern Theology*, edited by K. Vanhoozer, 3–25. Cambridge: Cambridge University Press, 2003.

THE QUEST FOR FULLNESS OF LIFE IN CONTEXTS OF SOCIETAL RENEWAL: A PERSPECTIVE FROM SPIRITUALITY STUDIES

Elisabeth Hense

Abstract

Spirituality understood as searching for quality of life, as "following intuitions that can lead to fullness of life"[1] is involved with human estimations and valuations. Human beings sense that alternative ways of living are possible, sense that certain activities or conditions may be fuller, richer, deeper, more inspiring, more admirable and more worthwhile than others. Although we all sense the possibility of alternative ways of living, we do not all have the same perspective on these ways nor do we all take the same decisions. Our esteem and appreciation inspire our factual discernments and choices. However, we realize that these decisions remain tentative and cannot be conceived as absolute. Any preference about what might be understood by 'fullness of life' remains subject to further critical reflection and evaluation. Scholarship in Christian spirituality has developed certain criteria for this reflection and evaluation during the last century and may need to think about further criteria in these days. These criteria can be seen as benchmarks within Christian spirituality and as points of reference in the debate of Christian theology with other worldviews. In addition to criteria of adequacy and criteria of appropriateness which have already been widely agreed upon in Christian spirituality, there might be a need for criteria of respondence, when quality of life is at stake.

I will first give a short introduction to spirituality studies as a normative discipline within Catholic theology and will explain what is meant by the aforementioned criteria for life enhancing spirituality. I will then answer the following questions: (a) What is seen as quality of life in spirituality studies?, (b) In what human conditions and practices do spirituality studies detect quality of life?, and (c) What suggestions do spirituality studies

1 Cf. E. Hense, "Present-day Spiritualities in Confessional, Popular, Professional and Aesthetic Contexts. Contrasts or Overlap?" in *Present-Day Spiritualities. Contrasts and Overlaps* (eds. E. Hense, F. Jespers and P. Nissen; Leiden: Brill, 2014), 1–17.

give in order to enhance these conditions and practices? I will conclude with some reflections on current initiatives of societal renewal concerning issues of food, care and money in the Netherlands, answering the questions whether we may consider these current forms of societal renewal as spirituality driven and whether spirituality is needed for these forms of societal renewal.

Introduction

Spirituality studies is the youngest subject of time-honored Catholic theology programs and is about to meet its first centennial.[2] The first chair of spirituality studies was established at the University of St. Thomas of Aquinas (Angelicum) in Rome in 1917. The holder of this chair was Reginald Garrigou-Lagrange, who studied systematic aspects of the spiritual path. In the same year, Benedict XV welcomed spirituality studies as important to the education of priests to prepare them for their duties as spiritual guides. From the very beginning of the Christian tradition, spiritual guidance means to accompany people to a fuller, richer, deeper, more inspiring, more worthwhile life. However, it was only at the beginning of the 20th century that training for this task became part of the study program.[3] Since the constitution *Deus scientiarum Dominus*, published in 1931 under Pius XI, spirituality studies has been rated as one of the ordinary subjects of theology programs.[4] This change was made, as Karl Rahner commented, because "spirituality should not only be a matter of practical experience, but should also be permeated by such critical reflection which we call scholarship".[5] After Vaticanum II (the second Vatican Council), spirituality studies were combined with ethics. In 1979, the constitution *Sapientia Christiana*, issued under John Paul II, spoke about *Theologia moralis et spiritualis*, classifying this subject immediately after dogmatic theology at the fourth position in the list of theological subjects.[6] Not everybody appreciated this position of

2 Cf. J. Weismayer, "Theologie und Spiritualität," in *Lasst euch vom Geist erfüllen (Eph 5,18). Beiträge zur Spiritualität* (Münster: Lit, 2001), 289–306; J. Weismayer, *Leben in Fülle, Zur Geschichte und Theologie christlicher Spiritualität* (Innsbruck-Wien: Tyrolia-Verlag, 1983), 17; O. Steggink and K. Waaijman, *Spiritualiteit en Mystiek* (Nijmegen: Uitgeverij B. Gottmer, 1985), 121–123; K. Waaijman, *Spiritualiteit* (Kampen: Kok, 2000), 390–394.

3 Congregatio de Seminariis et Studiorum Universitatibus, *Enchiridion Clericorum: Documenta Ecclesiae sacrorum alumnis instituendis* (Rome: Typis Polyglottis Vaticanis and Herder, 1938) no. 1110 and 1135.

4 Pope Pius XI, "Constitutio Apostolica Deus scientiarum Dominus," *AAS* 23 (1931): 241–260.

5 M. Viller and K. Rahner, *Aszese und Mystik in der Väterzeit* (Freiburg-Basel-Wien: Herder, 1989), 17.

6 Pope John Paul II, "Constitutio Apostolica Sapientia Christiana," *AAS* 71 (1979): 513.

spirituality studies. Especially some German theologians discussed an alternative meaning of this subject: Hans Urs von Balthasar considered spirituality studies as the subjective side of dogmatics,[7] Karl Rahner emphasized the anthropological dimension of spirituality,[8] and Joseph Sudbrack saw spirituality studies as a kind of crosspiece of theology which is connected to all other theological disciplines.[9]

Whatever is accepted as a suitable position of spirituality studies within the canon of theological disciplines, one thing is undisputed: Christian spirituality studies is viewed as a normative discipline. As regards the question of what criteria we have to decide what can be seen as Christian spirituality contributing to quality of life, many scholars sympathize with David Tracy, who speaks about criteria of adequacy and criteria of appropriateness.[10] Philip Sheldrake summarizes these criteria in his brief history of Christian Spirituality very sharply when he says: "Tracy suggests three broad criteria of adequacy. First, every religious interpretation of experience needs to be humanly meaningful. That is, it must be adequately rooted in common human experience. Second, the religious understanding of experience should be intellectually coherent. Third, any spiritual tradition needs to throw light on the underlying conditions of life. In other words, does it have anything to say about whether our human confidence in life is actually worthwhile?"[11] According to Tracy these criteria of adequacy should be applied to the first source of Christian spirituality, that is, "common human experience".[12] In current debates, these criteria can be helpful to focus on healthy and legally acceptable forms of spirituality, taking into account the results of scientific research and current developments in social spheres. The other source of Christian spirituality is "the Christian fact".[13] This source should be examined by criteria of appropriateness. Sheldrake recaps them as follows: the "understanding of Christian spirituality must relate in some way to the classic Christian beliefs. (...) Within the limits of legitimate diversity and of valid emphases, healthy spiritualities should generally reflect the whole Christian gospel rather than be selective in an unbalanced way. (...) Christian spirituality of its nature cannot avoid the question of tradition. So, in a particular spirituality, what is the role of scrip-

7 H.U. von Balthasar, "Spiritualität," *Geist und Leben* 31 (1958): 340–352.

8 K. Rahner, "Über den Versuch eines Aufrisses einer Dogmatik," *Schriften zur Theologie I* (Einsiedeln: Benziger, 1967): 9–47.

9 J. Sudbrack, "Möglichkeiten einer Theologie des Geistlichen Lebens," *Trierer Theologische Zeitschrift* 78 (1969): 49–59 (55).

10 D. Tracy, *Blessed Rage for Order* (New York: Seabury Press, 1975), 64–87.

11 P. Sheldrake, *Spirituality: a Brief History* (Malden-Oxford: Wiley-Blackwell, 2013), 19.

12 Tracy, *Blessed Rage for Order*, 64.

13 Ibid.

ture and of the wider tradition? Finally, an important question is whether a spiritual tradition has a developed sense of ultimate human purpose and destiny (what is known as eschatology), and specifically one that encourages an appropriate balance between 'the now' and 'the not yet'."[14]

Whereas criteria of appropriateness are used to give evidence of the Christian identity of a certain form of spirituality, criteria of adequacy are deployed to scrutinize the *aggiornamento* of this form of spirituality. The question, then, is not whether a concrete form of spirituality proves to be Christian, but whether this form proves to be Christian in accordance with "generally accepted developments in human knowledge".[15] Criteria of adequacy may potentially be applied to all forms of spirituality, whether Christian, Jewish, Muslim, Buddhist or otherwise.

In the following I argue that another set of criteria is needed to judge Christian spirituality and potentially all forms of spirituality, when quality of life is at stake. I call this third set of criteria 'criteria of respondence' and I understand them as an instrument to ascertain that a form of spirituality responds to the search for improvement of life in a specific socio-cultural context. Experiences of human suffering, shortcoming, and limitation are the starting point here. Each socio-cultural situation has its own challenges, its own problems, its own threats which we have to cope with. Forms of spirituality may contribute to resolve the stresses of a society and to transform its poor conditions and practices into more desirable ones. Real human needs are the source of these forms of spirituality. When something essential is missing, certain conditions feel wrong, or people suffer from miserable practices, looking for quality of life means to relate to this situation and to search for improvement in consonance with the possibilities given at that particular time and place. Forms of spirituality which have the ambition to contribute to the human search for quality of life will not be satisfied with being Christian or being in accordance with generally accepted developments in human knowledge. They also want to transform societies and make them part of a better world.

What is seen as quality of life in spirituality studies?

The way of living that is most appreciated in Christian spiritual tradition is what the mystic Jan of Ruusbroec called 'common life' (*ghemene leven*).[16] By 'common life' Ruusbroec meant a kind of flow between being absorbed in

14 Sheldrake, *Spirituality: a Brief History*, 19–20.

15 Ibid., 19.

16 J. van Ruusbroec, *Vanden blinckenden steen* (ed. G. de Baere; Tielt/Turnhout: Brepols, 1991), 181–182.

divine love at certain times and going out in love and mercy of one's neighbors and the world at other times. Ruusbroec described these two kinds of love as one unified graceful experience. It certainly was not a heavy duty which one had to fulfil toward God and toward one's neighbors. Both kinds of love were attractive to Ruusbroec's mind: being immersed in divine love was felt as a kind of refreshment for the self that strengthens it to go out to its neighbors to minister to their needs. Loving one's neighbors meant to enjoy human connectedness, to realize the good things of life, and to build up a better world. The answer to the question which side of the flow is the better one would not be 'refreshment in contemplation'. Works of mercy were seen as the better option and should be preferred to contemplative prayer when one is confronted with human needs. That is because God is loved in each work of mercy too. The Christian tradition has always rejected a one-sided contemplative life as quietist: that such a life fails not only one's neighbor but also God, who wants to be loved in his creatures.

Whereas Christian spirituality has always tried to find a balance between these two loves, social engagement and the practical service to people in need seems to have become more explicit in the statutes of congregations only from the 17th century onwards. Outstanding personalities were John Baptist de la Salle (1651–1719), who founded the congregation of teaching brothers; Vincent de Paul (1580–1660) and Louise de Marillac (1591–1660), who worked for orphans, slaves, victims of wars and the sick; and Francis de Sales (1567–1622) and Jeanne de Chantal (1572–1641), who assisted their fellows in need. Dedication to the distressed was naturally practiced along with dedication to God: personal prayer, spiritual conversation and the liturgical celebrations of the church remained essential and were still experienced as important moments of care of the self. Without these spiritual moments the self would dry up and get exhausted.

During the 20th century, however, it wasn't obvious any longer to experience prayer and contemplation as adequate forms of care of the self. More secular forms of care of the self as already known in ancient Greek as *epimelesthai sauto* ('to take care of yourself') revived in Western societies. Michel de Foucault pointed out that these practices were a type of "technologies of the self, which permit individuals to effect by their own means or with the help of others a certain number of operations on their own bodies and souls, thoughts, conduct, and way of being, so as to transform themselves in order to attain a certain state of happiness, purity, wisdom, perfection, or immortality".[17] Examples of these technologies of the self as described by Michel de Foucault are forms of ascesis (such as doing challenging sports, eating simple meals) or forms of coaching and spiritual guidance (such as

17 M. de Foucault, *Technologies of the Self* (eds. L.H. Martin, H. Gutman and P.H. Hutton; Amherst, Massachusetts: University of Massachusetts Press, 1988), 18.

speaking confidentially about one's own feelings and experiences, taking time for introspection). These practices still seem to be relevant to people who are responding to challenging situations. Thus quality of life continues to have these two sides: improvement of living conditions for the needy or those at the margins, and also attainment of a certain "state of happiness, purity, wisdom, perfection, or immortality" for those dedicating themselves to resolve the stresses of the needy and those at the margins. Insomuch this state is received by responding to real human problems, we can ascertain that a form of spirituality could indeed be seen as 'common life' in the sense attributed to this term by Ruusbroec.

In what human conditions and practices do spirituality studies detect quality of life?

In the long spiritual tradition of Christianity we can find many fascinating outlines of what is meant by improvement of 'common life'. Central to these outlines seems to be works of mercy. Important leaders of the Christian communities have therefore called attention to works of mercy time and again. Recently, Walter Kasper reasserted the key role of mercy in Biblical times and its function as a benchmark in Church practices of our times.[18] The Catechism (no. 2447) lists seven spiritual and seven corporal works of mercy. The spiritual works of mercy are:

"To admonish the sinner, to instruct the ignorant, to counsel the doubtful, to comfort the sorrowful, to bear wrongs patiently, to forgive all injuries, and to pray for the living and the dead".

In our days, to admonish the sinner can be understood as to awaken people about personal and societal structures of injustice and shortcomings. To instruct the ignorant signifies the requirement for training and instruction as to how we might work for something better than money. Because general standards for what it means to be a human seem to be lost in these times, the many doubtful should be advised about present-day possibilities for a better world so as not to let them fall into cynicism. The sorrowful should be strengthened when they have to cope with the 'wicked problems' of our days – that is, a mixture of social, economic, and environmental problems, such as unemployment, poverty and rising inequality, water and food shortages, increased numbers of political and economic refugees, and exhaus-

18 W. Kasper, *Barmherzigkeit, Grundbegriff des Evangeliums. Schlüssel christlichen Lebens* (Freiburg: Herder, 2012). Hereinafter, references to the Catechism follow Kasper's phrasing.

tion of natural resources.[19] To bear troublemakers and to forgive all injuries seem especially important in our pluralistic world, which sees many people under pressure or failing in their duties, feeling incapable of mutual tolerance. The Catechism enumerates the following corporal works of mercy:

"To feed the hungry, to give drink to the thirsty, to clothe the naked, to ransom the captive, to harbor the harborless, to visit the sick, and to bury the dead".

When we think about growing groups of people who have to live in poverty – especially children are more likely to belong to lower social classes – or when we think about those who don't have access to clean water or enough nourishment, those who come in small boats across the Mediterranean, those huge numbers of people who are captured in modern slavery etc., we realize that corporal works of mercy are also very essential in our times.

Practicing works of mercy is considered salutary to the whole body of a community. Those who need mercy in some respect at certain moments may be the ones who apply mercy in other respects at other moments. All works of mercy are interconnected with each other: each one of them supports the others. The spiritual ones become powerful through the corporal one's and vice versa. Together, works of mercy aim at improving the quality of life of each member of the community in an encompassing manner. This does not mean, though, that experiences of human suffering, shortcoming, and limitation will be driven away, but means that we have a repertoire enabling us to respond to these experiences. Jürgen Habermas considers such a repertoire as a "key resource for the creation of meaning and identity". [20] He says that "religious traditions have a special power to articulate moral intuitions, especially with regard to vulnerable forms of communal life". Not only Christians can pick up these intuitions; they are available to everybody, but those who take care of themselves are probably the only ones who are able to persevere, that is, to carry on with their works of mercy in the face of setbacks and complicated circumstances.

19 J. Conklin, *Dialogue Mapping: Building Shared Understanding of Wicked Problems* (Chichester: Wiley & Sons Ltd., 2006).

20 J. Habermas, "Religion in the Public Sphere," *European Journal of Philosophy* 14,1 (2006): 1–25.

What suggestions do spirituality studies give in order to enhance these conditions and practices?

Spirituality studies concentrate on works of mercy inspired by any religious or secular tradition and want to promote them right across the width of our society. By works of mercy we try to reshape our living together and to effect the survival of the needy and those at the margins. However, life is so complicated in our present world that we cannot practice strong works of mercy without sufficient knowledge about their practical implementation. The disciplines of sociology, management studies, and economics have joined our thinking about poor conditions such as poverty, low educational levels, exposedness to violence or environmental pollution etc. and they try to translate our concerns into practicable methods for improvement. In order to really enhance the quality of life in our times, works of mercy should show an indivisible unity of the spiritual-ethical urge for the 'common life' and the technical realization of it. This is why the discipline of spirituality studies looks for interdisciplinary approaches to enhance living conditions and practices. It is advantageous that other disciplines also share this concern. The sociologist Gabriel van den Brink[21], for example, conducted research into the spiritual motives and values in social sectors as diverse as medical care, the police force, sports, banking etc. in the Netherlands. He found that quite a lot of idealism can be found in these sectors. Although Van den Brink does not speak about works of mercy, such works were in fact part of what he found in the explored societal sectors. The current social engagement in these sectors offers a prospect of hope to everybody who does not want to reconcile himself/herself to the dominant cynical worldview in the Western world. Another scholar, the economist Niko Paech[22], wants to clear the way for more sustainability with regard to water and food, money, raw materials etc. He has thought about the many problems caused by the dogma of economic growth. Due to this dogma, many people in our world hunger and thirst, not only in the physical sense, but also in a figurative sense, after justice. Paech and others are critical of this situation and, looking for solutions to these problems, have actually advocated something similar to works of mercy, although without labeling them as such.

21 G. van den Brink, *De Lage Landen en het hogere. De betekenis van geestelijke beginselen in het moderne bestaan* (Amsterdam: University of Amsterdam Press, 2012).

22 N. Paech, "Wachstum – Aufstieg und Fall eines Dogmas," in *Universitas* 68 (2013): 26–35; N. Paech, *Befreiung vom Überfluss* (München: Oekom Verlag, 2012).

Current forms of societal renewal with regard to food, care, and money in the Netherlands

The current demand for societal renewal in the Netherlands confronts us with many intriguing topics, including questions such as: 'How do we treat food?', 'How do we want to reshape our care systems?', and 'How do we want to design our money?' Some of our contemporaries respond to these problems with promising projects. They do not want to wait for solutions from 'above', but claim that they can contribute from 'below'. I have interviewed nine initiators of such projects in 2013; three of them play a part in new ways of supplying food, three are concerned with new policies on healthcare, and three have come up with interesting ideas about alternative money systems. Details about these initiatives and an analysis of their central spiritual features are given elsewhere.[23] I will confine myself here to brief portraits of the nine initiatives.

1. Uit Je Eigen Stad (From your own town).[24]

In many Dutch cities human beings have become almost completely detached from food production, and food chains are precarious and non-transparent. These conditions have led to uncertainties about the quality of food, workplaces and the environment. With their city farm *From your own town* in Rotterdam, Huibert de Leede and Johan Bosman show that there are alternatives. By combining their farm with a shop, a conference room and a restaurant, they have embedded food production in other activities, showing the interdependence of various food variables. People start to realize where their food comes from and how it is cultivated; they get information about how to grow their own food; and they can taste new recipes with food from their own region. Huibert and Johan produce a great diversity of food – more than fifty vegetables – at prices people can afford and, besides agriculture, they also keep livestock – chickens, pigs and fish. By combining the cycles of production and waste in agriculture and livestock farming, they have made visible the natural abundance of food resources in Rotterdam. Huibert and Johan have set up their farm on an ugly abandoned rail yard in the city and so transformed a neglected part of

[23] E. Hense, *Vernieuwingsinitiatieven rond eten, zorg en geld in Nederland – Een kwestie van spiritualiteit* (Amsterdam: VU University Press, 2015).

[24] Hense, E. (Radboud Universiteit Nijmegen) (2013): *Data Spiritualiteit en Maatschappelijke Vernieuwing, interview met H. de Leede (initiatief Uit Je Eigen Stad).* DANS. www.dx.doi.org/10.17026/dans-x3a-76ks. See also "Uit je eigen stad," www.uitjeeigenstad.nl.

the city into a pleasant environment where people like to relax and to enjoy a luxuriant garden. All these aspects are part of the new sense of quality of life in Dutch cities.[25]

2. Hotspot Hutspot (Hot spot Hodge-podge).[26]

Many children in disadvantaged neighborhoods in Rotterdam struggle with low self-esteem. Bob Richters wants to give them a safe and happy place to develop themselves and to get positive experiences. He has set up small restaurants, called *Hot spot Hodge-podge*, where children can help with the growing of vegetables and with cooking and dishing up meals for their guests. Children can do so free of obligations; they can take part just for pleasure. So the restaurants promote children's development, bring them joy and also provide them with healthy meals. Together with their guests, the children build up an inclusive community. Bob Richters does not need huge amounts of money to carry out this project. From the boxes to grow vegetables to the furniture and crockery in the restaurants – he works with second-hand materials as much as possible. The overall look of the restaurants is nevertheless very trendy and vital because of well-chosen features; he goes for biological cultivation, a professional kitchen with new materials, nice chef's jackets and aprons for the children, a huge window that is decorated attractively, a nice color scheme and surprising dishes. *Hot spot Hodge-podge* creates room for resilience of marginalized children and thereby for more quality of communal life in their neighborhoods.

3. Thuisafgehaald (Shareyourmeal).[27]

This platform serving all parts of the Netherlands brings supply and demand of home-cooked meals directly together. The community of this platform wishes to avoid intermediary trade and to share meals without material profit. Many contemporaries only know this practice within their families and circles of friends. People living in the same street, neighbor-

25 C. Bronsveld, *Onze oogst. Sociale effecten van Rotterdamse stadslandbouwprojecten* (Rotterdam: Trichis, 2014).

26 Hense, E. (Radboud Universiteit Nijmegen) (2013): *Data Spiritualiteit en Maatschappelijke Vernieuwing, interview met B. Richters (over het initiatief Hotspot Hutspot).* DANS. www.dx.doi.org/10.17026/dans-24j-7c4m. See also "Hotspot Hutspot," www.hotspothutspot.nl.

27 Hense, E. (Radboud Universiteit Nijmegen) (2013): *Data Spiritualiteit en Maatschappelijke Vernieuwing, interview met M. Hart (over het initiatief Thuisafgehaald).* DANS. www.dx.doi.org/10.17026/dans-zhh-bd6u. See also "Thuisafgehaald, maaltijden delen met je buren," www.thuisafgehaald.nl.

hood or part of town have practically disappeared from most people's social networks. With this platform they come back in a surprising and casual manner. They do not only share meals, but the social and ecological side-effects often seem even more important and reflect different trends in society: giving more attention to local food and natural food; reduced food waste; preparing and sharing home-cooked meals; and looking for community in a contemporary manner. The platform focuses on sharing food, but quietly also wants to do something for a better world. It does not unfold ethical debates about food, but simply provides new possibilities for sharing. Co-founder Marieke Hart speaks about 'playful, sensible' dealing with food. The focus is on the desires and interests of people, but incidentally the platform also contributes to building up an inclusive society with special attention for people at the margins who cannot cook their own meals or who feel lonesome and useless.

4. Zorgcoöperatie Hoogeloon (Hoogeloon Care Cooperation).[28]

Certain values of the Dutch care system which are appreciated by modern citizens are under pressure. Especially self-determination, being in charge of one's own life, hominess, and security in one's own social environment are threatened. Elderly and disabled people are forced to move to big health care institutions in other places than where they used to live. The health care system is quite bureaucratic and unwieldy with the result that many people have problems to find their way. For example, people have to fill in many forms in order to get a wheeled walker, 'a rollator', or a mobility scooter. Moreover, client files are extensive and there are many rules to be followed. The Hoogeloon Care Cooperation, which is active in the Dutch village of Hoogeloon, takes an alternative view on care and refuses to accept these practices. It aims to preserve care nearby, to reduce the rules in the health care system, and to realize small-scale care. In this way the cooperation tries to retain self-determination, hominess and security for everyone. This is however only possible with the help of many dedicated volunteers and special efforts from the local government and the inhabitants of the village. According to those concerned, these efforts are paying off very well, providing a much higher quality of life to nearly every family in the village.

[28] Hense, E. (Radboud Universiteit Nijmegen) (2013): *Data Spiritualiteit en Maatschappelijke Vernieuwing, interview met J. van der Heijden (over het initiatief De Zorgcoöperatie Hogeloon).* DANS. www.dx.doi.org/10.17026/dans-xyp-ghu8. See also "Zorgcoöperatie Hoogeloon," www.zorgcooperatie.nl.

5. Unal zorg (Unal Care).[29]

This institution for health care of multi-problem families in Amsterdam aims at self-supporting functioning of minor disabled persons and their families, often from a migrant background. The care provided is strongly individualized and carefully geared to the limited possibilities of the individual clients. Each social worker tailors himself/herself to the needs of his/her clients and ensures appropriate security of his/her clients in order to enhance their self-development. Central to the employees of *Unal Care* are personal care of their clients, practical help, the improvement of communication between family members, and the increase of competencies of their clients. A big challenge in this kind of work is the fact that one does not know what exactly is the problem when one starts to work with a family. The common strategy – defining the problem, following well-established work practices and achieving the objectives – is of no use in these complicated cases. The social worker actually has to work the other way round; he/she becomes aware of what is wrong only while exploring a way out of the difficulties. Only open-end strategies appear suitable to improve the complex situations of multi-problem families.

6. Eigen Kracht Centrale (Own Strength Centre).[30]

The *Own Strength Centre* advocates that citizens who are in serious trouble should first be encouraged to use the strengths of their own private circle to solve their problems before calling in professional assistance. To make your own plan with the members of your family, your friends, your neighbors and members of your church community or your club is a world-wide strategy to overcome your troubles. But can this elementary strategy also work for children and youth in contact with children and youth services? Are they good observers of their own lives and are they able to think about adequate plans to improve their circumstances? Yes, says Fiet van Beek, director of the *Own Strength Centre*. Although confusing and unclear conditions may affect their ability to manage their own affairs, children, together with other stakeholders, can participate in the process of finding the right

[29] Hense, E. (Radboud Universiteit Nijmegen) (2013): *Data Spiritualiteit en Maatschappelijke Vernieuwing, interview met A. Disbudak (over het initiatief Unalzorg)*. DANS. www.dx.doi.org/10.17026/dans-z3w-r2d5. See also “Unalzorg, professionele zorg, aandacht voor de culturele achtergrond,” www.unalzorg.nl.

[30] Hense, E. (Radboud Universiteit Nijmegen) (2013): *Data Spiritualiteit en Maatschappelijke Vernieuwing, interview met F. van Beek (over het initiatief De Eigen Kracht Centrale)*. DANS. www.dx.doi.org/10.17026/dans-zqx-e47s. See also “Eigen Kracht Centrale, wij gaan voor samenredzaamheid,” www.eigen-kracht.nl.

solutions to their problems. The *Own Strength Centre* assists people to organize private circle conferences and to set up a plan with the members of their circle. That means more personal self-determination for those who are in trouble, more security in their own private circle, and more coherence in the help offered. Professionals have an assisting and supporting role. They provide relevant information and good arguments, but the person in trouble remains the leader of his or her own plan for change for the better.

7. STRO (Social Trade Organization).[31]

STRO started at the end of the 1960s as one of the first clubs for environmental policy. Since the 1990s, the organization has completely focused on alternative money systems, because it considers our current money system as one of the main factors that cause environmental pollution. Gradually, STRO has also become concerned with the problem of poverty and its connection with ordinary money systems and pollution problems. Up to now, *STRO* has been working on local alternative money systems, but it wants to come up with a universal coin in the near future. Its staff has the ambition to create such an attractive alternative to the current money systems that it will become more and more accepted all over the world and will really change our way of living. They think that they have already found a suitable model, but they still have to test it in the real world. With their coin, they want to contribute to social, cultural, ecological and economic purposes: they want their coin to connect people, to support their cultural contexts, to spare their environments and to keep them out of poverty. Bearing in mind the recent financial crises that caused a lot of trouble in our world and forced many countries to rethink their lifestyles, *STRO* hopes to contribute to a change of life by design, not by disaster.

8. Qoin (Qoin).[32]

This organization shares the concerns of *STRO*. *Qoin* wants to awaken people to the fact that money systems are constructions that are often damaging in social, environmental and cultural respects. But these systems can, and should, be changed; we can think about alternative arrangements. This

[31] Hense, E. (Radboud Universiteit Nijmegen) (2013): *Data Spiritualiteit en Maatschappelijke Vernieuwing, interview met J. Vink (over het initiatief Stichting Stro).* DANS. www.dx.doi.org/10.17026/dans-2b7-jdtz. See also "Social Trade Organisation," www.strohalm.nl.

[32] Hense, E. (Radboud Universiteit Nijmegen) (2013): *Data Spiritualiteit en Maatschappelijke Vernieuwing, interview met E. Kampers (over het initiatief Qoin).* DANS. www.dx.doi.org/10.17026/dans-zuk-sj6t. See also "Qoin, money that matters," www.qoin.org.

mind-blowing idea is spreading at the moment. Many people want to bring back the human aspect into the economy. They want to determine by themselves what is of value to them and they do not want to leave this choice to the highly abstract and obscure logic of stock markets. An alternative coin introduced by a small group of people with a vision of what quality of life might be can bring the actions, attitudes and insights of a whole community in clear harmony with its real values. Alternative money systems thus can help to solve the problems of a society. It becomes possible when people start using their money to establish common values and to realize life-enhancing objectives.

9. Dette Glashouwer's theatre productions (Dette Glashouwer: Money money money).[33]

Theatre producer and performer Dette Glashouwer has presented her own personal struggle with money in a theatrical production. Her autobiographical performances are revealing. She tells her audience how she lost her job because of the financial crisis and how it set her thinking about money. With a sense of humor and thought-provoking brain waves, she discusses many complicated aspects of money and uncovers what problems we have with our money system. Dette calls this form of theatre 'confessional theatre', because she lets spectators take part in her own ethical struggles with money, including her uncomfortable feelings about her retirement fund, the products she buys, the questionable wasting of energy and materials. Dette also combines her performances with shareholder meetings, led by the economist Helen Toxopeus, giving her shareholders an opportunity to strengthen the financial basis of her productions. The spectators become fellow actors to Dette: they join in Dette's search for ways in which we can reset our money system and bring about renewal of our society. In this way, people start thinking and become part of the movement that is looking for alternatives.

Evaluation of these initiatives

May we consider these nine initiatives of societal renewal with regard to food, health care, and money in the Netherlands as spirituality driven? Is spirituality needed for these forms of providing food to people in the

33 Hense, E. (Radboud Universiteit Nijmegen) (2013): *Data Spiritualiteit en Maatschappelijke Vernieuwing, interview met D. Glashouwer (over het initiatief Theaterprogramma 'Money, money, money').* DANS. www.dx.doi.org/10.17026/dans-z3f-guyu. See also "D. Glashouwer." www.detteglashouwer.com.

cities, to those in disadvantaged neighborhoods, and to those who want to enjoy meals cooked by someone else? Is spirituality needed for these forms of caring for elderly and enabled people and for children in problems? Is spirituality needed for these forms of creating and designing your own money and for giving insight in the many problematic aspects of money? I would answer 'yes', because spiritual discernment and choice come into play in these initiatives: they all follow 'intuitions of fullness of life' and want to contribute to what they consider 'a better world' and may therefore be understood as boosted by a spiritual quest. Are these initiatives rooted in common human experience and are they in accordance with Tracy's criteria of adequacy? Certainly yes, because fresh human knowledge is used to deal with experiences with food, health care and money, and these experiences are shared by many of our contemporaries. Are these initiatives Christian according to Tracy's criteria of appropriateness? Certainly not, because they don't relate to the 'Christian fact'. However, we might argue that these initiatives have arisen in a post-Christian culture that is still influenced by the sediment of Christian spirituality which has been accumulated over the centuries.[34] Do these initiatives meet real human needs and are they in accordance with criteria of respondence which I supplemented to Tracy's criteria? Certainly yes, because they all depart from experiences of human suffering, shortcoming, and limitation. In order to create for themselves and others more fullness, depth, and bloom in their lives, the initiators of these projects discern which practices and conditions would lead to a fuller, richer, deeper, more inspiring, more admirable and more worthwhile way of living. All of them show in a provisional way how quality of life could be increased in concrete socio-cultural contexts. None of them considers more money, more consumption of material goods or a wider availability of paid services as the solution. None of them believes in economic growth as the remedy for our problems – a belief that is unmasked by more and more scholars as a central superstition of the Western world in our times.[35] They all think that we have to restrain ourselves regarding economic growth and to commit ourselves to social, ecological and cultural well-being. A notable thing is that the initiators of these nine initiatives all tell us how refreshing, how well-spent and how pleasant they find their new way of life. Also their audiences enjoy the new configuration of values realized by these initiatives. New habits are cultivated in these initiatives; a new

34 See H. Arts-Honselaar, "Geestelijk leven in de twintigste eeuw" in *De Lage Landen en het hogere. De betekenis van geestelijke beginselen in het moderne bestaan* (ed. G. van den Brink; Amsterdam: University of Amsterdam Press, 2012), 127–167 (162).

35 T. Sedlacek, *Economics of Good and Evil: the Quest for Economic Meaning from Gilgamesh to Wall Street* (New York: Oxford University Press, 2011).

orientation of life is born. We might understand these initiatives as new forms of the 'common life' (the *ghemene leven* of Ruusbroec), as all of the initiators look for a balance between going out in love and mercy to one's fellows on the one hand and taking care of their selves on the other hand. They do not take care in a Christian, Jewish, Muslim or Buddhist way, as they do not describe their care of the self as contemplating God or nirvana. However, they do contemplate the well-known 'names of God' (in Jewish, Christian and Muslim traditions): empathy, connectedness, respect, love, responsibility, justice etc. They don't need to be mighty and wealthy for their commitment – and none of them is – but they do need to be sensitive to experiences of suffering, shortcoming and limitation. The remarkable thing is that they prove to be sensitive to these experiences without falling back on old religious traditions. They all seem to witness the graceful discovery of a secular form of 'common life'.

Bibliography

Arts-Honselaar, H., "Geestelijk leven in de twintigste eeuw". Pp. 127–167 in *De Lage Landen en het hogere. De betekenis van geestelijke beginselen in het moderne bestaan.* Edited by G. van den Brink. Amsterdam: University of Amsterdam Press, 2012.

von Balthasar, H.U., "Spiritualität." *Geist und Leben* 31 (1958): 340–352.

van den Brink, G., *De Lage Landen en het hogere. De betekenis van geestelijke beginselen in het moderne bestaan.* Amsterdam: University of Amsterdam Press, 2012.

Conklin, J., *Dialogue Mapping: Building Shared Understanding of Wicked Problems.* Chichester: Wiley & Sons Ltd, 2006.

de Foucault, M., *Technologies of the Self*. Edited by L.H. Martin, H. Gutman and P.H. Hutton. Amherst Massachusets: University of Massachusets Press, 1988.

Habermas, J., "Religion in the Public Sphere." *European Journal of Philosophy* 14,1 (2006): 1–25.

Hense, E., "Present-day spiritualities in confessional, popular, professional and aesthetic contexts: contrasts or overlap?" Pp. 1–17 in *Present-Day Spiritualities Contrasts and Overlaps.* Edited by E. Hense, F. Jespers and P. Nissen. Leiden: Brill, 2014.

—, (Radboud Universiteit Nijmegen) (2013): *Data Spiritualiteit en Maatschappelijke Vernieuwing, interview met A. Disbudak (over het initiatief Unalzorg).* DANS.

—, (Radboud Universiteit Nijmegen) (2013): *Data Spiritualiteit en Maatschappelijke Vernieuwing, interview met B. Richters (over het initiatief Hotspot Hutspot).* DANS.

—, (Radboud Universiteit Nijmegen) (2013): *Data Spiritualiteit en Maatschappelijke Vernieuwing, interview met D. Glashouwer (over het initiatief Theaterprogramma 'Money, money, money').* DANS.

—, (Radboud Universiteit Nijmegen) (2013): *Data Spiritualiteit en Maatschappelijke Vernieuwing, interview met E. Kampers (over het initiatief Qoin).* DANS.

—, (Radboud Universiteit Nijmegen) (2013): *Data Spiritualiteit en Maatschappelijke Vernieuwing, interview met F. van Beek (over het initiatief De Eigen Kracht Centrale).* DANS.

—, (Radboud Universiteit Nijmegen) (2013): *Data Spiritualiteit en Maatschappelijke Vernieuwing, interview met H. de Leede (over eten; initiatief Uit Je Eigen Stad).* DANS.

—, (Radboud Universiteit Nijmegen) (2013): *Data Spiritualiteit en Maatschappelijke Vernieuwing, interview met J. van der Heijden (over het initiatief De Zorgcoöperatie Hogeloon).* DANS.

—, (Radboud Universiteit Nijmegen) (2013): *Data Spiritualiteit en Maatschappelijke Vernieuwing, interview met J. Vink (over het initiatief Stichting Stro).* DANS.

—, (Radboud Universiteit Nijmegen) (2013): *Data Spiritualiteit en Maatschappelijke Vernieuwing, interview met M. Hart (over het initiatief Thuisafgehaald).* DANS.

—, *Vernieuwingsinitiatieven rond eten, zorg en geld in Nederland – Een kwestie van spiritualiteit.* Amsterdam: VU University Press, 2015.

Kasper, W., *Barmherzigkeit, Grundbegriff des Evangeliums. Schlüssel christlichen Lebens.* Freiburg: Herder, 2012.

Paech, N., *Befreiung vom Überfluss.* München: Oekom Verlag, 2012.

—, "Wachstum – Aufstieg und Fall eines Dogmas." *Universitas* 68 (2013): 26–35.

Rahner, K., *Über den Versuch eines Aufrisses einer Dogmatik.* Schriften zur Theologie I. Einsiedeln: Benziger, 1967.

van Ruusbroec, J., *Vanden blinckenden steen.* Edited by G. de Baere. Tielt/Turnhout: Brepols, 1991.

Sedlacek, T., *Economics of Good and Evil: the Quest for Economic Meaning from Gilgamesh to Wall Street.* New York: Oxford University Press, 2011.

Sheldrake, P., *Spirituality: a Brief History.* Malden-Oxford: Wiley-Blackwell, 2013.

Steggink, O., and K. Waaijman, *Spiritualiteit en Mystiek.* Nijmegen: Uitgeverij B. Gottmer, 1985.

Sudbrack, J., "Möglichkeiten einer Theologie des Geistlichen Lebens." *Trierer Theologische Zeitschrift* 78 (1969): 49–59.

Tracy, D., *Blessed Rage for Order.* New York: Seabury Press, 1975.

Viller, M. and K. Rahner, *Aszese und Mystik in der Väterzeit.* Freiburg-Basel-Wien: Herder, 1989.

Waaijman, K., *Spiritualiteit.* Kampen: Kok, 2000.
Weismayer, J., "Theologie und Spiritualität". Pp. 289–306 in *Lasst euch vom Geist erfüllen (Eph 5,18). Beiträge zur Spiritualität.* Münster: Lit, 2001.
—, *Leben in Fülle. Zur Geschichte und Theologie christlicher Spiritualität.* Innsbruck-Wien: Tyrolia-Verlag, 1983.

Church documents

Congregatio de Seminariis et Studiorum Universitatibus, *Enchiridion Clericorum: Documenta Ecclesiae sacrorum alumnis instituendis.* Rome: Typis Polyglottis Vaticanis and Herder, 1938.
John Paul II, Pope, "Constitutio Apostolica Sapientia Christiana." *AAS* 71 (1979): 513.
Pius XI, Pope, "Constitutio Apostolica Deus scientiarum Dominus." *AAS* 23 (1931): 241–260.

Websites

"Data spiritualiteit en maatschappelijke vernieuwing, interview met A. Disbudak (over zorg; initiatief Unal Zorg)." www.dx.doi.org/10.17026/dans-z3w-r2d5.
"Data spiritualiteit en maatschappelijke vernieuwing, interview met B. Richters (over eten; initiatief Hotspot Hutspot)." www.dx.doi.org/10.17026/dans-24j-7c4m.
"Data spiritualiteit en maatschappelijke vernieuwing, interview met D. Glashouwer (over geld; initiatief Money money money)." www.dx.doi.org/10.17026/dans-z3f-guyu.
"Data spiritualiteit en maatschappelijke vernieuwing, interview met E. Kampers (over geld; initiatief Qoin)." www.dx.doi.org/10.17026/dans-zuk-sj6t.
"Data spiritualiteit en maatschappelijke vernieuwing, interview met F. van Beek (over zorg; initiatief Eigen kracht centrale)." www.dx.doi.org/10.17026/dans-zqx-e47s.
"Data spiritualiteit en maatschappelijke vernieuwing, interview met H. de Leede (over eten; initiatief Uit je eigen stad)." www.dx.doi.org/10.17026/dans-x3a-76ks.
"Data spiritualiteit en maatschappelijke vernieuwing, interview met J. van der Heijden (over zorg; initiatief zorgcoöperatie Hoogeloon)." ww.dx.doi.org/10.17026/dans-xyp-ghu8.
"Data spiritualiteit en maatschappelijke vernieuwing, interview met J. Vink (over geld; initiatief Stro)." www.dx.doi.org/10.17026/dans-2b7-jdtz.

"Data spiritualiteit en maatschappelijke vernieuwing, interview met M. Hart (over eten; initiatief Thuis afgehaald)." www.dx.doi.org/10.17026/dans-zhh-bd6u.
Eigen Kracht Centrale. "Eigen Kracht Centrale, wij gaan voor samenredzaamheid." www.eigen-kracht.nl.
Glashouwer, D., "Dette Glashouwer." www.detteglashouwer.com.
Hotspot Hutspot. "Hotspot Hutspot." www.hotspothutspot.nl.
Qoin. "Qoin, money that matters." www.qoin.org.
Social Trade Organisation. "Social Trade Organisation." www.strohalm.nl.
Thuisafgehaald. "Thuisafgehaald, maaltijden delen met je buren." www.thuisafgehaald.nl.
Uit je eigen stad. "Uit je eigen stad." www.uitjeeigenstad.nl.
Unalzorg. "Unalzorg, professionele zorg, aandacht voor de culturele achtergrond." www.unalzorg.nl.
Zorgcoöperatie Hoogeloon. "Zorgcoöperatie Hoogeloon." www.zorgcooperatie.nl.

DISCERNMENT IN MANAGEMENT: A HERMENEUTIC APPROACH

Erik de Jongh

Abstract

Human beings have such experiences as vulnerability, a lack of control, fragmentation and indignation. They try to create for themselves and others more fullness, meaning and flourishing in their lives. Under proper conditions this may become a transformative experience. The word `discernment` refers to the human ability to make distinctions with respect to their inner world. This ability is addressed here in relation to the role of management in the context of societal renewal. It is considered as a way of proceeding with decision-making which draws on experience and subjective knowledge.

Based on Burrell and Morgan's organizational paradigms, discernment in managerial contexts is presumed to be problematic because the subjective approach of discernment does not sit well with the objectivist approach of organizations which is characteristic of the functionalist paradigm. Given that the functionalist paradigm is dominant, the practice of discernment in management is at risk of being accepted only on condition that it adjusts to the management perspective, which has also been perceived to happen with business ethics. Further, such an attempt is likely to be drawn in a reactive stance towards mainstream management.

The practice of discernment is concerned with the interpretation of experiences, events and situations. Two layers may be distinguished in this practice. The first layer could be characterized as factual in so far as it is concerned with describing problems within a managerial context as well as the alternatives which are available to resolve them. The other layer – and this is of special interest here – would involve the limitations which are imposed on managerial thinking as well as the values involved in managerial decision making and thereby open up a normative frame of reference. Therefore a hermeneutic approach is appropriate for gaining insight into the practice of discernment within the discipline of management. In order to explore how discernment may help managers to expand their hermeneutic horizon two approaches of discernment in the management literature will be studied.

The structure of this paper consists of an explanation of the hermeneutic mode of inquiry, an exploration of some high-profile examples of a limited hermeneutic horizon in the management literature, a cross-textual reading of two recent examples of discernment in the discipline of management, and an evaluation of the standards which are deemed mandatory for the practice of discernment in managerial contexts.

A hermeneutic approach to discernment in organizations

Management is a relatively new discipline within the academy. The institutional basis for the discipline was laid in the 19th century by schools for commercial and business education which were founded in the U.S. and Europe as a pragmatic response to the needs of the business world and national economies, facing increasingly complex modes of production in increasingly competitive environments.[1] The pragmatic approach of problems in the business world has moulded the way of thinking about organizations in management theory. Burrell and Morgan explain that the dominant framework for the study of organizations has been provided by their functionalist paradigm.[2] They observe that the majority of organizational theories within the functionalist paradigm are located within a relatively narrow range of academic theory, that is, social systems theory and objectivism.[3] As a result the academic debate around the study of organizations tends to focus on points of detail, while the big issues are rarely discussed. Among the big issues which remain hidden behind the commonality of perspective, they say, are charges of (a) an undue commitment to the models and methods of the natural sciences; (b) a complete disregard for the nature of the phenomena under investigation; (c) an overdeterministic view of human nature; and (d) an ideological bias in favour of a managerial view of organization.[4] The hermeneutic approach is bound to counter all these charges because it assumes that the social world does not exist independent of the minds of men, and acknowledges the positions and views of all organizational participants. In terms of Burrell and Morgan's organizational paradigms hermeneutics fits with the interpretive paradigm.[5] The interpretive paradigm seeks to un-

1 R.A. Gordon and J.E. Howell, *Higher Education for Business* (New York: Columbia University Press, 1959).

2 G. Burrell and G. Morgan, *Sociological Paradigms and Organisational Analysis* (Hants: Ashgate Publishing, 2008), 25–28.

3 Burrell and Morgan, *Sociological Paradigms*, 121–123.

4 Burrell and Morgan, *Sociological Paradigms*, 217–220.

5 Other theories consistent with the interpretive paradigm are phenomenology and ethnomethodology.

derstand and explain the social world primarily from the point of view of the actors directly involved.[6] The hermeneutic mode of inquiry is seldom used in the discipline of management. According to Burrell and Morgan all approaches outside the boundaries of the functionalist paradigm tend to be viewed by the dominant orthodoxy as critical perspectives whose aim and function is assumed to be exposure of the limitations reflected in the orthodoxy.[7] As a result these approaches are drawn into a reactive stance by the functionalist orthodoxy. One reason for this view may be that the hermeneutic mode of inquiry does not allow for the separation of facts and values, which is viewed as a basic requirement for the discipline of management,[8]

Hermeneutics is a school of thought which is concerned with understanding social and cultural phenomena as products of the human mind.[9] Among the products of the human mind are works of art, literature, languages, religions. Organizations may also be considered as such in so far as they are consciously constructed by human beings. Tennekes argues that organizations exemplify human culture, that is, the way human beings 'produce' their own existence.[10] Dilthey, who played an important part in the development of hermeneutics as a school of thought in social theory, argued that cultural artefacts can be understood and appreciated only in relation to the minds which created them and the inner experience which they reflected.[11] However, organizations cannot be understood only as the result of human action in the past, they are continually reshaped by human action. This is particularly clear when one takes an anthropological view of organizations.[12] Therefore it is not sufficient to understand the mind of those who created them. The observer of organizations must enter into a dialogue with those participating in contemporary organizational practices. Tennekes emphasizes that the logic of culture is an exchange of interpretations. There may be differences in the way that situations are interpreted and in what is considered as a legitimate of the frame of reference for interpretation. Tennekes draws explicit attention to the importance of

6 Burrell and Morgan, *Sociological Paradigms*, 227.

7 Burrell and Morgan, *Sociological Paradigms*, 396.

8 See for example H. Simon, *Administrative Behavior, A Study of Decison-Making Processes in Administrative Organization* (New York: The Free Press, 1976) and R.A. Giacalone and C.L. Jurkiewicz, "Towards a Science of Workplace Spirituality," in *Handbook of Workplace Spirituality and Organizational Performance* (eds. R.A. Giacalone and C.L. Jurkiewicz; London/ Armonk NY: M.E. Sharpe, 2003), 3–26.

9 Burrell and Morgan, *Sociological Paradigms*, 236.

10 J. Tennekes, *Organisatiecultuur. Een antropologische visie* (Leuven/Apeldoorn: Garant, 1995).

11 Burrell and Morgan, *Sociological Paradigms*, 229.

12 Cf. Tennekes, *Organisatiecultuur*, 22–25.

worldviews, values and norms underlying the arguments which are used in such discussions.[13] For this reason the observer of organizations must also reflect on his or her own assumptions and prejudices in the dialogue with organizational participants. In order to understand organizations, the participant perspective is therefore as important as the systems perspective. However, this insight is seldom reflected in the discipline of management.

Hermeneutics provides a mode of scientific inquiry which is appropriate to the nature of organizations as a cultural phenomenon. It complements the empirical mode in psychological and sociological investigation in organizational behavior.[14] The term hermeneutics refers to theoretical reflection on the question of how the interpretation of human expressions occurs.[15] The theoretical insights in the processes of interpretation can be applied in all disciplines which investigate the various expressions of the human mind. In the field of practical theology, for example, hermeneutics has been adopted as a way to gain insight into contemporary expressions of religion.[16] Students of theology and religious studies are made familiar with the hermeneutic mode of inquiry as part of their training in such professional fields as religious education, spiritual care, and leadership.[17] By attending to the processes of interpreting life they can engage organizational participants in conversations in which meaning is constructed.

It is rare to find an awareness of the need to attend to the process of constructing meaning in the management literature. One of the exceptions is Pauchant, who became aware of this need through his concern with the organizational response to the world's individual, social and ecological crises.[18] He argues that the suffering brought about by a crisis permits human beings to arrive at a better understanding of their situation, and to invent different ways of acting and being. In a few words he pinpoints the impor-

13 Tennekes, *Organisatiecultuur*, 27–28.

14 In the social sciences the positivist method of inquiry came to be seen as increasingly unsatisfactory and problematic, which led to a distinctive shift in attention towards the subjective dimension of human behavior. See Burrell and Morgan, *Sociological Paradigms*, 227–228.

15 H. de Wit, *"My God," she said, "ships make me so crazy." Reflections on Empirical Hermeneutics, Interculturality and Holy Scripture* (Amsterdam: VU University, 2008), 23. De Wit emphasizes that hermeneutics is not the interpretation itself, but the academic reflection on how the processes of interpretation work. In other words, the practice is guided by a theoretical framework. For the interpretation itself he recommends to use the concept of *hermeneuse*.

16 R.R. Ganzevoort, "Forks in the Road when Tracing the Sacred. Practical Theology as Hermeneutics of Lived Religion" (Chicago: presidential address to the International Academy of Practical Theology, August 3, 2009).

17 See for example A. Mulder and H. Snoek (eds.), *Werken met diepgang* (Zoetermeer: Meinema, 2012).

18 T.C. Pauchant, *La Quête du Sens. Gérer nos Organisations pour la Santé des Personnes, de nos Sociétés et de la Nature* (Montréal: Éditions Québec Amérique, 1996).

tance of a hermeneutic mode of inquiry by attending to the managerial experience of being unable to resolve a crisis:

"The crisis brings forth change because it leaves us empty-handed. It forces us, if we allow it, to forget our illusions for a moment and to communicate again with the hard and real issues of life."[19]

In the images of 'empty hands' and 'illusions' the subjective dimension of organizational behavior is ineluctable. In this connection Pauchant remarks that it is necessary for managers to communicate with the hard and real issues of life. The hardest issue which managers have to face, perhaps, is their vulnerability. Taylor argues that a sense of invulnerability is characteristic of the modern anthropocentric identity.[20] He speaks of a 'buffered' identity, by which he means a sense of self which is aware of the possibility of 'taking a distance from, disengaging from everything outside the mind'.[21] The 'buffered' self provides a sense of power over the external world, along with a sense of invulnerability. Taylor suggests a direct relation between the sense of invulnerability and the loss of meaning.

"One can hear all sorts of complaints about 'the present age' throughout history (...) But what you won't hear at other times and places is (...) that our age suffers from a threatened loss of meaning. This malaise is specific to a buffered identity, whose very invulnerability opens it to the danger that not just evil spirits, cosmic forces, or gods won't 'get to it', but that nothing significant at all will stand out for it."[22]

The 'buffered' self allows managers to remain unaffected by anything significant outside of themselves. To the extent that this happens, a loss of meaning is incurred. Managers must allow themselves to be concerned by the significant experiences of others, show their sensitivity and become vulnerable. Their own vulnerability is the key to meaning beyond rational explanations of organizational behavior. This insight is reflected in Pauchant's remarkable thought that the crisis *forces* communication with the hard and real issues of life only *if we allow it.*

In order to get a better grasp of the hermeneutic mode of inquiry two high-profile examples of attending to the process of interpretation in the management literature will be discussed in the next paragraph. Both exam-

19 Pauchant, *La Quête*, 15.

20 C. Taylor, *A Secular Age* (Cambridge, MA: The Belknap Press of Harvard University Press, 2007), 300.

21 Taylor, *A Secular Age*, 38.

22 Taylor, *A Secular Age*, 303.

ples will show that the manager's sense of self is involved in the process of interpretation.

The hermeneutic horizon of management

The concept of a hermeneutic horizon has been used by Verstraeten to explain why business ethics has had very little impact on management.[23] He observes that business ethics had to adjust to the rationality of managers in order to be accepted, while it was intended as a critical corrective of management. Referring to MacIntyre, he says that managers are subject to limits with respect to the questions which may and may not be asked about their behavior.[24] These limits constitute the hermeneutic horizon of management.[25] Two examples in the management literature will demonstrate how the hermeneutic horizon is operational in the discipline of management.

A. de Geus, The Living Company[26]

During a research project on long-living companies by the corporate planning department of the Royal Dutch/Shell group, De Geus became aware of some unquestioned assumptions about organizations. The research generated four factors which explained corporate longevity (sensitivity to the environment, cohesion and a strong sense of identity, tolerance and conservative financing). The research team noticed that economic criteria did not appear to determine corporate success in the long run, and that people seemed much more critical to a company than the economic lens suggests.[27] In other words, the organizational paradigm which De Geus had learned at business school was challenged. He says that he came to see these factors as abilities of living companies as distinct from economic companies: the ability to learn and adapt, to build a community and an identity,

23 J. Verstraeten, *Leiderschap met hart en ziel* (Tielt: Lannoo, 2003). See also J. Verstraeten, "Beyond Business Ethics: Leadership and Spirituality, and the Quest for Meaning," *Logos. A Journal of Catholic Thought and Culture*, 5/2 (2002): 17–39.

24 A. MacIntyre, "Corporate Modernity and Moral Judgment: Are They Mutually Exclusive?," in K. Goodpastor and K. Sayre, *Ethics and the Problems of the 21st Century* (Notre Dame: Notre Dame University Press, 1979). Quoted in J. Verstraeten, *Leiderschap*, 11.

25 In connection to Taylor's 'buffered' identity these limits may be understood as equipment of the buffer (such that the things beyond don't need 'to get to me'). See C. Taylor, *A Secular Age*, 38.

26 A. de Geus, *The Living Company* (Boston: Harvard Business School Press, 1997).

27 De Geus, *The Living Company*, 7 .

to build constructive relationships, and to govern their own growth.[28] The ability to learn and adapt appeared to be the most 'accessible', hence the decision to adopt a learning definition of success as opposed to an economic definition of success.

The first attempts at improving the ability to learn in the Royal Dutch/ Shell group by introducing new management instruments failed for various reasons. Then it dawned on the team that decision making itself could be a learning process. De Geus tells that it was not difficult to talk about a learning organisation in the executive boardroom, but talking about the board's decision-making as learning was off-limits. That is when he decided to leave the Royal Dutch/Shell group and started to talk 'from the outside in'.[29]

In terms of the process of interpreting the research findings, this example shows two instances of the research team expanding their hermeneutic horizon. First, the economic lens was exchanged for the lens of learning. Second, an instrumental approach to learning was abandoned and the members of the executive board were engaged in a conversation about their own decision-making process from the perspective of learning. The team repeatedly reconsidered its assumptions and habits until a problem occurred in the boardroom which could not be resolved. In this way the team showed that the hermeneutic horizon is not fixed – it can be expanded by attending to the process of interpretation.The final limitation in the hermeneutic horizon is evident when executive managers in the boardroom show an interest in 'building' a learning organization, but refuse to talk about their own decision making as learning. This moment reveals a peculiarity of the managerial perspective: the difficulty to consider themselves as participants in their own organization and the preference for an outsider perspective.

J.C. Collins and J.I. Porras, Built to Last[30]

The dominance of the outsider perspective in the discipline of management is also evident in the study of visionary organizations by Collins and Porras. They claim that a peculiar characteristic of visionary companies is to make things happen.[31] Their research indicates that the corporate capability to have an impact on its environment depends on the core ideology. Without such a core ideology, they say, companies are subject to the changing forces in their environment. The case that visionary companies adhere to a core ideo-

28 De Geus, *The Living Company*, 9.

29 De Geus, *The Living Company*, 73–74.

30 J.C. Collins and J.I. Porras, *Built to Last* (New York: HarperBusiness, 1997) .

31 Collins and Porras, *Built to Last*, 1.

logy attracted worldwide attention, and even developed into a management hype.[32] Observing the hype, Collins and Porras concluded that many executives and managers did not capture the meaning of the original research findings. Three years after the initial publication of their research they challenged the assumptions of their audience which they believed had led to the misinterpretation in an article in *Harvard Business Review*.[33] They explained that "You do not 'create' or 'set' core ideology. You *discover* core ideology. You do not deduce it by looking to the external environment. You understand it by looking inside. Ideology has to be authentic. You cannot fake it. Discovering core ideology is not an intellectual exercise.".[34]

This example shows that the authors attended to the process of interpretation of their research findings. The hermeneutic horizon of their audience first appears in the managerial response to the research by 'creating' mission and vision statements. This response even takes on the dimensions of a management 'hype'. Despite their *Harvard Business Review* article, Collins and Porras do not seem to have succeeded in broadening the hermeneutic horizon of their audience. Until the present time managers appear reluctant to embark on a journey of discovery and persist in creating mission and vision statements.

Discussion

These examples underline the importance of attending to the process of interpretation, particularly in the daily operations of management. Verstraeten argues that decision makers can confront the limitations in their hermeneutic horizon by relating directly to one's experience of reality, for which he refers to the encounter with other people, nature, and one's inner world. This implies a subjective turn in the discipline of management. The importance of this point is evident from a hermeneutical perspective, but hard to address in the field of management.[35] Many examples can be cited of companies which ran into difficulties in recent years as a result of executive behavior. At the global level executive behavior in the financial sector has been the most conspicuous. While 'the system' is often referred to for explaining the conduct of managers it is increasingly recognized that managers remain re-

32 Patrick Lencioni says that "The values fad swept through corporate America like chicken pox through a kindergarten class." See P. Lencioni, "Make Your Values Mean Something," *Harvard Business Review* 8/7 (2002): 113–117.

33 J.C. Collins and J.I. Porras, "Building Your Company's Vision," in *Harvard Business Review*, 74/5 (1996): 65–77.

34 Collins and Porras, *Built to Last* 71. Italics in the original text.

35 For a more extensive discussion see E. de Jongh, *Responding to the situation*, PhD diss. VU University Amsterdam (Leidschendam: Quist Publishing, 2011).

sponsible for their own conduct.[36] In this respect it is worthwhile to re-think the ways in which managers relate to their experience of reality.

Verstraeten argues that the ability of managers to relate to their own experience shapes the conditions for moral responsibility.[37] In this connection he draws attention to the importance of the language of metaphors, narratives and wisdom as opposed to the language of facts, calculation, competence, performance and control.[38] The importance of narratives for the construction of meaning has been recognized in such fields as ethics, psychology and practical theology.[39] A well-established narrative practice where people are invited to relate to their experience can be found in the Quaker tradition.[40] This practice is known as the clearness committee.

"Quakers can bring challenges they are facing [into the clearness committee], and other people will be with them in a prayerful, grounded way, and ask them questions, help them with what they are facing. That is a little community which holds them accountable and support them. It is both, I think you need both, a community where people feel known, and supported and loved, and there can be challenged. We have a severe lack of this kind of communities today."[41]

The clearness committee embodies the Quaker practice of discernment. As Benefiel explains, it plays a key role in upholding the Quaker sense of integrity: She argues that their deeply rooted reputation for honesty and integrity is sustained by the Quaker community:

"... who are you becoming when you are not living with integrity? If I am not living with integrity, then you care about that, you are going to challenge me. It is part of living in community, and sharpening each other."

36 See for example Commissie onderzoek financiële problematiek Amarantis, "Niet onwettig, wel onwenselijk," accessed May 20, 2014, https://zoek.officielebekendmakingen.nl/blg-208258.pdf.

37 Verstraeten, *Leiderschap*, 67.

38 J. Verstraeten, *Taal en stilte* (Averbode: Altiora, 2014).

39 See for example A. MacIntyre, *After Virtue* (Notre Dame: University of Notre Dame Press, 1984); T.R. Sarbin (ed.), *Narrative Psychology. The Storied Nature of Human Conduct* (New York: Westport/London: Praeser: 1978); C.V. Gerkin, *The Living Human Document. Re-visioning pastoral counselling in a hermeneutical mode* (Nashville: Abingdon Press, 1984).

40 Quakers are members of the Society of Friends, a religious movement dating from the 17th century by separating from the Church of England.

41 See the interview with Margaret Benefiel in the *Faith and Ethics in the Executive Suite series of Princeton University*, accessed June 9, 2014, http://www.princeton.edu/faithandwork/media/ethics-in-the-executive-suite/margaret-benefiel.

The Quaker practice of discernment shows how the ability to relate to one´s own experience is shaped by a community which can confront its members with their thoughts and actions only to the extent that it supports them. In this connection it is important to note that facts are inseparable from the normative frame of reference, including one's orientation in life, values and worldview.

We shall now look further into the practice of discernment within the discipline of management. With the limited hermeneutic horizon of managers in mind, it is to be expected that the invitation to relate directly to one's experience of reality will meet with resistance in mainstream management. The following paragraph will show that there are various ways to handle the normative frame of reference.

Discernment in managerial contexts

The discernment approach of decision making was initially presented to the Academy of Management by Benefiel, Delbecq and Falque.[42] In this paragraph we shall focus on the work of the latter two, which is rooted in the discipline of management.[43] Falque published on the practice of discernment together with the Jesuit and psycho-sociologist Robert Bougon.

In many respects Delbecq on the one hand and Falque and Bougon on the other seem to have a similar understanding of discernment, which is explained by the fact that they both draw upon the *Spiritual Exercises* of Ignatius of Loyola. Beneath the surface there are also profound differences, however, which are explained by the way they handle the normative frame of reference of the decision maker. Since Ignatius's *Spiritual Exercises* happens to be the source of both authors, this paragraph will bring us into the field of theology and religious studies. In the end it will appear, however,

42 A. Delbecq and M. Benefiel, "Awakened Spiritual Thirst Among Organizational Leaders. How Then Shall We Serve Them?" (Seattle: symposium at the Academy of Management annual meeting, August 4, 2003); A. Delbecq and L. Falque, "Practicing Discernment in Decision-making" (Honolulu: paper presented to the Academy of Management annual meeting, August 7, 2005).

43 Delbecq has shown an interest in discernment within the context of the MBA program at Santa Clara University. Observing that the business school curriculum is unlikely to provide space for spirituality beyond introductory courses, and being aware of the unfortunate precedents of business ethics and corporate social justice, he focused on post-MBA leadership formation program where alumni could practice discernment in peer group settings. Falque and Bougon started with a seminar on professional discernment in France, which was repeated several times per year over the next years. The desire of participants for on-going support and dissemination of the discernment approach led to the creation of the *Institut de Discernement Professionnel* (accessed June 9, 2014, http://www.discernement.org).

that the practice of discernment can be conducted with respect to any normative frame of reference, religious or otherwise.

In this paragraph we shall have a closer look at the similarities and differences in order to arrive at a better understanding of discernment in the context of management. The method to be used now is cross-textual reading. The term 'reading,' refers to the hermeneutical practice of analyzing a cultural artefact. This method intends to establish a critical and creative dialogue between two texts. Delbecq published his text in 2004 together with four other authors.[44] The text of Falque and Bougon was initially published in 2005, re-edited in 2009 and entirely rewritten in 2014.[45]

Discernment in relation to decision making

Delbecq argues that the complexity of the decision making process means that managers must confront the limits of bounded rationality. [D: 146][46] The concept of bounded rationality was introduced by Simon in 1945 and became very influential in the discipline of management.[47] By referring to this concept Delbecq says that there are limits to what the organizational environment can achieve in terms of rational behaviour. In his view this means that management must move beyond risk control into the domain of judgment and intuition. Falque and Bougon, who start their introductory chapter with the question 'Should we rely on intuition?', appear to concord. [FB: 1] They present discernment as a way to avoid the pitfalls of traditional approaches to decision making in management theory, for which they refer to the models of satisfactory choice, political game, garbage can and rational choice. Falque and Bougon emphasize that the decision maker is more or less absent in these models with the result that it looks like decisions can abstract from the subjectivity of decision makers. [FB: 11] Their view is comparable to Delbecq´s who presents discernment as a deep, broad and subjective approach when faced with complex choices. [D: 147]

For both authors discernment in the context of management refers to the importance of the decision maker whose subjective interpretation, ap-

44 A. Delbecq et al., "Discernment and Strategic Decision Making. Reflections for a Spirituality of Organizational Leadership," in *Spiritual Intelligence at Work* (ed. M.L. Pava; Amsterdam/London: Elsevier, 2004), 139–174.

45 L. Falque and R. Bougon, *Discerner pour décider* (Paris: Dunod, 2014).

46 The number between brackets refer to Delbecq et al., *Discernment and Strategic Decision Making* (preceded by D) or Falque and Bougon, *Discerner* (preceded by FB).

47 The aim of his administrative theory is to design the organizational environment in such a way that individuals will approach as close as practicable to economic rationality. In other words, the organization was to provide the boundaries of rational behaviour. See H. Simon, *Administrative Behavior*, 26–31.

preciation, and assessment of events and situations cannot be eliminated in the decision process. In terms of the hermeneutic horizon of management, Delbecq focuses on limitations of strategic decision making, while Falque and Bougon are primarily concerned with psychological, social and cultural pitfalls in the practice of professional decision making. I leave the differences between strategic and professional decisions aside. In both cases discernment is considered as an approach to decision making which gives full attention to the subjectivity of the decision maker.

The aim of discernment

Both authors say that the aim of discernment is greater freedom. But that doesn´t say much in itself. Falque and Bougon speak about helping individuals to become free from their attachments, by which they mean "a fundamental experience of changing viewpoints or to find greater freedom in one's way of thinking and acting". [FB: 109–110] The importance of such an experience lies in the context of professional work. Falque and Bougon are concerned with the deterministic view of human nature which has permeated organizations. What is at stake for professionals is to find in themselves an organizing principle instead of letting oneself be 'dictated' from outside. [FB: 216] By involving professionals and managers in the process of discernment they reclaim the importance of subjectivity in organizations.

Falque and Bougon emphasize that individuals are not expected to accept a shared foundation for making choices, but to understand and respect one another by clarifying their profound motivations. [FB: 127] They invite the participants in their discernment program to become aware of their normative frames of reference by asking questions about the choices they are facing with respect to work. [FB: 94] They start at the very beginning of their book: "We ask ourselves what we should do and this brings us to our many aspirations, to our relations and to our entire environment." [FB: ix] In this connection they ask their audience "... to remember those situations when we preferred the easy way, and then those in which we showed courage. And more precisely, at which moment did we show courage to contribute to a higher aspiration, a desire, a finality?"

The questions asked by Falque and Bougon pertain to the participants' relation to themselves, other people and their environment. Delbecq resonates with these questions when he says that the primary matter for discernment are questions of personal identity: "Who am I? Where am I going? What am I to do? How do I make sense of life, of my life? What will I leave behind as my inheritance to the next generation?". [D: 148] Questions such as these indicate that the material world, for both authors, is the place to make choices. However, Delbecq seems to be less interested in the actual personal experience of the material world. As he says, discernment is to be understood as "the process of developing eyes to see God in the midst of ordinary, finite, existence, to allow ourselves to be stirred by this God and called into a vocation of service in God´s creative project". [D: 147] In other words, Delbecq's normative frame of reference is 'God'. He considers 'the basic intentionality to choose God's will' to be ´the *sine qua non* for discernment'. [D: 157] The importance of this intention is underlined by his remark that the discernment process should pause when one loses this disposition, or at least the desire for it. The question is what God's creative project has to do with greater freedom in decision making.

Before getting to this question, it is important to note that Delbecq refers directly to Ignatius´s text.[48] In contrast, Falque and Bougon take some distance with respect to the text. As they say, they offer a 'lay' reading of the *Spiritual Exercises.* [FB: 8][49] In this reading they have translated the desire to advance in the search for God's will through the notion of finality, leaving everyone free to choose whatever transcends one's experience. [FB: 80, footnote 1] They postulate that "the quest for an ideal, for society, companies and every individual, is a challenge to be revealed" and "individual or group choices do not necessarily contribute to maintain this openness to the future". [FB: 216] They claim that Ignatius appeals to a profoundly human experience which is accessible to everyone if one accepts the ways in which one is interiorly touched and moved. [FB: 80] In order to make this experience accessible Falque and Bougon have reformulated the ignatian notions of a 'good spirit' and an 'evil spirit' in popular language. Instead of 'movements of the spirit', they talk about 'our internal meteo' (meteo being an abbreviation of meteorology). [FB: 76–78] By using the weather analogy, Falque and Bougon attempt to convey Ignatius's insight into the profound structures of human conscience to their lay audience without the need to adopt his religious frame of reference.

In order to legitimize this attempt to reframe Ignatius's insight in non-religious language Falque and Bougon claim that Ignatius remained prudent and evasive about the origin of these internal movements. [FB: 80] As they

48 *Spiritual Exercises*, 23. In the *Principle and Foundation* Ignatius refers to God's gifts of creation of which man should readily make use insofar as they do help him develop more as a loving person. As we shall see later there is no other way for Ignatius to relate to God than through their relations with the material world and the other people who are part of it. Therefore God's will is to be discerned in one's experience of the material world. In this connection it is interesting to note that Falque and Bougon as well as Verstraeten refer to the encounter with other people, nature, and one's inner world. For Delbecq, God is present in all these encounters.

49 In their usage the term 'lay' is inscribed in the French concept of 'laicité', which amounts to 'non-religious'.

say, his intention was primarily practical in the sense that the purpose of his *Spiritual Exercises* is "the conquest of self and the regulation of one's life in such a way that no decision is made under the influence of any inordinate attachment". This is, in fact, the complete title of the *Spiritual Exercises.* The question is whether Ignatius was indeed so prudent and evasive about the origin of the internal movements which are at the heart of discernment according to his *Spiritual Exercises.* The answer to this question will prove to be vital for understanding what God's creative project has to do with greater human freedom in decision making. We shall briefly suspend our hermeneutical reading of discernment in management for an excursion into theological reflection on Ignatian spirituality. Two contemporary commentators of the *Spiritual Exercises,* Fleming and Lucchetti Bingemer, will be our guides in this field.

Fleming appears to concord with Falque and Bougon about the meaning of the word 'spirits'.[50] In his view this word, used in the context of the Christian tradition, might be described as 'movements of one's heart or spirit', 'motions affecting one's interior life', 'a certain impetus in one's life', 'a feeling for or against some course of action', and so on. Just like Falque and Bougon he argues that the importance of the internal movements comes in the direction which they give to our lives. But he adds that "we are necessarily concerned about recognizing their good or evil source, especially in view of the possible deception of an apparently good direction".[51] The deception that Fleming refers to is not in the effects of the choice, but in the interpretation of the internal movements. This implies that the question about the source of the internal movements cannot be evaded so easily precisely because of the complexity of human motivations which Falque and Bougon intend to clarify.

Lucchetti Bingemer, our second commentator, observes that Ignatius had learned fairly early that it was dangerous to speak about the Holy Spirit, for which she refers to Ignatius's autobiography.[52] There he tells that the Spanish Inquisition questioned him on two occasions about his spiritual conversations.[53] Although he was never convicted, Ignatius decided to go to Paris to study theology, knowing that he would probably have been forbidden to speak any further about 'the things of God' if he had said that he was

50 D.L. Fleming, *A Contemporary Reading of the Spiritual Exercises. A Companion to St. Ignatius's Text* (St. Louis: The Institute of Jesuit Resources, 1976), 81.

51 Fleming, *Contemporary Reading* 81. In the *Guidelines for the discernment of spirits* Ignatius emphasizes that the 'good spirit' and the 'evil spirit' use the same tactics. The interpretation of their movements depends on whether one is 'intent upon living a good life' or is caught up in a life of sin'. See Fleming, *Spiritual Exercises,* 314–315 and 331.

52 M.C. Lucchetti Bingemer, *Em Tudo Amar e Servir* (São Paolo: Edicões Loyola, 1990), 43.

53 P. Divarkar, transl., *A Pilgrim's Testament. The Memoirs of Saint Ignatius of Loyola* (St. Louis: Institute of Jesuit Sources), 58–71.

inspired by the Holy Spirit. According to Lucchetti Bingemer this incident explains why Ignatius remained silent with respect to the Holy Spirit. But she explains that this does not mean that the Holy Spirit is absent in the *Spiritual Exercises.* She argues that "a guiding principle of the experience of the Holy Spirit can be searched and found between the lines of the text".[54] The guiding principle in question is the discernment of spirits, for which she refers to the coincidence of the fruits of the Holy Spirit with what Ignatius calls consolation.[55] A possible deception of an apparently good direction may be revealed by the lack of such fruits as joy and peace but also by a shortage of love, patience, kindness, goodness, faithfulness, humility and self-control. All these fruits are related to one's character and to the way one relates to the material world (including the other people who are part of it). Lucchetti Bingemer says that Ignatius has no need to *talk* about the Holy Spirit; it is much more important to him to *live* the Holy Spirit.[56] Based on her reading of the *Spiritual Exercises* it appears that Ignatius may have been prudent, but not evasive.

This brings us back to our hermeneutical reading of discernment in management.

Finding a general sense of correctness of the choice

If there is no need for Falque and Bougon to talk about the Holy Spirit, they should be concerned about the source of the internal movements which provided Ignatius with a general sense of correctness of choices. In fact, they do not seem to be concerned at all with the possibility that decision makers may be deceived while taking an apparently good direction. The overall experience of consolation in their lay reading of the *Spiritual Exercises* is "a dynamism which gives a more profound or more intense feeling of what I am living, which comforts me in my finality". [FB: 79] As the sign of consolation they mention contentment, serenity and clarity. Desolation, on the other hand, is marked by "little taste, or even distaste, of the tasks at hand, driving me away from what is right and good or from my own finality". [FB: 79] As the signs of desolation they mention discouraging thoughts, idleness, grumpiness, discontentment with self and others, sadness, and feelings of confusion, loneliness and abandonment. In view of the com-

54 Lucchetti Bingemer, *Amar e Servir,* 43.

55 Lucchetti Bingemer, *Amar e Servir,* 46. The fruits of the Holy Spirit are named in Paul's letter to the Galatians: 'love, joy, peace, patience, kindness, goodness, faithfulness, humility and self-control.' (Gal. 5,22). For Ignatius's definition of consolation see Fleming, *Spiritual Exercises,* 316.

56 Lucchetti Bingemer, *Amar e Servir,* 43–46. Italics by the author.

plexity of human motivations the question is how Falque and Bougon are able to gain a general sense of correctness about what is right and good to choose by the mere distinction of contentment or discontentment. The problem will be clarified by taking an excursion into the life of Ignatius.

Ignatius knew the importance of attachments in the lives of human beings from personal experience, first when his ideal as an *hidalgo* (knight) in the service of the Spanish court was shattered and later as a spiritual counselor to other people and general superior of the Jesuit Order. In the search for what really matters to us and in making the best choice, he considered both reason and feelings important as well as an objective point of reference. In the context of the 'discernment of spirits' he was particularly concerned with feelings. In the process of making a decision, he found that reason and feelings may be at odds. In order to make the best choice, he considered that it was important to pay attention to one's attachments. The Spanish word *afecto*, which Ignatius uses, is related to the heart, intimacy, being moved, inclined, attracted, attached, touched.[57] Attachments play a role in what human beings feel and want. The issue is not that human beings have attachments, but that they may be misguided by their attachments. Ignatius considered that individuals need to be free of any disordered attachments in order to make the right choice.[58] He calls this 'indifference', that is, a state of mind in which one is prepared to do anything provided that it helps one to grow in love.[59] In contrast to the popular meaning of indifference as 'not caring' (where one has no strong feelings about the values involved in the matter) in the ignatian sense it is the expression of a personal commitment to the ultimate value one perceives, understood as a process of growth.

We can understand from this excursion that Ignatius was primarily concerned with human growth. This brings us back to the discernment of spirits, which Lucchetti Bingemer indicated as the guiding principle in the *Spiritual Exercises*. As we have seen, in ignatian thought, consolation is marked by the fruits of the Holy Spirit as described in the letter of Paul to the Galatians. For Delbecq freedom is about the same fruits of the Holy Spirit. [D: 137] These fruits are consistent with the intention expressed in the *Principle and Foundation* to desire and choose whatever brings us closer to God (the ultimate horizon for Christians).[60] In other words human

57 I. of Loyola, "Trefwoorden," in *Geestelijke Oefeningen* (trans. M. Rotsaert; Averbode/Baarn: Averbode / Gooi en Sticht, 1994).

58 J. García de Castro, *Diccionario de Espiritualidad Ignaciana* (Bilbao/Santander: Ediciones Mensajero/Sal Terrae, 2007), 92–93.

59 Fleming, *Spiritual Exercises*, 23. See also W. Lambert, *Aus Liebe zur Wirklichkeit* (Mainz: Matthias-Grünewald-Verlag, 1991).

60 See Fleming, *Spiritual Exercises*, 23.

growth may be stifled by acting in accordance with one´s inclinations and personal preferences. This brings us to the importance of making a distinction between the material world and the ultimate horizon.

THE WAY OF RELATING TO THE MATERIAL WORLD

We have seen that the questions asked by Falque and Bougon as well as Delbecq indicate that the material world is the place to make choices. However, in contrast to Delbecq, Falque and Bougon do not make a distinction between the material world and an ultimate horizon. In this respect their concept of finality is of key importance. As we have seen, in their lay reading, 'finality' replaces the desire to advance in the search for God's will. Finality is understood as 'an orientation which animates the decision maker'. [FB: 66] It is framed in terms of a horizon of concern, a contribution to society, or a mission and vision. [FB: 15] Falque and Bougon complement this move with the need for everyone to be free in choosing 'whatever transcends one's experience'. Although it is understandable that they want to do away with the assumption that spiritual discernment requires a religious frame of reference, their line of thinking is confusing. Transcendence is not a matter of human choice.[61] In terms of Taylor's 'buffered' self their approach of discernment fits with a sense of power over the external world, which is illustrated by their criterion for making a choice: any personal finality must meet the requirements of a deep and authentic 'taste of life'. [FB: 80] The question is how a sense of vulnerability may be upheld in the practice of discernment without necessarily invoking a religious frame of reference.

Lucchetti Bingemer observes that Ignatius recognizes, in the *Principle and Foundation*, that there is no other way for human beings to relate to God than through their relations with the material world and the other people who are part of it.[62] She calls this material world (which is also sign of God's presence and action) the 'horizonte penúltimo' or horizon-before-the-last. In other words, God transcends the material world as well as revealing and presenting himself through the material world.[63] However, this mediation of the material world is ambiguous and partial. One could easily stumble in the pitfall of mistaking the material world for the ultimate horizon. Luc-

61 Transcendence is described in terms of God, the absolute, mystery, other, other as other or alterity. Various types of transcendence may be distinguished, which have in common that transcendence is revealed. See W. Stoker, "Culture and Transcendence – a typology", in *Culture and Transcendence. A typology of transcendence* (eds. W. Stoker and W.L. van der Merwe; Leuven: Peeters, 2012).

62 Lucchetti Bingemer, *Amar e Servir*, 173.

63 In Biblical terms this understanding of the material world is called creation.

chetti Bingemer explains that the distinction between the ultimate and the penúltimo was not evident for Ignatius. Whether God is found in the material world depends, in ignatian thought, on how individuals make use of it.

When this insight is related to Falque and Bougon's requirement of a deep and authentic 'taste of life', we can see that the process of discernment is concerned not so much with the taste of life as with the way that one tastes it. It matters, for example, whether one has patience to engage with the hard issues of work, and whether one 's way of learning is marked by love and humility.

Conclusion

Hermeneutics provides a way of scientific inquiry which is appropriate to the nature of organizations as a cultural phenomenon. It seeks to understand organizations as products of the human mind. The hermeneutic mode of inquiry complements the empirical mode in the psychological and sociological investigation of organizational behavior. In contrast to empirical research, this mode of inquiry can engage organizational participants in conversations in which meaning is constructed and helps them to arrive at a better understanding of their situation. This is particularly important with respect to organizational and societal renewal where a change of perspective is required.

The practice of discernment is concerned with interpretation of experiences, events and situations. The aim of discernment is greater freedom from disordered attachments in order to make appropriate decisions in view of human growth. The hermeneutic horizon of mainstream management does not stand in the way of the practice of discernment, provided that decision makers allow themselves to relate directly to their experience of reality and to attend to the process of interpretation.

Discernment is inevitably bound up with a normative frame of reference in the sense of one's orientation in life, values, worldview or religion. The normative frame of reference can enter into the practice of discernment in various ways. Delbecq speaks of *Christian* discernment, and Falque and Bougon speak of discernment *according to finality*. Delbecq shows that Christian discernment can help managers who take their reference from the Christian tradition to serve their organization by finding greater freedom in their own decision making process and their relation with other organizational participants who do not need to share the Christian worldview. Falque and Bougon, on the other hand, engage all organizational participants in the process of discernment. Therefore they need to give room to various worldviews within the process of discernment. The big advantage of Falque and Bougon is that their approach allows for a *shared* process of discernment.

Based on our cross-textual reading of both authors, the following standards are deemed mandatory for the practice of discernment in managerial contexts:

- the recognition that organizational behavior is not only determined by external factors and that organizational participants, including managers, remain responsible for their own conduct;
- a reflective inner disposition which enables decision makers to relate to their own experiences, sustained by a community of accountability and support (either within the organization or elsewhere);
- a commitment to human growth, or at least the desire for it;
- patience in the process of discovering the question relating to the choice, and continued listening that always recognzes that the deeper questions or issues may not emerge until one is further on in the process;
- awareness of the internal movements and attention to the interpretation of these movements in order to get a general sense of the correctness of any choice;
- remaining attentive to one's experience of events and situations following the decision to act.

It is important to remember that, in the *Spiritual Exercises*, the 'discernment of spirits' is only one of three ways to decide on a course of action, along with rational decision making and 'instant clarity'. Discernment of spirits is indicated when feelings play a role in the decision making process, as is the case when decision makers have to communicate with underlying issues in order to invent better ways of acting and being. Against this background discernment and rational decision making are complementary approaches. In the context of management these approaches may be viewed as a continuous circle in determining the corporate course of action. This circle could become part of the governance code as a decision making practice which will strengthen the organizational authority and its mandates for action.

Bibliography

Burrell, G., and G. Morgan, *Sociological Paradigms and Organisational Analysis.* Hants: Ashgate Publishing, 2008, originally published in 1979.

Collins, J.C., and J.I. Porras, *Built to Last.* New York: HarperBusiness, 1997.

—, "Building Your Company's Vision." in *Harvard Business Review*, 74/5 (1996): 65–77.

Delbecq, A., and M. Benefiel, "Awakened Spiritual Thirst Among Organizational Leaders. How Then Shall We Serve Them?" Seattle: Symposium at the Academy of Management annual meeting, August 4, 2003.

Delbecq, A., and L. Falque, "Practicing Discernment in Decision-making." Honolulu: paper presented to the Academy of Management annual meeting, August 7, 2005.

Delbecq, A., E. Liebert, J. Mostyn, P. Nutt, and G. Walter, "Discernment and Strategic Decision Making. Reflections for a Spirituality of Organizational Leadership." in *Spiritual Intelligence at Work*, edited by M.L. Pava. Amsterdam/London: Elsevier, 2004, pp. 139–174.

Divarkar, P. (transl.), *A Pilgrim's Testament. The Memoirs of Saint Ignatius of Loyola*. St. Louis: The Institute of Jesuit Sources, 1983.

Falque, L., and R. Bougon, *Discerner pour décider*. Paris: Dunod, 2014.

—, *Pratiques de la décision*. Paris: Dunod, 2005/2009.

Fleming, D.L., *A Contemporary Reading of the Spiritual Exercises. A Companion to St. Ignatius's Text*. St. Louis: Institute of Jesuit Resources, 1976.

Ganss, G.E., *The Spiritual Exercises of Saint Ignatius*. St. Louis: The Institute of Jesuit Sources, 1992.

Ganzevoort, R.R., "Forks in the Road when Tracing the Sacred. Practical Theology as Hermeneutics of Lived Religion." Chicago: Presidential address to the International Academy of Practical Theology, August 3, 2009.

García de Castro, J., *Diccionario de Espiritualidad Ignaciana*. Bilbao/Santander: Ediciones Mensajero/Sal Terrae, 2007.

Gerkin, C.V., *The Living Human Document. Re-visioning pastoral counselling in a hermeneutical mode*. Nashville: Abingdon Press, 1984.

Geus, A. de, *The Living Company*. Boston: Harvard Business School Press, 1997.

Giacalone, R.A., and C.L. Jurkiewicz, "Towards a Science of Workplace Spirituality." Pp. 3–26 in *Handbook of Workplace Spirituality and Organizational Performance*, edited by R.A. Giacalone, and C.L. Jurkiewicz, London/Armonk NY: M.E. Sharpe, 2003.

Gordon, R.A., and J.E. Howell, *Higher Education for Business*. New York: Columbia University Press, 1959.

Jongh, E. de, *Responding to the situation*. PhD diss. VU University Amsterdam. Leidschendam: Quist Publishing, 2011. Online access: http://dare.ubvu.vu.nl/handle/1871/32143.

Lambert, W., *Aus Liebe zur Wirklichkeit*. Mainz: Matthias-Grünewald-Verlag, 1991.

Lencioni, P., "Make Your Values Mean Something." *Harvard Business Review* 80/7 (2002).

de Loyola, I., "Trefwoorden." in *Geestelijke Oefeningen*, translated by M. Rotsaert. Averbode/Baarn: Averbode / Gooi en Sticht, 1994.

Lucchetti Bingemer, M.C., *Em Tudo Amar e Servir*. São Paolo: Edicões Loyola, 1990.

MacIntyre, A., *After Virtue*. Notre Dame: University of Notre Dame Press, 1984.

—, "Corporate Modernity and Moral Judgment: Are They Mutually Exclusive?" in K. Goodpastor and K. Sayre. *Ethics and the Problems of the 21st Century*. Notre Dame: Notre Dame University Press, 1979.

Mulder, A., and H. Snoek (eds.), *Werken met diepgang.* Zoetermeer: Meinema, 2012.

Pauchant, T.C., *La Quête du Sens. Gérer nos Organisations pour la Santé des Personnes, de nos Sociétés et de la Nature.* Montréal: Éditions Québec Amérique, 1996. Originally published as *In Search of Meaning: Managing for the Health of Our Organizations, our Communities, and the Natural World.* San Francisco: Jossey-Bass, 1995.

Sarbin, T.R. (ed.), *Narrative Psychology. The Storied Nature of Human Conduct.* New York: Westport/London: Praeser: 1978.

Simon, H., *Administrative Behavior, A Study of Decison-Making Processes in Administrative Organization.* New York: The Free Press, 1976.

Stoker, W., "Culture and Transcendence – a typology." In *Culture and Transcendence. A typology of transcendence,* edited by W. Stoker and W.L. van der Merwe (Leuven: Peeters, 2012).

Taylor, C., *A Secular Age.* Cambridge, MA: The Belknap Press of Harvard University Press, 2007.

Tennekes, J., *Organisatiecultuur. Een antropologische visie.* Leuven/Apeldoorn: Garant, 1995.

Verstraeten, J., *Leiderschap met hart en ziel.* Tielt: Lannoo, 2003.

—, "Beyond Business Ethics: Leadership and Spirituality, and the Quest for Meaning." in *Logos. A Journal of Catholic Thought and Culture,* 5/2 (2002): 17–39.

—, *Taal en stilte.* Averbode: Altiora, 2014.

Wit, H. de, *"My God", she said, "ships make me so crazy." Reflections on Empirical Hermeneutics, Interculturality and Holy Scripture.* Amsterdam: VU University, 2008.

Websites

Commissie onderzoek financiële problematiek Amarantis. *Niet onwettig, wel onwenselijk.* Accessed May 20, 2014. https://zoek.officielebekendmakingen.nl/blg-208258.pdf.

Institut de Discernement Professionnel. Accessed June 9, 2014. http://www.discernement.org.

Interview with Margaret Benefiel. *Faith and Ethics in the Executive Suite series of Princeton University.* Accessed June 9, 2014. http://www.princeton.edu/faithandwork/media/ethics-in-the-executive-suite/margaret-benefiel.

BANKING AND SPIRITUALITY? AN EXPLORATION

Aloys Wijngaards

Introduction

In the years after the financial crisis of 2008, intense debates have arisen on the causes of this crisis. Both in politics and in public opinion, bankers have often been identified as the main perpetrators. It is believed that because of their greedy and irresponsible behavior, bankers were at the root of the problems that brought the financial system close to a breakdown, and made the real economy suffer. In other words, according to politicians and the public, bankers are to blame ('banker-bashing'). The causes of the crisis are far more complex, as has been elaborated by Raghuram Rajan: systemic aspects of the financial sector, macroeconomic developments, and decisions by politicians (for instance, policies aimed at supplying cheap credit to people with low incomes in order to enable them to buy a house) created 'fault lines', that created a context in which a crisis was bound to happen.[1] Interestingly, however, the public debate on the crisis is framed as a question of *morality*: it is the bankers' alleged amoral, or even immoral behavior that caused discontent in society.

As the value-judgments on the behavior of bankers illustrate, this debate is an evaluative debate. This could be interpreted as a debate on social norms, e.g. the implicit or explicit evaluative expectations on behavior. Yet, the questions that are at stake in these debates go beyond debates on social norms in terms of 'right vs wrong'. On a more profound level, the questions that are discussed could be paraphrased as: "what do we want bankers (or more broadly, the financial sector in general) to contribute to our society?", "towards which desirable future society are bankers' activities to be directed?". These are also evaluative questions, but on a deeper level than morality. These questions refer to the evaluative orientation of the 'heart' of banking itself: they are about what makes it meaningful to be a banker within the context of a free democracy in the 21st century. However, this question has yet rarely been addressed.

1 See R. Rajan, *Fault Lines: How Hidden Fractures Still Threaten the World Economy* (Princeton: Princeton University Press, 2010). Rajan was the chief economist at the IMF in the years before the crisis, and was one of the very few people who predicted the crisis and tried to warn his fellow policymakers for the negative consequences.

In this article, an exploration is made of the question of the meaningfulness of banking, by using the concept of spirituality. To this effect, we first discuss the economic activities of banks. Second, the concept economic spirituality is elaborated, as a starting point for the relation between banking and spirituality. Third, we take a first step in connecting banking and spirituality by focusing on trust and societal responsibility. Fourth, financing a sustainable society is explored as a possible way for connecting banking and spirituality. In the concluding section, some reflections are offered on the possible impact of connecting banking and spirituality.

(1) Banking as an economic activity

Banking might seem a matter of 'mechanics' only, a calculation of risks and profits. But this is only one side of the activities of banking. In the decisions of bankers, evaluative orientations play an important role as well. That is, bankers can choose to serve different interests. For instance, in the early 2000s, most of the banks chose to focus on maximizing shareholder value. This meant maximizing the profits of the bank, and, in doing so, maximizing shareholder value by paying out dividends and raising the value of the shares. The interests of the shareholders were the main focus of the banks. As a result, other interests – the interests of customers, employees, and the environment, the stakeholders, so to say – were neglected. The decisions of bankers to focus on one interest only was an evaluative decision: they chose to let the interests of one specific group prevail over the interests of others. It was not merely a matter calculation, it was an evaluative choice between different interests.

Bankers fulfill an important role in our societies by engaging in economic activities. What are the primary economic activities of a bank? First, and most importantly, banks intermediate between people and companies that have money to spare, and others who are in need of money. By taking deposits, and lending this money to others (by giving 'credit'), banks finance new economic opportunities, and thus enable innovation and economic growth. By 'fractional-reserve banking',[2] the possibility to supply credit is greatly magnified. Second, and less important for the topic of this article, is that banks can match the different periods of time that peo-

[2] Fractional-reserve banking means that a bank only has to hold a fraction of the deposits, and can use the rest to finance loans. For instance, someone puts 100 euros in the bank, and the bank keeps 10 euros (10%) and lends the remaining 90 to a company. This 90 euros that was lent to the company finds its way back to the bank as a deposit (i.e. the company spends it, and the receiver brings it back to the bank). Of the 90 euros that are deposited, the bank holds 9 euros, the remaining 81 euros it can lend again. This is often referred to as creating "leverage".

ple and companies entrust the banks with their money, or lend it from the bank (e.g. long-term loans can be financed by several short-term deposits). Third, banks (together with central banks) provide the infrastructure for making payments.

From the perspective outlined in the introduction, the evaluative questions of the contribution of bankers to society, it is most useful to focus on the first role of banks: making loans (with the savings/deposits of the public). Cowton has provided us with a distinction of several evaluative considerations that are at stake here.[3]

First, a banker has to make sure whether an investment is both profitable and safe, that is, it will pay enough money to interest and profit. In other words, an investment made by a banker needs to have an appropriate balance between risk and return.

Second, according to Cowton, a banker has to engage in 'responsable lending'. This, Cowton explains, entails lending fairly, not being too hasty to foreclose, and not lending too much.[4]

Both these points, the proper balance between risk and return, and lending responsibly, are fundamental evaluative aspects of banking. These two points appear to be focused on 'prudence', on what it means to be a 'proper' banker. Yet, the evaluative dimension can be further elaborated. A question that provides a broader evaluative horizon for the day-to-day actions of a banker, is which evaluative orientations provide direction in the longer term. This question involves choices in focus and policy. What is the 'value' that a banker by engaging in economic activities wants to add to society in the longer term? This of course includes, but is not solely defined by, financial value. What does the bank want to (help) achieve – in terms of adding *societal* value –, for instance, with regard to innovation, sustainability, service to clients, and (financial) inclusion? To rephrase these questions: which evaluative orientation directs a banker in his or her work, and how is this directed at achieving societal value? These questions refer to the increasing demands from society about the role of banking in general, and, more specifically, to the decisions of bankers (to invest in certain projects or firms, or not). By focusing on these questions, the evaluative orientation of bankers may provide a possible starting point for a reflection on banking and spirituality. But in order to do so, we must first elaborate an approach to spirituality that enables this.

3 C.J. Cowton, "Integrity, responsibility and affinity: three aspects of ethics in banking," *Business ethics: A European Review*, 11/4 (2002): 393–400.

4 Cowton, Integrity, 395.

(II) Economic spirituality as the foundation for a spirituality of banking

In previous work, I have elaborated a concept of 'economic spirituality'.[5] Economic spirituality can be conceived as *the enactment of a transcending evaluative orientation in everyday economic practices.* As was argued in the previous section, banking is in its core an economic activity. For this reason, the concept economic spirituality can be applied to it. In this section, the main aspects of the concept of economic spirituality are highlighted.

Spirituality is often argued to reflect a meaningful framework as an ultimate horizon in a person's everyday life.[6] The *ultimate horizon* indicates that it encompasses the things that are most valuable and worthy of pursuit for a person, and places these as a beacon on the horizon of someone's life – the direction in which someone wants to go in the longer term of her life. By means of giving a direction or 'beacon', it provides a meaningful framework in a person's everyday practices. Meaning is constituted by the directedness towards what is ultimately valuable, which is an evaluative orientation.[7] As a person tries to contribute to the realization of this evaluative orientation through her everyday activities, these everyday activities become part of a journey towards this meaningful horizon – the horizon that ultimately encompasses her life in its totality. As such, spirituality can be argued to grasp the (ultimate) evaluative orientation that someone 'stands for', and which provides meaningful direction in her life.

Can this generic elaboration of spirituality in terms of an evaluative orientation be given more substance? The specific content of spirituality as a meaningful direction can differ from person to person, and in part depends on historical context and social and cultural surroundings. Yet, as all spiritualities are the spiritualities of human beings, they refer to *human* ideals and values. This allows us to provide a general delineation of what spirituality as an evaluative orientation refers to. For spirituality, the evaluative orientation is directed to 'the fullness of humanity' or the 'full-

5 For an elaborate discussion of the concept *economic spirituality*, see A. Wijngaards, "Economic Spirituality," *Studies in Spirituality*, 23 (2013): 302–309.

6 See, for instance, C. Kourie, "The 'Turn' towards spirituality," in *The Spirit that moves: Orientation and Issues in Spirituality* (eds. P. de Villiers, C. Kourie and C. Lombaard; Bloemfontein: Publications Office of the University of the Free State, 2006), 19–38.

7 Meaning can be defined in different ways, see M. Csikszentmihalyi, *Flow: the Psychology of Optimal Experience* (New York: Harper, 1990). For a discussion of the concept 'meaning of life', see A. Wijngaards, *Worldly Theology: on Connecting Public Theology and Economics* (Nijmegen: Radboud University, 2012).

ness of life'.[8] This means life in its most truthful, beautiful and good way – a reality that is yet far removed from everyday life as it is experienced. Elisabeth Hense has provided us with a helpful elaboration of what 'the fullness of life' encompasses: flourishing, dignity, wellbeing, wholeness, and purpose. These are general categories that allow for a specific interpretation or meaning, but which taken together indicate what a genuinely meaningful state of being human comprises.

As the definition of economic spirituality indicates, this evaluative orientation is a *transcending* evaluative orientation. Transcendence can be interpreted in various ways, and is often thought to refer to a different realm of existence, a higher or 'otherworldly' reality. This is *not* what transcendence seeks to capture in the definition of economic spirituality. Transcendence is understood here in a 'this-worldly' sense. By engaging in human interactions and exchanges, our lives as human beings become interrelated with the lives of other human beings, with traditions and previous generations, and, as the impact of our present decisions stretches out through a web or rippling of causations, to future generations as well. Our everyday, individual actions, and their evaluative import, can be reflected upon as an (explicit or implicit) connectedness to an evaluative horizon. This horizon, which connects the everyday and individual actions to a social and temporal space beyond these actions, can be reflected upon as a shape of transcendence, as Toine van den Hoogen has explained:

"transcendere means that we humans broaden and expand our relationship with the world and ourselves by rising above our spatio-temporal situation and embarking on a journey that opens up ever new horizons. (...) The infinitude and boundlessness of the journey brings us face to face with the infinitude and boundlessness of humans and their reality, which many people believe to be the true meaning of infinity."[9]

Transcendence, in this interpretation, is anchored in human existence, and stretches out towards infinitude and boundlessness. Therefore, it goes beyond 'being human' in the sense of the life of a human being, that is finite and limited in its possibilities. Applied to economic spirituality, transcendence means that in someone's everyday economic activities, the meaningful evaluative orientation provides a 'beacon' that is 'larger than life'.[10] The evaluative import of economic spirituality, the ultimate end that

8 E. Hense, "Present-day spiritualities in confessional, popular, professional and aesthetic contexts: Contrasts or overlap?," in *Present-Day Spiritualities. Contrasts and Overlaps* (eds. E. Hense et al.; Leiden: Brill, 2014), 1–17.

9 T. van den Hoogen, *A Taste of God: on spirituality and reframing foundational theology* (Münster: Lit Verlag, 2011), 58–59.

10 This interpretation of 'larger than life' was inspired by reading Nicholas Rescher, *Issues in the Philosophy of Religion* (Berlin: De Gruyter, 2007).

drives it, is not limited to the time and location of the specific economic activities that he or she is engaged in. Economic spirituality expands the meaning of everyday economic activities to an imagination of how life can be in its fullest – a meaningful imagination that goes 'beyond' everyday life, and therefore says something about how 'all of life' should reflect a certain flourishing, dignity, wellbeing, wholeness, and purpose.

(III) A first step in connecting banking and spirituality: trust and societal responsibility

How can we connect the evaluative considerations that are at stake in banking to a(n) (economic) spirituality? As was argued above, the activities of bankers do not merely comprise technical and calculative decisions, but also evaluative considerations. Let us now go back to the activities of banks, and reflect on the way these could be used to serve evaluative orientations that are directed at a fullness of life, in the sense of flourishing, dignity, well-being, etc. and the interests that are at stake in banking, the interests that bankers want to serve.

As was argued above, one of the key functions of a bank is safeguarding money for people who have money to spare and lending money to people or companies that need it. Keeping money safe and using that money to invest and lend is the distinctive characteristic of a bank. Both of these activities are basically matters of trust. The first requires the trust that your money will be handled well and returned when needed, it has to do with the trustworthiness of a bank. The second requires some further elaboration. When a banker considers to give a loan to a company or entrepreneur, he or she has to assess whether the company or entrepreneur is credit-worthy. Is, for instance, the investment a farmer wants to make by buying new farming equipment going to pay off? Or will, for example, the money that a banker lends to a start-up internet company be paid back? Will the loan lead to a successful new project? Here, the meaning of 'credit' is clearly connected to its ancient forbear, the Latin 'credere': to believe, to trust, to adhere to. It is not merely trust about getting the money they lend back, it is also trust in new opportunities, new and better products, that will contribute to society by 'adding value'.[11] Here, adding value does not only mean financial value, but also *societal value*, as the credit supplied by banks will enable projects and innovations that have an impact on society.

[11] Of course, this is not to argue that *every* banker will reflect on his or her actions in a deliberate way. It is merely to argue that there is an evaluative space that is available in every banker's daily actions to broaden the orientation of his/her actions. On the other hand, one might argue that if a banker decides to only care about 'getting the money', this reflects an *implicit* evaluative orientation as well.

In this way, the decisions of bankers reflect a *responsibility*: a banker – being entrusted with money by depositors – has a key role to play in 'putting this money to work', and in doing so, creating a societal impact. As Cowton's concept of responsible lending indicated, this first entails a prudent decision on the (financial) trade-off between risk and return. However, by including the societal value that is inextricably linked to the bankers' decisions on giving 'credit', Cowton's concept of responsible lending can be expanded. Responsible lending in this interpretation means both financially prudent decision-making *and* reflecting on the societal impact of the investment. Will an investment lead to a high financial payoff, but does it have negative societal side-effects (such as loss of jobs, or ecological damage)? Does a new start-up enterprise, which has not yet financially proven its merit, show potential as it seeks to answer a societal problem?

The societal impact of the investment decisions of bankers creates an evaluative space in which bankers can reflect on the question whether their activities contribute to a 'fullness of life'. Questions such as, for instance, 'do these activities contribute to flourishing, dignity, and well-being? And how are the financial payoff and societal 'payoffs' balanced?' can be asked here. By connecting the activity of lending to the trust a banker needs to have when providing 'credit' in the value that is created, and relating this to the responsibility for the societal impacts of the credit, we create a possibility for discussions on how banking could – or should – be directed at flourishing, dignity, etc. In doing so, a space for the bankers' own 'intuitions on the fullness of life', for connecting banking to spirituality, is opened. In the next section, an example of how this might be put into practice is elaborated.

(IV) Financing a sustainable society

It is clear that the development of our societies over the last two centuries has led to several great challenges with regard to safeguarding the sustainability of our way of living for both the current and future generations. Pollution, degradation of rain forests and oceans, global warming and rising sea levels, increasing inequality, the growing world population in need of food and clean water: these are just a handful of the problematic issues that threaten the sustainability of our current way of living. In other words: if we continue this way of development, a future society in which we have come closer to realizing a 'fullness of life' – in whatever more specific interpretation – is difficult to imagine. Flourishing, dignity, and well-being will likely be more difficult to attain, especially in 'developing countries'.

As an important part of these problematic developments is caused by our economic activities, banks might be able to play a role in changing these developments. As banks are the most important providers of credit to companies, they can either enable sustainable investments with the money that is entrusted to them, or finance companies that hamper sustainable development. Of course, this 'all or nothing' statement is a simplification of the questions that banks actually face: there are different approaches possible, and other considerations at stake (such as competition for deposits, the riskiness of certain sustainable investments, etc.). With regard to sustainability, at present, some banks choose for a 'clean-hands' policy, selecting only 'green' and 'social' investments. Other banks opt for an 'engagement' approach, which means that they choose to invest in a company that is not yet at the desired level of sustainable conduct, with which they engage in a dialogue on how to improve the situation. Also, several banks have developed new financial instruments to foster the financing of green and social enterprises, such as, for instance, 'green' and 'social' bonds.[12]

By extending credit, banks enable innovation and growth. This is a vital function for our society, a key process that allows for societal renewal. Therefore, the functioning and growth of our economy is related to the societal responsibility of the banker to decide whether to give 'credit' to an entrepreneur or company. In this way, the decisions of bankers can thus be considered as an evaluative space which enables them to direct the economic impact of their work towards a meaningful contribution to society and a sustainable future. As these (everyday) decisions are directed towards a future state of 'fullness of life', – in terms of flourishing, dignity, etc. – , they can be understood as the enactment of a transcending evaluative orientation.

Of course, contributing to a sustainable society is only one possible way in which banking might be connected to a meaningful end, there are other evaluative orientations that can be a guiding framework for bankers. For example, in a collaborative effort between the Dutch banking association, Duisenberg School of Finance and Vrije Universiteit Amsterdam, a 'cultural map' was developed that displays the core values of banking and what may be expected of bankers based on these values.[13] Ambition, trustworthiness, integrity, and client-centeredness are conceived as the core evaluative orientations of bankers. By striking a balance between different interests, these values can be argued to direct the decisions bankers make – decisions that impact the way our society will develop, and therefore, the flourishing of people in our society.

12 Green bonds are bonds of companies that comply with certain criteria regarding their ecological footprint. Social bonds are a pay-for-performance way of financing projects or enterprises that succeed in reducing government spending on social issues (such as youth unemployment).

13 See Nederlandse Vereniging van Banken, "Cultuurkaart financiële sector," www.nvb.nl/media/document/001365_cultuurkaart-financiele-sector.pdf.

(IV) Conclusion

This article started with the observation that in the years after the financial crisis of 2008, there have been many fierce debates about banking, in which evaluative arguments on the shortcomings of bankers often focused on moral questions. This article has made some first steps in shifting these debates from a focus on morality to the question of the end and meaning of banking, by using the concept spirituality. This might reflect a more forward-looking, deeper, and constructive approach than continuing the 'banker-bashing' (as still many politicians and NGOs continue to do). *Forward-looking*, because it focuses on the orientation towards a 'fullness of life' (in terms of human flourishing), that is to be achieved in the future by means of concrete decisions by bankers. *Deeper*, as it is not confined to bickering about social norms, but allows a focus on overarching values and meaning. This is not to say that social norms are not relevant, important, or interesting, but focusing on spirituality may prove to cause a more profound change in attitudes and actions than mere 'compliance' with norms. *Constructive*, as continued banker-bashing – scolding bankers for their alleged misbehavior – may actually lead to apathy and indifference amongst bankers. Instead, opting for connecting banking to spirituality may lead bankers to a renewed orientation on what their fundamental drivers and overarching values are.

The central question for bankers then becomes a question of 'soul searching': which evaluative orientation do I (either implicitly or explicitly) serve by my actions as a banker? To what intuitions of 'fullness of life' means – what future state of flourishing and living together in society – are my decisions to finance projects by giving them 'credit', directed? These questions refer to the question on what 'quality of life' actually means, which is a topic that transcends the scope of this article[14]. This requires a longer term perspective – something bankers are not necessarily used to. Banking activities often focus on a short term, ranging from days to months, to a couple of years maximum[15]. By focusing more on long-term investments with a positive future societal impact, such as investments in infrastructure and sustainable energy and production, the trust of society in banks may return.

[14] Within the context of economic decision-making, an interesting discourse has been developed by A. Sen (amongst others), on the "capabilities" that people require in order to live a fulfilling life. See, for instance, A. Sen, *Development as Freedom* (New York: Anchor Books, 1999).

[15] The greatest direct threat to a bank – a 'bank run' in which people massively withdraw their deposits – can happen anytime on a short notice.

Bibliography

Cowton, C.J., "Integrity, responsibility and affinity: three aspects of ethics in banking." *Business ethics: A European Review*, 11/4 (2002): 393–400.

Csikszentmihalyi, M., *Flow: the Psychology of Optimal Experience.* New York: Harper, 1990.

Hense, E., "Present-day spiritualities in confessional, popular, professional and aesthetic contexts: Contrasts or overlap?" Pp. 1–17 in *Present-Day Spiritualities. Contrasts and Overlaps.* Edited by E. Hense et al.; Leiden: Brill, 2014.

Hoogen, T. van den, *A Taste of God: on spirituality and reframing foundational theology.* Münster: Lit Verlag, 2011.

Kourie, C., "The 'Turn' towards spirituality." Pp. 19–38 in *The Spirit that moves: Orientation and Issues in Spirituality.* Edited by P. Villiers, C. de Kourie and C. Lombaard. Bloemfontein: Publications Office of the University of the Free State, 2006.

Rajan, R., *Fault Lines: How Hidden Fractures Still Threaten the World Economy.* Princeton: Princeton University Press, 2010.

Rescher, N., *Issues in the Philosophy of Religion.* Berlin: De Gruyter, 2007.

Sen, A., *Development as Freedom.* New York: Anchor Books, 1999.

Wijngaards, A., "Economic Spirituality." *Studies in Spirituality*, 23 (2013): 302–309.

Wijngaards, A., *Worldly Theology: on Connecting Public Theology and Economics.* Nijmegen: Radboud University, 2012.

Websites

"Cultuurkaart financiële sector." *Nederlandse Vereniging van Banken.* www.nvb.nl/media/document/001365_cultuurkaart-financiele-sector.pdf.

HALF HER KNEE: A DESCRIPTION OF THE SPIRITUAL DIMENSION OF A PHYSIOTHERAPEUTIC CASE

Willem Marie Speelman

Abstract

Ms. Alberts had an operation in which half her knee was replaced by an artificial joint. But the rehabilitation didn't go as expected. Her body rejected the prosthesis and it had to be removed. In preparation for her second operation, Ms. Alberts had to become as fit as possible. She was trained and advised by a physiotherapist; her husband prepared for her return home. How did she cope with this situation spiritually?[1]

The question of spiritual coping is becoming very strong in the practice of care in recent years.[2] The background of this question is complex. For one, there is a growing interest in the role that spirituality plays in people coping with their diseases, especially when they suffer from chronic or terminal disease.[3] Second, the attitude of society towards health care is changing. What kind of health can society offer to the people? Should disease be the main focus of care? Are we dealing with patients or with people? What is a person's role in their own practice of care? All these questions have a spiritual dimension, for spirituality is about people's relationship with the self and that which transcends it. The description of this spiritual dimension is a matter of discussion. Is it about Ms. Alberts' faith in God? About

1 This article is part of a project in which the spiritual method of Speelman is applied to physiotherapeutic cases. The project is a collaboration of N. van Meeteren, E. Oosting, J. Dronkers, T. Hoogeboom and W.M. Speelman. See W.M. Speelman, "A spiritual method for daily life practices," in *Towards a Theory of Spirituality* (eds. E. Hense and F. Maas; Leuven: Peeters, 2011), 55–71; W.M. Speelman, *Levende franciscaanse spiritualiteit. Een spirituele methode* (Heeswijk: Berne Media, 2013).

2 See, for example, the reviews of M.O. Harrison et al., "The epidemiology of religious coping: A review of recent literature," in *International Review of Psychiatry* 13 (2001): 86–93; M. Hermanns et al., "Biopsychosocial and Spiritual Aspects of Parkinson Disease: An Integrative Review," *Journal of Neuroscience Nursing* 44/4 (2012): 194–205.

3 M.A. Perry et al., "Older adults' experiences regarding discharge from hospital following orthopaedic intervention: A metasynthesis," in *Disability and Rehabilitation* 34/4 (2012): 267–78.

her engaging in spiritual practices like fasting, retreating, and praying? About whether or not these practices have influence on her condition? Or is it possible to dig deeper into the nature of the spiritual dimension, and develop a way to describe her spirituality as it is silently working in her life even without the traditional names and rituals that culture provides? For it may be that she does not believe in God or pray or fast, and yet develops ways to relate to the same realm of transcendence that religious traditions have given names of divinity.

Status quaestionis in the realm of spiritual studies

Spirituality is people's involvement with the transcendent in view of the destination of their lives.[4] The transcendent is usually referred to as 'divine' or 'eternal'. In all cultures, the transcendent forces in life have been given a narrative reality, beyond the present day reality, in which these forces are personified in divine figures. In this way, people relate their situation to eternity, thus making the finiteness of their lives bearable. It is therefore understandable that spirituality has been developed in the realm of religion. A theological critique of this narrative approach to transcendence could be that, by definition, it is impossible to grasp the transcendent in words or stories. This critique would lead to a tendency to use abstract words such as 'otherness' or simply 'transcendence' in an attempt to adequately approach the transcendent dimension of spirituality. However, the *principle* impossibility to grasp the transcendent in adequate words – even the term 'transcendence' has proven to be debatable[5] – has led Kees Waaijman to return to the use of the name "God" as an inclusive term of otherness in his definition of spirituality.[6] He describes the field as a relational process between God and human, whereby both poles of the relationship are being mutually transformed.[7]

However, if we choose to describe "God" or transcendence as it is working in our lives, many forms of otherness and many "names for God" may

4 The question of defining spirituality has been discussed by E. Hense, who proposes specifying spirituality as 'following intuitions in the quest for fullness of life,' E. Hense, "Present-day spiritualities in confessional, popular, professional and aesthetic contexts: Contrasts or overlap?," in *Present-Day Spiritualities. Contrasts and Overlaps* (eds. E. Hense et al.; Leiden: Brill, 2014), 1–17; In the field of health care, spirituality is received as 'the quest for connectivity with a higher or deeper reality or the sacred,' in H.G. Koenig et al., *Handbook of religion and health* (Oxford: Oxford University Press, 2001); quoted in S. Körver, *Spirituele coping bij longkankerpatiënten* (Eindhoven, 2013), 129.

5 M. Henry, *Incarnation: Une philosophie de la chair* (Paris: Seuil, 2000).

6 K. Waaijman, *Spirituality. Forms, Foundations, Methods* (Leuven: Peeters, 2002), 430.

7 Waaijman, *Spirituality*, 426.

be found. For example, a patient may ask why "God" is doing this to him; a nurse can be "an angel" to him; a disease may be "a demon." And when one's own body is not working properly, or when "my knee doesn't feel like *my* knee!" one can even be confronted with oneself as an *other*.[8] It is important to realize that we cannot grasp this otherness or measure it, for it transcends us and each of our systems. But we can *relate* to it, for example, by giving it a name and including it in our stories. By relating to it, we will enter with the transcendent in a process of mutual transformation. For example, by relating to one's disease, one may enter into a process of spiritual growth (or decline). The ultimate destination of people's involvement with the transcendent is their reconciliation with it or Him. Opposites – like health vs. disease, oneself vs. the other, ability vs. inability – are being transformed into a relation: disease as a form of health, oneself as an other, the ability to live with a disability. Finally, this relation becomes a communion: one can live *with* it. This is what spiritual coping is ultimately aiming at.

An inductive approach to spirituality, in which the names and stories of people form the basis, simply postpones the questions about new forms of religiosity or the relation between traditional and new forms of spirituality. We just start with what people say they are experiencing, doing, and longing for. Later on we may ask, for example, to what extent do the values that people say they are longing for in their lives resemble the virtues with which religious traditions describe the good life? In the end, it may very well be that traditional names for God, like Love, Faith, Hope, Communion, Life, Potency, Peace, etc., are very much the same as the names people use to describe their coping with health care. From a theological point of view, this would lead to the thesis that, religious or not, people do meet "God" in the very immanent situation of their bodily existence.

This approach is closely related to our proposition to describe the spiritual dimension as it is functioning in societal contexts as a question of quality of life. I hope to be able to answer the three questions formulated in our introduction on the basis of my analysis of a therapeutic practice: 1) What is seen as quality of life in spiritual studies? 2) In which human conditions and practices do spiritual studies detect quality of life? 3) What suggestions do spiritual studies give in order to enhance these conditions and practices?

Status quaestionis in the realm of health care

In the specific context of health care, the spiritual dimension or process is somehow functioning in the way people cope with situations of complaint. They want to become healthy again. But what is health, and what is the sort

8 P. Ricoeur, *Oneself as Another* (Chicago: University of Chicago Press, 1992).

of health that people really want? The *International Classification of Functioning, Disability and Health* (ICF) of the World Health Organization (WHO) defines health in terms of functioning: the functioning of the body as an organism, capable of functioning in a natural and social environment.[9] Note that health is not described as a state of living without pain, sorrow, deformities, and disabilities; one can live a healthy life with all these deviations from perfection. Machteld Huber describes health as "the ability to adapt and to self-manage."[10] Yvonne Heerkens distinguishes four dimensions of health: physical, mental, social and spiritual. The spiritual dimension is distinguished in four aspects: meaningfulness, striving for goals, future prospects, and acceptance.[11]

Let us focus on these four aspects and try to connect them to our description of spirituality.

Meaningfulness is a narrative effect; people are able to experience something as meaningful when they turn it into a story: "What happened to you?" "Well, doctor ...." According to Ruard Ganzevoort and Judith Visser, the story is a form of transcendence for it transcends the reality of the real life.[12] The spiritual dimension, then, could be described by studying people's stories, not by asking what is really the case *behind* the story, but by asking what meaning they form *in* and *through* that story.

Striving for goals is a force connecting a person with his or her destination. This destination is another form of transcendence; it is a calling voice or a driving force ('Spirit') that destines or motivates people to do what is to be done. The analysis of people's stories should reveal traces of these 'destining' or driving forces, and how they cause or inhibit people to act. The aspect of striving is interpreted here in its most active form.

Future prospects is an ability to see beyond the finiteness of the present situation; it puts the present life in the perspective of a life to come. The analysis of people's stories should reveal traces of faith and ability or the lack of them.

Acceptance is the ability to see the present situation as it is, recognizing its values as true and good. The analysis of people's stories should reveal traces of evaluation, hopefully positive.

9 See: "ICF Browser," www.apps.who.int/classifications/icfbrowser.

10 Huber, M. et al., "How should we define health?" *British Medical Journal* (2011): 343:d4163. https://digitalcollections.anu.edu.au/bitstream/1885/17067/1/f5625x-PUB9012_2011.pdf [visited January 2016].

11 Y. Heerkens et al., Factsheet *A dynamic concept of health and its relation with the ICF*, presented on the *WHO – Family of International Classification Network Annual Meeting*, 12–18 October 2013, Beijing, China. http://www.louisbolk.org/downloads/2882.pdf [visited January 2016].

12 R. Ganzevoort and J. Visser, *Zorg voor het verhaal. Achtergrond, methode en inhoud van pastorale begeleiding* (Zoetermeer: Meinema, 2007), 56.

Having offered a description of spirituality, and having connected this description with the four aspects of the spiritual dimension of health care, we now need a way to analyze this spirituality in people's stories. I would like to offer a method of narrative analysis, which allows for the description of the generation of meaning in people's stories, traces of their motivating forces, traces of their faith and abilities, and traces of their evaluations. This method is based on the semiotic analysis of the Paris School of A.J. Greimas, elaborated in the Netherlands by Gerard Lukken et al.[13] A very short introduction may show that the method can help us describe the spiritual dimension as proposed by Heerkens.

A short introduction in the analytical method

A semiotic analysis of stories describes how meaning has been/is being generated in the process of reading/writing. In semiotics meaning is not approached as a given or thing, but as an effect of a process of interpretation. The main question, then, is not what the meaning of the story *is*, but what traces the writer has left and the reader is following to come to their interpretation. There are many traces in a story, many threads to follow, but they form one chord, one route. Although different readers may be arriving from different angles, the final destination will bring them together. One thread, the so-called 'red thread', forms the theme connecting all the different actions. This is the main program of the story. The narrative program tells about a performance, which changes an initial situation into a final one. This change of the situation can be described as the realization of one or more values. A story about curing a patient may, for example, be described as the realization of the value / health/ in his body. (The stories will reveal that the reality of health care is more complicated than that.) The analysis tries to discern the main program from the other programs in the story, and the intended value(s) realized.

A program is framed by the so-called narrative scheme (*schéma narratif*), which describes the story in four subsequent phases. It begins with the question of what or who motivates the action: what or who wants this program to be executed? In the analysis we look for traces of motivation (*destination*), forces that influence that action by the modalities of /want-

13 A.J. Greimas and J. Courtés, *Sémiotique. Dictionnaire raisonné de la theorie du langage. Tome 1* (Paris: Hachette, 1979), translated as *Semiotics and language: an analytical dictionary* (Bloomington: Indiana University Press, 1982); Semanet, *Semiotiek en christelijke uitingsvormen. De semiotiek van A.J.Greimas en de Parijse School toegepast op bijbel en liturgie* (ed. G. Lukken; Hilversum: Gooi & Sticht, 1987); W.M. Speelman, *The generation of meaning in liturgical songs* (Kampen: Kok Agora; Leuven: Peeters, 1995).

ing/ or /having to/. For example, did the woman come to see the therapist in order to be rehabilitated? Does the story tell us this somewhere? Or are there other motivating forces (*destinateurs*) sending her to the therapist?

The second phase is the question of competence (*compétence*), for no action can be done if the ability to do is lacking. If the competence of the main program is lacking, the story remains unfinished. However, the story itself will lead us to a 'second best' program, which is realized instead. For example, if the rehabilitation does not succeed, is it because of the knee, or because everybody is only focusing on her knee and not on the woman? And, if so, can the woman gain self-confidence to become the active subject of the rehabilitation? The third phase is the performance itself (*performance*), which is described as a change from one situation into another. Motivated by a destinator (Dr), a competent subject of doing (Sd) transforms a situation in which a subject of state (S) is disjoined from an object of value (Ov) into a situation in which that subject is conjoined with that object. When a subject is in conjunction with an object of value, this value is said to be realized. The value forms the connection between the destinator, the subject of doing, and the subject of state in the following formula:

$$\mathrm{Dr} \Rightarrow \mathrm{Sd} \Rightarrow [(\mathrm{S} \vee \mathrm{O_v}) \rightarrow (\mathrm{S} \wedge \mathrm{O_v})]$$

It is often difficult to describe exactly which value(s) is/are realized, but, ultimately, that is what the story is about. Knowing that our human reality is formed by stories, we can conclude that every practice, including the therapeutic one, is about the realization of values. For example, by lack of ability to rehabilitate, the woman may be able to adapt to a new reality and conjoin herself with the object *life* in which the value /acceptance/ is invested.

The fourth and last phase of the narrative scheme is the evaluation (*sanction*), which is the task of the destinator or motivating force. The one who motivates the action must also evaluate its success, as if she recognizes herself in the realized value (cf. Genesis 1,4: "He saw that it was good"). This implies that if the main destinator does not express his or her consent, the work remains unfinished. It is important to notice that a narrative analysis only measures the program's success by the evaluation given by the destinator of that story. The whole world of health care may be very happy with the result of the operation, but the only thing that matters to the patient is whether the motivating force of his or her program is happy.

Analysis of the stories of Ms. Alberts, Mr. Alberts, and the Therapist

In order to trace the spiritual dimension of a therapeutic situation, we asked the people directly involved to write or tell a story about the therapy. Any story will do for the moment, for any story reveals what the story-teller intends to tell.[14] Of course, if he or she intends to keep things secret, the story will contain empty spots. In later phases we may discuss the meaning of such empty spots; for now, we just want to be able to describe spiritual processes on the surface.

As the social dimension is part of the health process it seems apt to analyze the stories of (at least) three roles in this situation: the patient, her husband, and the therapist. It may be, and I actually expect it to be, that these three positions have different motivations and perhaps even different values to be realized. In other words, it may be expected that the physiotherapist wants something different than the patient, and that her husband wants something different again. I will come back to the question of relating the different stories: how do they relate and how should they relate?

The physiotherapist

The story of the therapist begins by explaining that Ms. Alberts came under treatment after a knee operation, but that the rehabilitation didn't go "according to the protocol." The artificial knee was rejected by the body, and "the patient was informed about the policy to be followed. The prosthesis will be removed and a TKP revision will take place. This operation will take place on 23 April 2014." The patient's reaction is negative.

"She says that she is fed up with the way things happened. But she doesn't have the idea that she is not heard, because verification photos have been made. However, the patient indicates that after the operation a doctor made a visit; he asked her to bend her knee as far as possible. When this didn't go well, the doctor gave a blow to the leg, which hurt considerably."

The therapist continues her story by telling about the patient's strong motivation

[14] For the moment one story suffices because we only want to know if and how the method can be applied to therapeutic cases. In the follow-up of this research project more stories will be analyzed, because the research question focuses on the changes between the pre-operative and post-operative situation.

"to train for the operation. She wants to be as fit as possible when the TKP revision takes place."

The goals of the treatment aim at the functioning in daily life. The patient, however, indicates that she is afraid of the operation. The first operation went wrong, which may happen in the second one too. She is uncertain, but

"I have the impression that the patient herself has a great intrinsic motivation to work on her recovery. She dearly wants to perform all her activities in daily life. However, during the last rehabilitation it appeared that the other bodily complaints were sometimes a hindrance to work optimally on the recovery of the knee. (...) As far as I can estimate the patient, she is indeed a stickler."

She is very faithful to the therapy and has a good coping style. Moreover, she is already familiar with the exercises.

"What role the negative experiences will play is still uncertain, and the advices must be clear so that the patient will not experience uncertainties. If there are uncertainties, there may be fear, and this would be a possible hindrance to the recovery."

This story tells about a program ("protocol") of a complex health care institution and the resistance of the body to cooperate with that program. The effect is a division between the protocol and the body. As the patient reluctantly follows the protocol, however, the consequence is a double division: between the patient and her body on the one hand, and between the patient and the health care institution on the other. The physiotherapist finds herself in the middle of this complex conflict, mediating between the health care institution and the patient, and between the patient and her body. The theme of the story is that the physiotherapist tries to motivate the patient to heal the relations with her body and with the health care institution by gaining trust in herself and accepting the role of a competent subject of doing, so that she will be able to function in her domestic situation again. The most important value that is to be realized is /trust/. It is the physiotherapist who implicitly indicates that the patient is the first destinator (motivator) of this program, by stressing her intrinsic motivation and by indicating that she evaluates the initial situation negatively. The program intended by the patient has not been realized yet in this story; but trust has been given by the physiotherapist.

Let us come back to the questions with which we started, in particular the one about quality of life in the theory of spiritual studies. As indicated, we are involved in an inductive approach in which we describe what people say they are hoping for. In this first story we find the value of /trust/ or / faith/. The physiotherapist considers it as her ('destining') role to enhance the patient's faith in her role as a subject of doing. In this case of rehabilitation therapy, the physiotherapist – seemingly in addition to the protocol of the health care institution – considers it her role to communicate trust and faith to her patient. Thus she appears to see this patient to be more than just a patient; she motivates her to become the responsible subject of doing in her own health process. She tries to heal this woman by enhancing her "ability to adapt and to self-manage."[15] A first answer to the first question concerning quality of life would be that the values that the physiotherapist is trying to communicate constitute the qualities of a good life as she sees it. A first answer to the second question is, of course, already given in the choice of a therapeutic situation, which is in itself a quest for quality of life. In this quest, however, the good life is a remembered life; it is how life was before Ms. Alberts became in need of help. In order to answer the third question, we need to analyze the other stories and compare them.

The patient

The story of the patient is about her

"struggle to get better (...). You want to walk, you want to do – things which you think you have to do. But that is getting heavier and heavier."

She has had the idea that things would become better by following the therapy, and the doctor had done "what was necessary and possible": "placing half a knee." But neither the operation nor the therapy has made her better. She doesn't blame the doctor, though, and she finds the physiotherapist's care

"extremely good. (...) She has given me tasks to do what was best and she also says 'you're a stickler', and I want to be that. You have to do it yourself... and... together we are going to rebuild it towards the operation (...) so that the tendons and muscles, the strength will get in still, because that is what I need then. Because the fear of this moment will get out, the fear that it will happen again, and then... I am afraid for that. (...) Everybody, the people that I know, a new knee... you don't walk well, but that is what I feel too, I don't walk well (...) and then I feel a little bad, because I thought, I should be able to do it too, until I found out that it wasn't me. (...) Everything went fine, the care, the precaution, the explanation, nothing wrong with that...."

15 Huber, *How should we define health?*.

And then she tells about this doctor who unexpectedly pushed her leg too hard.

"I was sitting next to the bed and then this group entered, the ward doctor and the whole team and all that, and they came to ask how the patients were doing... And now how are you doing and all that, and I said all right, yes.... How far can you stretch? And I did stretch that leg as far as I could and he was standing in front of me and gives a blow against the slipper with his shoe, and that leg comes backwards. That did hurt. I said fine thank you, and I thought, man, how can you do this? (...) I found this humiliating... and he should have asked me to try a bit harder and then I would have done it myself. Because I found this so rude, and humiliating...."

The patient ends her story by repeatedly telling that everybody is trying hard.

"The strength must come from yourself, nobody can do that for you. She is a very good therapist, I have had others, but she is doing very good, I have no complaints for that matter...."

The red thread of this story can be indicated by three quotations: "you have to regain strength," "so that the tendons and muscles, the strength will get in still," and "the strength must come from yourself." But the theme is that the rehabilitation does not go well. Everybody has the best intentions and does their best. But the strength must come from the patient herself. This is to say that the patient is trying to regain the position of a competent subject of doing (which in her eyes was robbed from her by the ward doctor). In order to regain this position she has to get rid of her fear. The value realized in this story is not /health/ but /self-confidence/. The explicitly positive evaluation of the therapist indicates that the patient has been looking for a therapist who could help her regain self-confidence, and that this program has succeeded. The programs of the physiotherapist and Ms. Alberts are related as auxiliary program and main program.

Coming back to the second question concerning quality of life, about the human conditions and practices in which quality of life may be detected, both the analyzed stories suggest that the good life may not be so far away, or at least in daily life people seem to make steps toward it: a life in which people share faith and trust, thus gaining self-confidence. With respect to the third question, we can confirm that the physiotherapist and Ms. Alberts work together, the one in an auxiliary program (helping) and the other in the main program. But we shall return to the questions after the story of Mr. Alberts.

Her husband

Mr. Alberts wrote a concise report about what happened and what must be done from his point of view.

"In November 2012 my wife had to undergo an operation to her left knee. Half a knee would be put in. This has not been taken lightly. My wife found it dreadful, but pursued it still. Operation succeeded."

Then the story of the ward doctor who kicked against her foot.

"Now half her knee is loose and a new one must be put in. The follow up at home has been great. The home based care has been perfect, so no complaints about that."

And his story closes with:

"We have well adapted the house, so after the operation she can abide well at home with the help of neighbor-based care."

However concise the story is, fourteen lines, it shows that Mr. Alberts is hardly present himself and that his wife is not really involved in the trajectory. And although everybody in the complex health care institution has done his or her best, except for the ward doctor who apparently made a mistake, the hospital is not the place where Ms. Alberts can regain her health. Actually, analysis shows that the hospital is described as a kind of service station: necessary, strange, cool, lonely. The program realized is that "we" have prepared the house so that "after the operation, she can abide well at home with the help of neighbor-based care." Just by putting home in opposition to the hospital Mr. Alberts pictures home as a place of hope: not strange but familiar, not cold but warm, not individual but communal.

The good life, as it is implicitly depicted in the three stories, is to be found in daily life where people are capable of adapting to their situation – even if it is with infirmities – and self-manage. The program of the physiotherapist is auxiliary, for she helps Ms. Alberts to regain self-confidence and eventually rehabilitate; Mr. Alberts depicts the place where the good life is to be found: not in the health care institutions, but here at home. The main values actualized and sometimes realized in the stories are trust and self-confidence, guilt and forgiveness, hope and communion.

The third question concerning quality of life, what suggestions spiritual studies might give in order to enhance the conditions and practices of a good life, may be combined with another question: that about the relation between the three stories. In the therapeutic practice there seem to be three different programs: the one of the therapist, the one of the patient, and the program of her partner. The question is, of course, what would help them to cooperate in the creation of a new daily life as a trustful, confident, hopeful, and shared life. Actually, our answer to this question is that we can see how people and their stories cooperate. The role of this spiritual analysis may be one of making clear how far people indeed cooperate.

The spiritual dimension of the health process as revealed in the stories

We have described spirituality as involvement with the transcendent in view of the destination of life. The images of life's destination are sometimes made explicit in people's stories, but more often they are silently present and active. Technically speaking, there are always implicit destinators motivating people's actions. Yet, it is believed that these implicit destinators leave their traces in people's stories, for example, in the form of values. It is possible, and to be honest it is my conviction, that the implicit destinators form the transcendent realm which religious stories refer to as "God" and "the divine." In my experience of analyzing stories, values such as / communion/, /faith/, /love/, /integrity/, etc ., are very often found as traces of this implicit destinator.[16] Another form of implicit destination is an image or story of the good life, playing in the background of the story told, like home as it is implicitly presented in the story of Mr. Alberts. Let us re-read the stories in the light of this question of implicit destination.

For the physiotherapist, the implicit destination may be pictured as the idea or faith that this woman should have access to a world in which everybody is fit to independently lead her daily life. This image of a good life motivates her actions. We could add to this that her own role is one of leading this patient away from incompetence towards competence. She wants to help people, give them access to this good life. Ms. Alberts, however, has a slightly different implicit destinator, a little more modest: instead of a fit and independent life, she wants to regain her own strength, and be reconciled with her body, disabled or not, just fit enough to be capable of living her own social life. Mr. Alberts is quite clear in his future prospect: fit or not, his wife should come home as soon as possible. It is interesting to notice that for these people – and perhaps they are many – the image of a

16 Perhaps this implicit destinator in people's stories – claimed to be of ultimate significance for "me" and any other human being – refers to the universal truth claim proposed by C. Hübenthal in this volume.

good life is not so different from their own daily life, that is: as it was *before* it went wrong. A spiritual approach to health care may lead to a critical discussion about the targets that the health care institutions have set themselves. Are they making people better, or are they helping people to adapt to their new situation and live their old and lost life again in a new way?

In our stories the health care institution appears as a form of transcendence, with its agencies of the hospital, the medical staff, the knee prosthesis, and the therapies. On the whole, the implicit destination is pictured as a normal, daily, but good life. Several forces – motivating and hindering – have an effect on the normal life of the patient: the one is calling and helping to live life as a good life, the other is hindering people to reach it. The spiritual involvement with these forces transforms the involved, both the transcendent (health care institution) and the immanent I-here-now (Ms. Alberts). In this case, the physiotherapist – representing the transcendent – is being transformed from a servant and guard of the protocol into a human being communicating trust. Ms. Alberts is being transformed from a patient into a human being taking control over her own life. Mr. Alberts – representing the good life at home – is transforming their home into a place where his wife can abide well.

How is this meaningful? Meaning is generated by telling and reading stories. In the story, the transcendent (otherness) – divine or demonic – is related to the self. This relationship is brought into a process in which they are reconciled as different roles in a shared program. In this shared program shared values are being realized, values that belong to the destination, values of the good life. And even if the intended program has not been realized, as is partly the case in the stories that we have been reading here, meaning has been generated because the otherness and the self are being related in the stories; they are joined instead of opposed. Here, the fourth term of Heerkens, acceptance, comes to the front. A patient can come to live with his or her diseases and still find the good life.

The relevance of a spiritual approach to health processes

Entering the therapeutic process as a theologian, one will immediately be confronted with suspicion: "Are you going to Christianize our work?" Is it possible to adapt a spiritual approach in a non-religious environment without colonizing it and foisting on it one's theological words and, with these words, one's religion? How can I talk about "transcendence," "otherness," "God" with people who do not relate to these words? The path we choose in adapting spiritual studies to the physiotherapeutic practice is that we search for values and roles in which people in fact invest their hope and faith. In this way, we are reading the traditional religious story in people's individual stories. If we know what people do believe in and are hoping for, we may relate these relevant words to the spiritual realm and knit the loose ends of people's individual stories to the bigger religious story. Are we converting them or are they converting us? In a certain way both questions can be answered positively, for we are conversing with each other. We discover how the religious story is being incarnated in and/or is being generated by people's life stories, and people may discover how their daily experiences are part of a bigger story about the good life.

Bibliography

Ganzevoort, R. and J. Visser, *Zorg voor het verhaal. Achtergrond, methode en inhoud van pastorale begeleiding.* Zoetermeer: Meinema, 2007.

Greimas, A.J. and J. Courtés, *Sémiotique. Dictionnaire raisonné de la theorie du langage. Tome 1.* Paris: Hachette, 1979. Translated as *Semiotics and language: an analytical dictionary.* Bloomington: Indiana University Press, 1982.

Harrison, M.O. et al., "The epidemiology of religious coping: A review of recent literature." *International Review of Psychiatry*, 13 (2001): 86–93.

Y. Heerkens et al., Factsheet *A dynamic concept of health and its relation with the ICF*, presented on the *WHO – Family of International Classification Network Annual Meeting*, 12–18 October 2013, Beijing, China. http://www.louisbolk.org/downloads/2882.pdf [visited January 2016].

Henry, M., *Incarnation: Une philosophie de la chair.* Paris: Seuil, 2000.

Hense, E., "Present-day spiritualities in confessional, popular, professional and aesthetic contexts: Contrasts or overlap?" Pp. 1–17 in *Present-Day Spiritualities. Contrasts and Overlaps.* Edited by E. Hense et al. Leiden: Brill, 2014.

Hermanns, M. et al., "Biopsychosocial and Spiritual Aspects of Parkinson Disease: An Integrative Review." *Journal of Neuroscience Nursing*, 44/4 (2012): 194–205.

Huber, M. et al., "How should we define health?" *British Medical Journal* (2011): 343:d4163. https://digitalcollections.anu.edu.au/bitstream/1885/17067/1/f5625xPUB9012_2011.pdf [visited January 2016].

Koenig, H.G. et al., *Handbook of religion and health.* Oxford: Oxford University Press, 2001.

Körver, S., *Spirituele coping bij longkankerpatiënten.* Eindhoven: Tilburg University, 2013.

Perry, M.A. et al., "Older adults' experiences regarding discharge from hospital following orthopaedic intervention: A metasynthesis." *Disability and Rehabilitation* 34/4 (2012): 267–278.

Ricoeur, P., *Oneself as Another.* Chicago: University of Chicago Press, 1992.

Semanet, *Semiotiek en christelijke uitingsvormen. De semiotiek van A.J. Greimas en de Parijse School toegepast op bijbel en liturgie.* Edited by G. Lukken. Hilversum: Gooi & Sticht, 1987

Speelman, W.M., "A spiritual method for daily life practices." In *Towards a Theory of Spirituality,* edited by E. Hense and F. Maas, 55–71. Leuven: Peeters, 2011.

—, *Levende franciscaanse spiritualiteit. Een spirituele methode.* Heeswijk: Berne Media, 2013.

—, *The generation of meaning in liturgical songs.* Kampen: Kok Agora. Leuven: Peeters, 1995.

Waaijman, K., *Spirituality. Forms, Foundations, Methods.* Leuven: Peeters, 2002.

Websites

"ICF Browser." http://apps.who.int/classifications/icfbrowser.

CONCEPTS AND IMAGES

THE CHOICE OF DE-OWNERSHIP AND THE OWNERSHIP OF VIRTUE: A FRANCISCAN PERSPECTIVE

Krijn Pansters

Abstract

This paper deals with the ethical problems of personal property in today's world, the benefits of an individual ethics of 'virtue ownership', and the promising translation of the concept of 'de-ownership' from corporate to individual ethics. From a perspective of Franciscan moral spirituality, we will focus on the following aspects: the *possession of poverty* as a virtue of self-renunciation; the *spiritual capital* of personal virtue and conscience as the capacity to know and to choose the good; the cultivation of personal goodness as a prerequisite for *the good life*; the *virtue of temperance* as a new disposition of self-restraint in the face of modern saturation and excess; the necessity of *personal choice* and accountability; the *art of living* a respectful, responsible, and sustainable life; the characteristics of the *care for creation*; and the *choice of de-ownership* as a spiritual strategy. Our point of departure is the traditional (Franciscan) idea of conscience: turning within in order to behave well. This requires disappropriation, roots in a spiritual attitude, brings forward personal virtue, shapes the human character, and refers to the goodness of God. From the inner order of the human being springs the choice of *de-ownership*: individual disappropriation and personal renunciation of things on the basis of modesty and humility. The de-owner employs goods without possessing them, gives them back to their rightful owner, enjoys their use, and is grateful for them. The *use* of worldly things thus frees the spirit and connects the 'user' to his 'Provider'. A Franciscan strategy of de-ownership stresses the development of good intentions, striving for the goodness that lies within, and the preservation of inner purity and integrity. It calls for 'alacrity, austerity, and benignity' – the triple condition for a good conscience that earns us the ownership of virtue.

The Problem of Property – Introduction

The problem of property and possession that determines so many of the 'wicked problems' of today's world is not a matter of things, but of right measure in accordance with right desire:

"For if you desire these things in order to be sustained by them, be they your own or those of others, you keep the middle way. If you overestimate them as if happiness were to be found in them, you are at one extreme; if you spurn them as being wicked, you are at the other."[1]

With his stress on proper discernment as a personal duty, the Franciscan minister general and theologian Bonaventure (1221–1274) here shows that in the sphere of possessions "conscience is key."[2] Had the Seraphic Doctor visited the 'Big Challenges, Radical Changes' National Sustainability Congress in Rotterdam on November 21, 2013, he would have been struck by at least three things: the continuing actuality of the 'big challenge' that 'property' poses; the total absence of (an awareness of) *individual* ethics as an 'agent' for 'radical change'; and the surprising solution that lies in a strategy for sustainability proposed by *business* and *legal* ethicists, namely:

1 Bonaventure, *Collationes in Hexaemeron* 5,4 (ed. C.M. Cullen; Oxford: Oxford University Press, 2006), 100.

2 On conscience, see: Bonaventure, *De triplici via* 1,1,8–9 ("As soon as these three [alacrity, austerity, benignity] are attained, the conscience becomes good and straight"), J. de Vinck (transl.), *The Works of Bonaventure* 1 (Paterson: St. Anthony Guild Press, 1960), 67–68; Bonaventure, *Apologia pauperum* 3,3 ("This betokens in reality a threefold act of love: avoiding evil, pursuing good, and bearing with adversity. For as regards the avoidance of evil, charity is said to be from a pure heart; as regards the pursuit of good, from a good conscience; and as regards the bearing of adversity, from a faith unfeigned"), J. de Vinck (transl.), *The Works of Bonaventure* 4 (Paterson: St. Anthony Guild Press, 1960), 38–39. On conscience, see further: R. Bernet, *Conscience et existence. Perspectives phénoménologiques* (Paris: PUF, 2004); H. Katchadourian, *Guilt. The Bite of Human Conscience* (Stanford: Stanford General Books, 2010); J. Keating and D.J. Billy, *Conscience and Prayer. The Spirit of Catholic Moral Theology* (Collegeville: Liturgical Press, 2001); W. Koops et al. (eds.), *The Development and Structure of Conscience* (Hove: Psychology Press, 2010); D.C. Langston, *Conscience and Other Virtues. From Bonaventure to MacIntyre* (University Park: Pennsylvania State University Press, 2001); M. Ojakangas, *The Voice of Conscience. A Political Genealogy of Western Ethical Experience* (New York: Bloomsbury, 2013); S. Overman, *The Conscience Economy. How a Mass Movement for Good is Great for Business* (Boston: Bibliomotion, 2014); R. Sorabji, *Perception, Conscience, and Will in Ancient Philosophy* (Farnham etc.: Ashgate, 2013); L.A. Stout, *Cultivating Conscience. How Good Laws Make Good People* (Princeton: Princeton University Press, 2011); P. Strohm, *Conscience. A Very Short Introduction* (Oxford: Oxford University Press, 2011); F.B.M. de Waal et al. (eds.), *Evolved Morality. The Biology and Philosophy of Human Conscience* (Leiden and Boston: Brill, 2014); J. White, *Honesty, Morality & Conscience. Making Wise Choices in the Gray Areas of Life* (Carol Stream: NavPress, 1996).

'de-ownership.'[3] These three seraphic observations – the cons of 'property,' the pros of 'conscience,' the 'de-' of ownership – are also what concern us here. Starting from the idea that modern-day problems related to issues of inequality and immorality essentially ask for a renewed reflection on *virtue*, in particular environmental virtue,[4] I present a Franciscan-inspired model of material poverty and spiritual wealth that corresponds with, or complements, popular notions of ethical living, in particular 'spiritual capital,' 'the good life,' 'the art of living,' 'care for creation,' and 'the new economy.'

The Possession of Poverty

From a Franciscan point of view, most possessions present a spiritual problem, but not all of them. Virtues, for example, are possessions (*possit habere*) of the one who is predisposed to good behavior, 'fundamental characteristics' of the servant of God.[5] Yet it is exactly in the *most exalted poverty* that the Franciscan brothers are "made poor in temporal things (*pauperes rebus fecit*) but exalted in virtue (*virtutibus sublimavit*)."[6] In this paradox lies the

3 Among the specific themes were: the Netherlands as leading exporting country, the transition of energy, sustainable food, circular economy, the 'people' aspect, and sustainable business cases. The general theme of the NSC in 2014 was "Changing the Game with Technology."

4 See especially: R. Sandler, *Character and Environment: A Virtue-Oriented Approach to Environmental Ethics* (New York: Columbia University Press, 2007); R. Sandler and P. Cafaro (eds.), *Environmental Virtue Ethics* (New York: Rowman and Littlefield, 2005); B. Treanor, *Emplotting Virtue: A Narrative Approach to Environmental Virtue Ethics* (New York: SUNY Press, 2014); L. van Wensveen, *Dirty Virtues: The Emergence of Ecological Virtue Ethics* (Amherst, NY: Prometheus Books, 2000).

5 Francis of Assisi, *Salutatio virtutum* 5–6 (*possit habere, omnes habet*); Francis of Assisi, *Epistola ad fideles* 2,30 (*habeamus*); Francis of Assisi, *Regula bullata* 10,9 (*et habere*); Bonaventure, *De triplici via* 3,3 (*ad habendum habere*); Bonaventure, *De perfectione* 8,8 (*possideas*); Bonaventure, *Regula novitiorum* 10,2 (*in corde et opere habere*). See also: R.J. Armstrong et al. (transl.), *Francis of Assisi. Early Documents* 1 (New York etc.: New City Press, 1999), 137; K. Pansters, *Franciscan Virtue. Spiritual Growth and the Virtues in Franciscan Literature and Instruction of the Thirteenth Century* (Leiden and Boston: Brill, 2012), 38–39, 269–280.

6 Francis of Assisi, *Regula bullata* 6,4 in Armstrong, *Francis* 1, 103; *Admonitiones* 18,2 (Everything good should be given back to God, the rightful owner of all earthly things). See also: K. Esser and E. Grau, *Antwort der Liebe. Der Weg des franziskanischen Menschen zu Gott* (Werl: Dietrich-Coelde-Verlag, 1967), 153: "Um die Anerkennung der Eigentumsrechte Gottes am Besitz des Menschen geht es bei der Entäußerung des franziskanischen Menschen, wenn er auf allen irdischen Besitz verzichtet." On Franciscan poverty, see further: V.-M. Breton, *La pauvreté* (Paris: Editions Franciscaines, 1959); G. Barone, *La povertà del secolo XII e Francesco d'Assisi. Atti del II Convegno Internazionale. Assisi, 17–19 ottobre 1974* (Assisi: Studi Francescani, 1975); A. van Corstanje, *Gottes Bund mit den Armen. Biblische Grundgedanken bei Franziskus von Assisi* (Werl: Dietrich-Coelde-Verlag, 1964), 41–80; M. Geulen, *Die Armut des heiligen Franz von Assisi im Lichte der Wertethik* (diss. Köln: 2005); M.D. Lambert, *Franciscan Poverty. The Doctrine of the Absolute Poverty of Christ and the Apostles in the*

richness of poverty (as opposed to the power of the purse denounced by Francis of Assisi) that affects the whole person and all areas of his life.[7] It is 'external' in its call for disappropriation (dispossession), begging, and the renunciation of money. It is 'internal' when it amounts to a spiritual attitude – being willing to follow the model of the 'poor' Christ in a total and unqualified way and observe the Gospel spiritually.[8] Never an aim in itself, poverty primarily serves *kenosis*: the renunciation of oneself for the sake of God's dwelling within.[9] Bonaventure equally emphasizes the spiritual quality of poverty: voluntary poverty is the beginning and foundation of evangelical perfection, the foundation of Christian religion, and the primary foundation of "the whole spiritual edifice."[10]

The Spirituality of Capital

Focusing on the possession of spiritual things, I would like to turn here to the notion of 'spiritual capital.'[11] Standing in the socio-economic tradition of

Franciscan Order 1210–1323 (St. Bonaventure: Franciscan Institute, 1998); G. Melville and A. Kehnel (eds.), *In proposito paupertatis. Studien zum Armutsverständnis bei den mittelalterlichen Bettelorden* (Münster etc.: Lit-Verlag, 2001); J. Micó, "Franciscan Poverty," *Greyfriars Review* 11 (1997): 257–300; N. Senocak, "The Making of Franciscan Poverty," *Revue Mabillon* nouv. ser. 24–85 (2013): 5–26; A.A. Tils, *Der heilige Franziskus von Assisi und die Armut. Eine genetische Darstellung seiner religiösen Anschauung von der Armut im Lichte der Quellen des 13. Jahrhunderts* (diss. Brixen: Weger, 1961).

7 K. Esser, "Die Armutsauffassung des hl. Franziskus," *Poverty in the Middle Ages* (ed. D. Flood; Werl: Dietrich-Coelde-Verlag, 1975), 60–70 (69). See further: G. Todeschini, *Ricchezza francescana. Dalla povertà volontaria alla società del mercato* (Bologna: Il Mulino, 2004); L. Lehmann, "„Arm an Dingen, reich an Tugenden". Die geliebte und gelobte Armut bei Franziskus und Klara von Assisi," in *Gelobte Armut. Armutskonzepte der franziskanischen Ordensfamilie vom Mittelalter bis in die Gegenwart* (eds. H.-D. Heimann et al.; Paderborn etc.: Schöningh, 2012), 37–65; W.M. Speelman, *Rijk leven zonder bezit. Franciscaanse spiritualiteit als bron van vernieuwing* (Zoetermeer: Meinema, 2013); K.B. Wolf, *The Poverty of Riches. St. Francis of Assisi Reconsidered* (Oxford: Oxford University Press, 2003).

8 "Er versteht die Armut als eine Gesamthaltung des ganzen Menschen, so daß die äußere, tatsächliche Armut der Ausdruck für eine viel tiefer greifende und weiter reichende innere Armut ist." K. Esser, "Mysterium paupertatis. Die Armutsauffassung des hl. Franziskus v. Assisi," *Wissenschaft und Weisheit* 14 (1951): 177–189 (177). See also: Lambert, *Franciscan Poverty*, 59–60; Pansters, *Franciscan Virtue*, 138–143.

9 Esser, "Mysterium," 187.

10 Bonaventure, *Apologia pauperum* 7,3 (De Vinck, *The Works* 4, 126); *Apologia pauperum* 9,29; *Constitutiones Narbonensis* 1; *Regula novitiorum* 16,1. See also: Pansters, *Franciscan Virtue*, 143–149.

11 On spiritual capital, see for example: T.R. Malloch, *Doing Virtuous Business. The Remarkable Success of Spiritual Enterprise* (Nashville etc.: Thomas Nelson, 2008), 17–24; S.D. Rima, *Spiritual Capital. A Moral Core for Social and Economic Justice* (Farnham etc.: Ashgate, 2012); M. O'Sullivan and B. Flanagan (eds.), *Spiritual Capital. Spirituality in Practice in Christian Perspective* (Farnham etc.: Ashgate, 2012); D. Zohar and I. Marshall, *Spiritual Capital.*

the 'capital' concept, in particular social capital ("the accumulated social resources inherited by each new generation from its predecessor") and human capital ("skills, experience, and knowledge, embodied in human beings"), it may be defined as "the fund of beliefs, examples, and commitments that are transmitted from generation to generation through a religious tradition, and that attach people to the transcendental source of human happiness."[12] Spiritual capital theory covers areas such as spirituality, economic poverty, ecology, and business.[13] What interests us here is both its methodological foundation, which can be defined as "authentic subjectivity in knowing and choosing,"[14] and its principal manifestation, which "lies in the virtues of individual people."[15] It is the subjective element of "knowing and choosing" – conscience – that I would like to draw attention to here, as well as the immediate result of personal virtue(s) as spiritual capital: "the shaping of the human character, which in turn transforms culture."[16] What connects 'knowledge and choice' with 'character and culture' is goodness, for to know the good and to choose it (the good of 'morality-in-spirituality') is to be good and to do it (the good of 'individuality-in-community').

The Goodness of Life

Correlating with the idea of the possession of virtue(s) as personal goodness is the notion of 'the good life,' a term associated with Aristotle's teaching on ethics and used "for the life that one would like to live, or for

Wealth We Can Live By (San Francisco: Berrett-Koehler Publishers, 2004). Spiritual capital is now part of a new theory called 4Capital Theory. According to this theory, four capitals "need to be taken into account in measuring a society's wellbeing and in working for social transformation:" material capital (funds, properties, physical resources), intellectual capital (knowledge, skills, abilities), social capital (relationships, networks, good reputation), and spiritual capital (spiritual and religious resources) (M. O'Sullivan, "Spiritual Capital and the Turn to Spirituality," in O'Sullivan and Flanagan, *Spiritual Capital*, 43–59 (43).

12 Malloch, *Doing Virtuous Business*, 11, 17, 18.

13 O'Sullivan, "Spiritual Capital," 43–49; J. Kennedy, "The Ecological Crisis and Spiritual Capital," in O'Sullivan and Flanagan, *Spiritual Capital*: 61–77; W. O'Brien, "Spiritual Capital in a Competitive Workplace," in O'Sullivan and Flanagan, *Spiritual Capital*: 97–109.

14 O'Sullivan, "Spiritual Capital," 43.

15 Malloch, *Doing Virtuous Business*, 23. See also: L. Bruni, *The Genesis and Ethos of the Market* (Basingstoke: Palgrave MacMillan, 2012).

16 O'Sullivan, "Spiritual Capital," 44–47; Malloch, *Doing Virtuous Business*, 24. See also: J.A. Jacobs, *Choosing Character. Responsibility for Virtue and Vice* (Ithaca: Cornell University Press, 2001). A good example is the motto at the Consultancy for Leadership Development and Organizational Transformation, www.zijnwerkt.nl: "We believe that true transformation within and through teams, groups and organisations only takes place when we ourselves are willing to make an 'inner shift' of perspective."

happiness".[17] Fundamental questions related to the good life may be the following:

"Does it make sense to talk about *the* good life or *the* human good, or are there many human goods and many ways of leading a good life? If there are many goods, then how are they related, and how are we to determine whether one good outweighs another? Does living one's life well leave room for concern for the well-being of others? Are there other, nonmoral concerns that may sometimes take precedence over moral values?"[18]

17 "The good Life", last modified on October 26, 2015, http://en.wikipedia.org/wiki/The_good_life. On the good life and morality, see for example: T.L. Carson and P.K. Moser (eds.), *Morality and the Good Life* (New York and Oxford: Oxford University Press, 1997); J. Cottingham, *Philosophy and the Good Life. Reason and the Passions in Greek, Cartesian and Psychoanalytic Ethics* (Cambridge: Cambridge University Press, 1998); J. Kazez, *The Weight of Things. Philosophy and the Good Life* (Malden etc.: Blackwell, 2007); M.W. Martin, *Happiness and the Good Life* (Oxford: Oxford University Press, 2012); E.F. Paul et al. (eds.), *The Good Life and the Human Good* (Cambridge: Cambridge University Press, 1992); C. Smith, "The Good," in C. Smith, *What is a Person? Rethinking Humanity, Social Life, and the Moral Good from the Person Up* (Chicago and London: University of Chicago Press, 2010), 384–433; R. Veenhoven, "The Four Qualities of Life. Ordering Concepts and Measures of the Good Life," *Journal of Happiness Studies* 1 (2000): 1–39. For Christian perspectives, see for example: H. McCabe, *The Good Life. Ethics and the Pursuit of Happiness* (London and New York: Bloomsbury, 2005); R. Gula, *The Good Life. Where Morality and Spirituality Converge* (New York: Paulist Press, 1999); S.J. Jensen, *Living the Good Life. A Beginner's Thomistic Ethics* (Washington: The Catholic University of America Press, 2013); M. Sarot and W. Stocker (eds.), *Religion and the Good Life* (Leiden and Boston: Brill, 2004); J. Pieper, *Living the Truth. Reality and the Good. The Truth of All Things* (San Francisco: Ignatius Press, 1989). On Christianity and goodness, see for example: P.A. Bertocci, *The Goodness of God* (Washington: U.P. of America, 1981); M.Viller, et al , "Bonté," in *Dictionnaire de spiritualité* 1 (Paris: Beauchesne, 1937): 1860–1868; W. Kasper, "Gut, das Gute," in *Lexikon für Theologie und Kirche* 4 (Freiburg: Herder, 1995): 1113–1116; C.H. Hollencamp, *«Nemo bonus nisi unus Deus». The Divine Attribute of Goodness Studied According to St. Thomas* (Rome: Pontificia Studiorum Universitas a S. Thoma Aq. In Urbe, 1987); D.S. Long, *The Goodness of God. Theology, Church, and the Social Order* (Grand Rapids: Brazos Press, 2001); S. MacDonald (ed.), *Being and Goodness. The Concept of the Good in Metaphysics and Philosophical Theology* (Ithaca and London: Cornell University Press, 1991); B. Strack, "Das bonum Gottes," in *Pax et bonum. Studientage der Franziskanischen Arbeitsgemeinschaft 1983* (Werl: Dietrich-Coelde-Verlag, 1983); J.W. Wenham, *The Goodness of God* (London: Inter-Varsity Press, 1974).

18 *The Good Life*, eds. Paul et al., vii. Lawrence Becker formulates a list of seventeen 'criterial' (distinct, necessary, definitive) goods with respect to a good life: the material conditions necessary for sustaining life and consciousness; the quality of consciousness; understanding; self-command; the harmonization of reason, desire and will; the exemplification of goodness-of-a-kind; meaningful opportunity; meaningful activity; meaningful necessity; self-love; benevolence; mutual love; sexuality; achievement; rectitude; integrity; a life as an aesthetic object (L.C. Becker, "Good Lives: Prolegomena," in *The Good Life*, eds. Paul et al., 15–37 (18–23)).

Franciscan answers to these questions would imply a religious orientation[19] and be unequivocal in their emphasis on the highest good that lies in God, who is "all good, supreme good, totally good," and the human good as a derivative good aimed at the realization of the Good that is God.[20] According to Bonaventure, the three divine attributes are unity (*unitas*; the Father), truth (*veritas*; the Son), and goodness (*bonitas*; the Holy Spirit).[21] As a consequence, supreme love and supreme sweetness are found wherever supreme goodness is united to the divine will.[22] God is the origin and end of all good.[23] For humankind there lies great consolation in the fact that God's goodness is infinite and even extended unto the wicked and unworthy.[24] He is a Good so great as to exceed every possible request, desire, or surmise.[25] His generosity cannot deplete his infinite perfection, his goodness.[26] He deems us worthy of his good so great if we love and desire Him above all else, and for his own sake; therefore, He should be loved with perfect love.[27] Moreover, one is perfectly just (justified) when one, accordingly, "assents to all truth, supports all goodness, and opposes to all evil by thought and word and deed."[28] One is good insofar as one participates in the supreme Good (*summum bonum*) itself,[29] since human goodness, unlike divine goodness, may still be destroyed at any time by some defective circumstance or improper intention.[30] But as the natural, created, inner order

19 A spiritual ethos based on individual choice (see below), which nowadays can no longer be taken for granted.

20 Francis of Assisi, *Laudes ad omnes horas dicendae* 11 (Armstrong, *Francis* 1, 162); *Expositio in Pater Noster* 2. See also: Pansters, *Franciscan Virtue*, 82–85.

21 Bonaventure, *De triplici via* 3,7,12. Two corresponding categories consist of power (*potestas*), wisdom (*sapientia*), and will (*voluntas*); and loftiness (*altitudo*), beauty (*pulcritudo*), and sweetness (*dulcedo*). Consequently, the Spirit is sweet (*dulcedo*) because of His goodness (*bonitas*) and His will (*voluntas*). On Bonaventure and goodness, see also: Pansters, *Franciscan Virtue*, 85–86; A. Speer, *Triplex veritas. Wahrheitsverständnis und philosophische Denkform Bonaventuras* (Werl: Dietrich-Coelde-Verlag, 1986), 95, 202–207.

22 Bonaventure, *De triplici via* 3,7,12 (De Vinck, *The Works* 1, 92).

23 Bonaventure, *De triplici via* 1,2,14 (De Vinck, *The Works* 1, 70); *Lignum vitae* 12,48.

24 Bonaventure, *De praeparatione ad missam* 2,5 (De Vinck, *The Works* 3, 238).

25 Bonaventure, *De triplici via* 1,2,14 (De Vinck, *The Works* 1, 70).

26 Bonaventure, *Soliloquium* 2,3,19 (De Vinck, *The Works* 3, 93).

27 Bonaventure, *De triplici via* 1,2,14 (De Vinck, *The Works* 1, 70); *Soliloquium* 4,5,27. See also: V. Brümmer, "Ultimate Happiness and the Love of God," in *Religion* (eds. Sarot and Stocker), 241–265; T. Hurka, "Virtue as Loving the Good," in *The Good Life* (eds. Paul et al.), 149–168.

28 Bonaventure, *De regimine animae* 9 (De Vinck, *The Works* 3, 245); *De sex alis seraphim* 2,1.

29 Bonaventure, *Apologia pauperum* 2,12 (De Vinck, *The Works* 4, 30).

30 Bonaventure, *Apologia pauperum* 1,7 (De Vinck, *The Works* 4, 13); *Apologia pauperum* 6,1; *De sex alis seraphim* 6,2.

of the human being is fundamentally good, one is able to reach a *rectus ordo* by way of virtue.[31]

The Virtue of Temperance

In order to "go from strength to strength" (Ps. 84,7) and demonstrate (with the philosopher Josef Pieper) "the unsound overvaluation of moderation that has made contemporary morality a hollow convention and point out the true significance of the Christian virtues,"[32] we now move from the possession of virtue(s) – the good – in relation to the possession of material things – goods – to the conventional scheme of the four cardinal virtues: prudence (*prudentia*), justice (*justitia*), temperance (*temperantia*), and fortitude (*fortitudo*).[33] The traditional virtue of temperance, in particular, shows us a new 'habit' as disposition (*possit habere*) in the face of modern saturation and excess. It is the ability to restrain oneself by control over excess. Essentially a "saving and defending realization of the inner order of man" by way of "selfless self-preservation," it upholds chastity, continence, humility, gentleness, mildness, and the like.[34] According to Bonaventure, the virtue of temperance (in a definition taken from Cicero's *De rhetorica*) "is the firm and measured dominion of reason over passion and over other movements

31 Bonaventure, *Quaestiones disputatae de perfectione evangelica* 1 ("virtue is a habit of mind in harmony with the order of nature and of reason"), T. Reist and R.J. Karris (transl.), *Works of St. Bonaventure* 13. *Disputed Questions on Evangelical Perfection* (Saint Bonaventure: Franciscan Institute, 2008), 37. See also: J.A.W. Hellmann, *Ordo. Untersuchung eines Grundgedankens in der Theologie Bonaventuras*, Münchener Universitätsschriften. Neue Folge 18 (München etc.: Schöningh, 1974): 78–80, 105.

32 J. Pieper, *The Four Cardinal Virtues. Prudence, Justice, Fortitude, Temperance* (Notre Dame: University of Notre Dame Press, 1965), back cover blurb.

33 Theodore Rooseveldt Malloch, who focuses on the virtues of faith, hope, charity, leadership, courage, patience, perseverance, discipline, justice, forgiveness, compassion, humility, and gratitude, also mentions the cardinal virtues (Malloch, *Doing Virtuous Business*, 27–28). On the tradition of the cardinal virtues, see: I.P. Bejczy, *The Cardinal Virtues in the Middle Ages. A Study in Moral Thought From the Fourth to the Fourteenth Century* (Leiden and Boston: Brill, 2011); R. Cessario, *The Moral Virtues and Theological Ethics* (Notre Dame: University of Notre Dame Press, 2009); R.E. Houser, *The cardinal virtues. Aquinas, Albert, and Philip the Chancellor* (Toronto: Pontifical Institute, 2004); A. MacIntyre, *After Virtue. A Study in Moral Theory* (Notre Dame: Notre Dame University Press, 1984); Pieper, *The Four Cardinal Virtues.* On the relevance of the cardinal virtues today, see for example: E. Drewermann, *Ein Mensch braucht mehr als nur Moral. Über Tugenden und Laster* (Düsseldorf and Zürich: Walter, 2001); P. Kreeft, *Back to Virtue. Traditional Moral Wisdom for Modern Moral Confusion* (San Francisco: Ignatius Press, 1992); D. Mieth, *Die neuen Tugenden. Ein ethischer Entwurf* (Düsseldorf: Patmos, 1984); H.B. Streithofen, *Macht, Moneten und Moral. Die Kardinaltugenden als Normen für Politik und Wirtschaft* (Aachen: MM Verlag, 2005).

34 Pieper, *The Four Cardinal Virtues*, 150–151. See also: Cullen, *Bonaventure*, 100: "sobriety with regard to taste, chastity with regard to touch, and modesty with regard to the other senses."

of the soul that are not righteous."[35] This means that *temperantia* "rectifies the positive appetite"[36] so that one "rightly desires external goods on the basis of an accurate judgment about their value."[37]

The Necessity of Choice

Temperance refers the individual primarily to himself. The virtue of the right measure "implies that man should look to himself and his condition, that his vision and his will should be focused on himself."[38] By rectifying the positive appetite, it "affects human free choice," which essentially consists of the rational faculty and the negative and positive appetites of the will (*voluntas*).[39] From a *Franciscan* perspective, the human will on its own expresses itself in sinful wishes but can be bent and aimed back at the good.[40] There are three ways to start doing this: renounce the will, for the sake of God and by voluntary obedience, for that of a superior;[41] substitute the will, by setting all desires and wishes rightly upon loving God, for His will;[42] and order the will, by developing good intentions (*fervor bonae voluntatis*), to "move in accord with a legitimate judgement."[43] For the current purpose this would mean: personal accountability and choosing to adopt a respectful, responsible, and reasonable lifestyle.[44]

35 Bonaventure, *Collationes in Hexaemeron* 6,15 (Cullen, *Bonaventure*, 100).

36 Bonaventure, *Breviloquium* 5,4 (D.V. Monti (transl.), *Works of St. Bonaventure* 9. *Breviloquium* (Saint Bonaventure: Franciscan Institute, 2005), 185).

37 Cullen, *Bonaventure*, 100.

38 Pieper, *The Four Cardinal Virtues*, 147.

39 Monti, *Works of St. Bonaventure* 9, 185 n.45.

40 Francis of Assisi, *Regula non bullata* 22,6; *Officium passionis Domini* 5,15,8 (cfr. Lc 2,14). See also: Pansters, *Franciscan Virtue*, 184–185.

41 E.g., Bonaventure, *Apologia pauperum* 3,15; Francis of Assisi, *Regula non bullata* 5,14; *Admonitiones* 3,3–4; *Testamentum* 28.

42 E.g., Bonaventure, *Regula novitiorum* 14,3; Francis of Assisi, *Epistola ad fideles* 2,10; *Regula non bullata* 23,8.

43 E.g., Bonaventure, *Collationes in Hexaemeron* 6,15; David of Augsburg, *Profectus religiosorum* 3,59; 3,27 (D. Devas (transl.), *Spiritual Life and Progress* 2 (London: Burns Oates & Washbourne, 1937), 54).

44 On personal accountability and responsibility, see for example: N. Branden, *Taking Responsibility. Self-Reliance and the Accountable Life* (New York: Touchstone, 1997); R. Connors et al., *The Oz Principle. Getting Results Through Individual and Organizational Accountability* (New York: Penguin, 2010); L.P. Hartman et al., *Business Ethics. Decision Making for Personal Integrity & Social Responsibility* (New York: McGraw-Hill, 2013); J. Hollender and B. Breen, *The Responsibility Revolution. How the Next Generation of Businesses Will Win* (San Francisco: Jossey-Bass, 2010); Jacobs, *Choosing Character*, W. Sinnott-Armstrong

The Art of Living

When a person of good will gives up the 'thoughtless' lifestyle and takes up a 'temperate' one, he or she can become a respectful, responsible, and reasonable individual. Like medieval forms of moderation, modern ones ask for a conscious choice, a firm commitment, and careful consideration.[45] In order to show how these can be made or given, we will follow the ten "aspects" of the "lifestyle of the ecological self" that Wilhelm Schmid gathered together in his *Ökologische Lebenskunst. Was jeder Einzelne für das Leben auf dem Planeten tun kann.*[46] Schmid proposes the following "subjectively chosen elements of lifestyle" ("die vom Subjekt der Lebenskunst gewählten Stilelemente") for a "free life, in-formed by an individual on the basis of his prudence" ("ein freies Leben, dem das Individuum aus Gründen der Klugheit die Form gibt"):[47] greater self-understanding as the ability to perceive one's own existence in a broader context; living a deliberate and moderate life, in particular with respect to resources and techniques; asceticism as self-formation by way of subjective (willful, deliberate, moderate, calculated) techniques; self-reflection with regard to customs, the adoption of changed habits, and the avoidance of thoughtless choice; an awareness of the many life cycles and knowledge of the cyclicity of things and elements; a sustainable and durable lifestyle as a positive affirmation of life; a 'corporal ecology' as an expression of the mindful and careful treatment of the self; the enjoyment of the inner resources of life and the unfolding of the senses; and equanimity and the capacity to renounce things, wishes, and actions. We may add to this list of essential elements the observation that whereas deliberation and interiorization can lead to a respectful, responsible, and durable lifestyle, temperance of outward behavior may, in turn, have "a strengthening repercussion on the inner order of man."[48]

(ed.), *Moral Psychology 4. Free Will and Moral Responsibility* (Cambridge: MIT Press, 2014); W. Schweiker, *Responsibility & Christian Ethics* (Cambridge: Cambridge University Press, 1995).

45 On moderation, see for example: H. Clor, *On Moderation. Defending an Ancient Virtue in a Modern World* (Waco: Baylor University Press, 2008); M. de Geus, *The End of Over-Consumption. Towards a Lifestyle of Moderation and Self-restraint* (Utrecht: International Books, 2003); C. Hartshorne, *Wisdom as Moderation. A Philosophy of the Middle Way* (Albany: State University of New York Press, 1987).

46 W. Schmid, *Ökologische Lebenskunst. Was jeder Einzelne für das Leben auf dem Planeten tun kann*, Suhrkamp Taschenbuch 4034 (Frankfurt: Suhrkamp, 2008), 67–75.

47 Schmid, *Ökologische Lebenskunst*, 67.

48 Pieper, *The Four Cardinal Virtues*, 204.

The Creation of Care – Excursion

By way of contrast as well as complement to the individual and interior perspective of virtuous living, we need to address the more secular and exterior perspectives that are highly authoritative today. In *The Sustainability Revolution*, Andres Edwards describes the seven themes "that together paint a comprehensive portrait of the Sustainability Revolution today."[49] These are: *stewardship* and the importance of establishing an ecological ethic for managing and preserving the biological integrity of ecosystems; *respect for limits* and living within nature's means by preventing waste, pollution, and unsustainable resource depletion; *interdependence* and the awareness of the ecological relationships between species and nature as well as the economic and cultural ties at the local, regional, and international levels; *economic restructuring* and the need for expanding employment opportunities while safeguarding ecosystems; *fair distribution* and the importance of social justice and equity in areas such as employment, education, and healthcare; *intergenerational perspective* and the need for a long-term rather than a short-term view to guide the critical choices facing society; and *nature as a model and teacher* and the acknowledgement of 3.5 billion years of evolution of living systems and nature's significance as a reservoir of 'expertise.' A *Franciscan* perspective would stress the centrality of evangelical spirituality, fraternal harmony, and relational responsibility (in what is nowadays called the 'care for creation'), and possibly add the following seven characteristics of 'Franciscan durability:'[50] *vitality* and the impetus of spiritual inspiration;

[49] A.R. Edwards, *The Sustainability Revolution. Portrait of a Paradigm Shift* (Philadelphia: New Society, 2006), 128–130. On modern (management) issues of sustainability, see further: A. AtKisson, *The Sustainability Transformation. How to Accelerate Positive Change in Challenging Times* (London etc.: Earthscan, 2011); I.G. Barbour, *Western Man and Environmental Ethics* (Reading etc.: Addison-Wesley, 1973); W.R. Blackburn, *The Sustainability Handbook. The Complete Management Guide to Achieving Social, Economic and Environmental Responsibility* (London: Environmental Law Institute, 2007); B. Doppelt, *Leading Change Toward Sustainability. A Change-Management Guide for Business, Government and Civil Society* (Sheffield: Greenleaf, 2010); A.R. Edwards, *Thriving Beyond Sustainability. Pathways to a Resilient Society* (Gabriola Island: New Society, 2010); T. Flannery, *Here On Earth. A New Beginning* (London: Allen Lane, 2011); C. Gifford, *Sustainable Development* (Oxford: Heinemann Library, 2003); N. Harre, *Psychology for a Better World. Strategies to Inspire Sustainability* (Auckland: University of Auckland, 2011); S.M. Koger and D. DuNann Winter, *The Psychology of Environmental Problems* (Mahwah: Psychology Press, 2010); P. Senge, *The Necessary Revolution. How Individuals and Organizations are Working Together to Create a Sustainable World* (New York: Broadway Books, 2008); S. Sernau, *Global Problems. The Search for Equity, Peace, and Sustainability* (Boston: Pearson, 2012).

[50] K. Pansters, "Duurzaamheid: bronnen en structuren van gemeenschappelijk leven," *Franciscaans Leven* 96 (2013): 100–111. See also: E.A. Armstrong, *Saint Francis: Nature Mystic. The Derivation and Significance of the Nature Stories in the Franciscan Legend* (Berkeley etc.: University of California Press, 1973); J.J. Boersema, "Why is Francis of Assisi the Patron Saint of Ecologists?," *Science & Christian Belief* 14 (2002): 51–77; R. Dubos,

regularity and constitutions for the provision of care, control, and correction; *solidity* and the community as a continuum with certain unalterable traits rooted in spirituality; *sustainability* and the all-encompassing program for the maintenance and support of the good for all; *integrity* and the interior purity of the social fabric; *universality* and the all-inclusive search for salvation; and *sacramentality* and the acknowledgement that "all created things point beyond themselves to their Creator."[51]

The Choice of De-Ownership

With the personal possession ('*possit habere*') of virtue ('poverty-goodness-temperance') as spiritual property ('conscience') in mind, I would now like to introduce the notion of 'de-ownership.' In *Zakendoen in de nieuwe economie* (*Doing Business in the New Economy*), strategic management specialist Marga Hoek describes the "seven windows to success," seven busi-

"Franciscan Conservation versus Benedictine Stewardship," in *Ecology and Religion in History* (eds. D. and E. Spring; New York: Harper & Row, 1974), 114–136; T.J. Johnson, "Francis and Creation," in *The Cambridge Companion to Francis of Assisi* (ed. M.J.P. Robson; Cambridge: Cambridge University Press, 2012), 143–158; E. Leclerc, *The Canticle of Creatures. Symbols of Union. An Analysis of St. Francis of Assisi* (Chicago: Franciscan Herald Press, 1977); R.D. Sorrell, *St. Francis of Assisi and Nature. Tradition and Innovation in Western Christian Attitudes Toward the Environment* (New York and Oxford: Oxford University Press, 1988). For Christian and Franciscan theologies of the environment, see: T. Berry, *The Dream of the Earth* (San Francisco: Sierra Club Books, 1998); I. Delio et al., *Care for Creation. A Franciscan Spirituality of the Earth* (Cincinnati: St. Anthony Messenger Press, 2008); D. Edwards, *Ecology at the Heart of Faith. The Change of Heart That Leads to a New Way of Living on Earth* (Maryknoll: Orbis Books, 2006); M. Fox, *A New Reformation. Creation Spirituality and the Transformation of Christianity* (Rochester: Inner Traditions 2006); D.T. Hessel and R.R. Ruether, *Christianity and Ecology. Seeking the Well-Being of Earth and Humans* (Harvard: Harvard University Press, 2000); B.R. Hill, *Christian Faith and the Environment. Making Vital Connections* (Maryknoll: Orbis Books, 1998); G. Liedke, *Im Bauch des Fisches. Ökologische Theologie* (Stuttgart: Kreuz-Verlag, 1988); M.S. Northcott, *The Environment & Christian Ethics* (Cambridge: Cambridge University Press, 1996); D.M. Nothwehr, *Franciscan Theology of the Environment. An Introductory Reader* (Quincy: St. Anthony Messenger Press, 2002); M. Vonk, *Sustainability and Quality of Life. A Study on the Religious Worldviews, Values and Environmental Impact of Amish, Hutterite, Franciscan and Benedictine Communities* (Amsterdam: Buijten en Schipperheijn, 2011); J. Willis, *Ecologies of Grace. Environmental Ethics and Christian Theology* (Oxford: Oxford University Press, 2008). For critiques of the Christian environmental ethic, see: Barbour, *Western Man*; A. Toynbee, "The Religious Background of the Present Environmental Crisis," *International Journal of Environmental Studies* 3 (1972): 141–146; L. White Jr., "The Historical Roots of Our Ecologic Crisis," *Science* 155 (1967): 1203–1207.

51 Armstrong, *Saint Francis*, 11. See also: Bonaventure, *In Quartum Librum sententiarum* 1,1; *Catechism of the Catholic Church* (Vatican city: Editrice Vaticana, 1993), 1131 ("efficacious signs of grace, instituted by Christ and entrusted to the Church, by which divine life is dispensed to us").

ness principles to promote sustainable enterprise.[52] The first of these is a *performance-based* new economy, in which customers buy "light, not lamps; mobility, not cars; warmth, not heaters."[53] Property is "no longer functional," as the sale of products is substituted by the use of things.[54] There are thus four stages of de-ownership: financial lease (the sale of the *use* of products); circular use (the *return* of products after their use); full operational use (*services* to support the use of the product); and diversified use (the combination and *expansion* of services).[55] Here, we suggest that what is essentially a business strategy that requires new arrangements and a new framework of thought[56] can be 'owned' and thus interiorized as virtue. Consequently, a 'spiritual consumer' would choose to de-own (disappropriate) goods by only using them (stage 1), by returning them (stage 2), by enjoying the service and the use, instead of the ownership of them (stage 3), and by profiting from the provider's additional services (stage 4). The corresponding *Franciscan* strategy would be to employ goods without having them (stage 1), to give them back (*reddamus* – stage 2), to enjoy their use and the service provided (stage 3), and to acknowledge "all good" and receive "everything" (stage 4).[57] The key element here is trust.[58] In the style of Bonaventure, these stages together would entail true (evangelical) poverty, wherein one "is sustained by what is not his" and all ownership (*dominium*) and property rights (*proprietas*) of earthly things are renounced, "but not necessarily their use (*usus*)."[59] Their nature would be material (*abdicatio mundi*; *abdicatio potes-*

52 M. Hoek, *Zakendoen in de nieuwe economie. Zeven vensters op succes* (Alphen aan den Rijn: Vakmedianet, 2013): customers, value cycle, scale, innovation, businesscase, finance, and leadership.

53 Hoek, *Zakendoen*, 55.

54 Hoek, *Zakendoen*, 55.

55 Hoek, *Zakendoen*, 72–78.

56 Hoek, *Zakendoen*, 72.

57 "Let us refer (*reddamus*) all good to the Lord, God Almighty and Most High, acknowledge that every good is His, and thank Him, from Whom all good comes, for everything" (Francis of Assisi, *Regula non bullata* 17,17; Armstrong, *Francis* 1, 76); *Laudes ad omnes horas dicendae* 11; *Officium passionis Domini* 1, Oratio; *Officium passionis Domini* 1,5,14; *Officium passionis Domini* 4,13,6; *Expositio in Pater Noster* 2; *Admonitiones* 18,2; Bonaventure, *Apologia pauperum* 11,5 (De Vinck, *The Works* 4, 241); *Apologia pauperum* 3,8; *Apologia pauperum* 9,22; *Expositio super Regulam fratrum minorum* 4,9. To these goods belong knowledge and wisdom: "Even if you were so skillful and wise that you possessed all knowledge [...] you could not boast in these things" (Francis of Assisi, *Admonition* 5; Armstrong, *Francis* 1, 131); See also: "We go from having knowledge to knowing knowledge" (Hoek, *Zakendoen*, 154).

58 "It is precisely the relationship of trust between user and provider that makes it possible for the provider to make changes in his supply in order to meet the specific need of his buyer" (Hoek, *Zakendoen*, 72; my translation).

59 Bonaventure, *Apologia pauperum* 7,3–7,5 (De Vinck, *The Works* 4, 127–129); *Apologia pauperum* 7,13; *Apologia pauperum* 8,4. I quote here a full paragraph in order to illustrate the technicality of the discussion: "Hence, the nature of evangelical perfection may be seen: it is the virtue

tatis possidendi proprium) as well as spiritual (*abdicatio concupiscentiae eius; abnegatio propriae voluntatis*);[60] their means "the experience of real poverty";[61] and their aim "freedom of spirit."[62] The renouncer would disappropriate all worldly things as well as all desires for them,[63] and during the *whole period of use* remain a user fully connected to the Provider of a "complete arrangement."[64]

The Interiority of Strategy – Conclusion

Modern-day problems related to issues of inequality and immorality essentially ask for a renewed reflection on individual virtue. This reflection would show that a simple dispossession of all things and desires (however difficult) does not result in the possession of virtue, for example *as* spiritual capital. The realization of the good requires a strategy and a system, producing a practice and a sense of achievement.[65] One example of such a

which renounces temporal goods and by which a man lacking private property is sustained with things he does not own. Since the dominion over temporal goods may be given up in two ways, there are two ways of being sustained with what is not one's own. Correspondingly, there is a double mode and perfection in evangelical poverty. Since the dominion over things is twofold, that is, it may consist either in private or in common ownership, the one relating things to a person and the other to a group, and since it is possible to disclaim the former while retaining the latter, it is also possible to disclaim the latter together with the former. Hence, in parallel with this twofold mode of poverty, there will be two kinds of perfect possession of poverty. In the one, a man renounces all private and personal dominion over temporal goods and is sustained by things he does not own, things that are not his but are shared with a community. In the other, a man renounces all dominion over temporal goods, both private and common, and is sustained by things that are not his but someone else's: his sustenance is kindly and justly provided by an outsider." Bonaventure, *Apologia pauperum* 7,4 (De Vinck, *The Works* 4, 127–128); See also Pansters, *Franciscan Virtue*, 146. We are also reminded here of the sharing-principle as discussed, for example, in F. Kinzelmann & B. Priemer, "Ist Teilen das neue Haben? Tschüs, eigenes Auto! Der Sharing-Gedanke verändert unseren Alltag – in allen Bereichen," *Auto Motor Sport* 2 (2015): 108–111.

60 Bonaventure, *Apologia pauperum* 7,3 (De Vinck, *The Works* 4, 126); Bonaventure, *Apologia pauperum* 7,22.

61 Bonaventure, *Apologia pauperum* 12,28 (De Vinck, *The Works* 4, 280); *Apologia pauperum* 12,33; *Epistola de tribus quaestionibus* 3.

62 Bonaventure, *Apologia pauperum* 12,28 (De Vinck, *The Works* 4, 280).

63 Bonaventure, *Apologia pauperum* 7,3 (De Vinck, *The Works* 4, 126); *Apologia pauperum* 9,24. See also Cullen, *Bonaventure*, 100.

64 "By consequence, the 'seller' and the 'buyer' during the whole period of use remain connected to each other" (Hoek, *Zakendoen*, 73; my translation); "The final stage in the transition from product to service is a complete arrangement" (Hoek, *Zakendoen*, 76; my translation).

65 See especially the well-known definitions of 'virtue' and 'practice' by A. MacIntyre: "A virtue is an acquired human quality the possession and exercise of which tends to enable us to achieve those goods which are internal to practices and the lack of which effectively

practice-oriented strategy would be Theodore Roosevelt Malloch's pursuit of a spiritual entrepreneurship (*doing* virtuous business); another is Willem Marie Speelman's spiritual (and Carthusian-inspired) method of *lectio, meditatio, oratio, operatio,* and *contemplatio.*[66] What counts most in committing and conforming to the good in life, however, is the choice behind the conduct and the resolution behind the rationale – the *interior* component. It is associated, by both ethical strategists and spiritual teachers, to personal responsibility. Bonaventure, for example, tells his brothers to "preserve purity of heart and body, to be zealous for most holy poverty, and to strive eagerly towards the heights of perfection."[67] He also reminds them of what Francis told his brothers: "that poverty is the special way to salvation, as the stimulus of humility and the root of perfection, whose fruit is manifold but hidden."[68] In the same vein, Pope Gregory IX, in his bull *Quo elongati* (1230), reminded the lesser brothers of "the goodness and integrity with which you offered to the Lord a total holocaust by your contempt of all that pertains to this world."[69] What we can take from these morally-minded men is the promising thought of a spiritual capital that lies *within,* hidden but manifold. It is *acquired* by purity and zeal, by poverty and humility, and by goodness and integrity. What commits us to it is an *interior* striving, stimulus, and strategy. Corresponding with it, finally, is the *act* of alacrity, austerity, and benignity[70] – Bonaventure's triple condition for the goodness of conscience that earns us the ownership of virtue.

prevents us from achieving any such goods" (MacIntyre, *After Virtue,* 191); "By a 'practice' I am going to mean any coherent and complex form of socially established cooperative human activity through which goods internal to that form of activity are realized in the course of trying to achieve those standards of excellence which are appropriate to, and partially definitive of, that form of activity, with the result that human powers to achieve excellence, and human conceptions of the ends and goods involved, are systematically extended" (MacIntyre, *After Virtue,* 187). See also K. Waaijman, *Spirituality. Forms, Foundations, Methods* (Leuven etc.: Peeters Publishers, 2002): 666–667 ("The practice of the virtues").

66 Malloch, *Doing Virtuous Business,* 43–45; W.M. Speelman, "A Spiritual Method for Daily Life Practices," in *Towards a Theory of Spirituality* (eds. E. Hense and F Maas; Leuven etc.: Peeters Publishers, 2011), 55–71.

67 *Constitutiones Narbonensis* 1,8, Monti, *Works of St. Bonaventure* 5, 78.

68 Bonaventure, *Legenda S. Franci* 7,1, *Bonaventure. The Soul's Journey into God. The Tree of Life. The Life of St. Francis* (transl. E. Cousins; New York etc.: Paulist Press, 1978), 240; *Lignum vitae* 2,8.

69 *Quo elongati* 51–54 (Armstrong, *Francis,* 572).

70 See footnote 2 (Bonaventure, *De triplici via* 1,1,8–9; De Vinck, *The Works* 1, 67–68).

Bibliography

Armstrong, E. A., *Saint Francis: Nature Mystic. The Derivation and Significance of the Nature Stories in the Franciscan Legend.* Berkeley etc.: University of California Press, 1973.

Armstrong, R.J. et al. (transl.), *Francis of Assisi. Early Documents 1.* New York etc.: New City Press, 1999.

AtKisson, A., *The Sustainability Transformation. How to Accelerate Positive Change in Challenging Times.* London etc.: Earthscan, 2011.

Barbour, I.G., *Western Man and Environmental Ethics.* Reading etc.: Addison-Wesley, 1973.

Barone, G., *La povertà del secolo XII e Francesco d'Assisi. Atti del II Convegno Internazionale. Assisi, 17–19 ottobre 1974.* Assisi: Studi Francescani, 1975.

Becker, L.C., "Good Lives: Prolegomena" (1992): 15–37.

Bejczy, I.P., *The Cardinal Virtues in the Middle Ages. A Study in Moral Thought From the Fourth to the Fourteenth Century.* Leiden and Boston: Brill, 2011.

Bernet, R., *Conscience et existence. Perspectives phénoménologiques.* Paris: PUF, 2004.

Berry, T., *The Dream of the Earth.* San Francisco: Sierra Club Books, 1998.

Bertocci, P.A., *The Goodness of God.* Washington: U.P. of America, 1981.

Blackburn, W.R., *The Sustainability Handbook. The Complete Management Guide to Achieving Social, Economic and Environmental Responsibility.* London: Environmental Law Institute, 2007.

Boersema, J.J., "Why is Francis of Assisi the Patron Saint of Ecologists?" *Science & Christian Belief* 14 (2002): 51–77.

Bonaventure, *Apologia pauperum.* Translated by J. de Vinck, *The Works of Bonaventure* 1. Paterson: St. Anthony Guild Press, 1960.

—, *Breviloquium* 5,4. Translated by D.V. Monti, *Works of St. Bonaventure* 9. *Breviloquium.* Saint Bonaventure: Franciscan Institute, 2005.

—, *Collationes in Hexaemeron* 5,4. Edited by C.M. Cullen. Oxford: Oxford University Press, 2006.

—, *Collationes in Hexaemeron.* Translated by J. de Vinck, *The Works of Bonaventure* 1. Paterson: St. Anthony Guild Press, 1960.

—, *Constitutiones Narbonensis.* Translated by D.V. Monti, *Works of St. Bonaventure* 5. *Writings Concerning the Franciscan Order.* Saint Bonaventure: Franciscan Institute, 1994.

—, *Constitutiones Narbonensis.* Translated by J. de Vinck, *The Works of Bonaventure* 1. Paterson: St. Anthony Guild Press, 1960.

—, *De perfectione.* Translated by J. de Vinck, *The Works of Bonaventure* 1. Paterson: St. Anthony Guild Press, 1960.

—, *De praeparatione ad missam.* Translated by J. de Vinck, *The Works of Bonaventure* 1. Paterson: St. Anthony Guild Press, 1960.

—, *De regimine animae.* Translated by J. de Vinck, *The Works of Bonaventure* 1. Paterson: St. Anthony Guild Press, 1960.

—, *De sex alis seraphim.* Translated by J. de Vinck, *The Works of Bonaventure* 1. Paterson: St. Anthony Guild Press, 1960.
—, *De triplici via.* Translated by J. de Vinck, *The Works of Bonaventure* 1. Paterson: St. Anthony Guild Press, 1960.
—, *Epistola de tribus quaestionibus.* Translated by J. de Vinck, *The Works of Bonaventure* 1. Paterson: St. Anthony Guild Press, 1960.
—, *Expositio super Regulam fratrum minorum.* Translated by J. de Vinck, *The Works of Bonaventure* 1. Paterson: St. Anthony Guild Press, 1960.
—, *In Quartum Librum sententiarum.* Translated by J. de Vinck, *The Works of Bonaventure* 1. Paterson: St. Anthony Guild Press, 1960.
—, *Legenda S. Francisci.* Translated by E. Cousins, *Bonaventure. The Soul's Journey into God. The Tree of Life. The Life of St. Francis.* New York etc.: Paulist Press, 1978.
—, *Lignum vitae.* Translated by E. Cousins, *Bonaventure. The Soul's Journey into God. The Tree of Life. The Life of St. Francis.* New York etc.: Paulist Press, 1978.
—, *Lignum vitae.* Translated by J. de Vinck, *The Works of Bonaventure* 1. Paterson: St. Anthony Guild Press, 1960.
—, *Quaestiones disputatae de perfectione evangelica.* Translated by T. Reist and R.J. Karris, *Works of St. Bonaventure 13. Disputed Questions on Evangelical Perfection.* Saint Bonaventure: Franciscan Institute, 2008.
—, *Regula novitiorum.* Translated by J. de Vinck, *The Works of Bonaventure* 1. Paterson: St. Anthony Guild Press, 1960.
—, *Soliloquium.* Translated by J. de Vinck, *The Works of Bonaventure* 1. Paterson: St. Anthony Guild Press, 1960.
Branden, N., *Taking Responsibility. Self-Reliance and the Accountable Life.* New York: Touchstone, 1997.
Breton, V.-M., *La pauvreté.* Paris: Editions franciscaines, 1959.
Brümmer, V., "Ultimate Happiness and the Love of God." Pp. 241–265 in *Religion and the Good Life.* Edited by Sarot and Stocker. Leiden and Boston: Brill, 2004.
Bruni, L., *The Genesis and Ethos of the Market.* Basingstoke: Palgrave MacMillan, 2012.
Carson, T.L., and P.K. Moser (eds.). *Morality and the Good Life.* New York and Oxford: Oxford University Press, 1997.
Catechism of the Catholic Church. Vatican city: Editrice Vaticana, 1993.
Cessario, R., *The Moral Virtues and Theological Ethics.* Notre Dame: University of Notre Dame Press, 2009.
Clor, H., *On Moderation. Defending an Ancient Virtue in a Modern World.* Waco: Baylor University Press, 2008.
Connors, R. et al., *The Oz Principle. Getting Results Through Individual and Organizational Accountability.* New York: Penguin, 2010.
Cottingham, J., *Philosophy and the Good Life. Reason and the Passions in Greek, Cartesian and Psychoanalytic Ethics.* Cambridge: Cambridge University Press, 1998.

David of Augsburg, *Spiritual Life and Progress* 2.Translated by D. Devas. London: Burns Oates & Washbourne, 1937.

Delio, I. et al., *Care for Creation. A Franciscan Spirituality of the Earth*. Cincinnati: St. Anthony Messenger Press, 2008.

Doppelt, B., *Leading Change Toward Sustainability. A Change-Management Guide for Business, Government and Civil Society*. Sheffield: Greenleaf, 2010.

Drewermann, E., *Ein Mensch braucht mehr als nur Moral. Über Tugenden und Laster*. Düsseldorf and Zürich: Walter, 2001.

Dubos, R., “Franciscan Conservation versus Benedictine Stewardship.” Pp. 114–136 in *Ecology and Religion in History*. Edited by D. and E. Spring. New York: Harper and Row, 1974.

Edwards, A.R., *The Sustainability Revolution. Portrait of a Paradigm Shift*. Philadelphia: New Society, 2006.

—, *Thriving Beyond Sustainability. Pathways to a Resilient Society*. Gabriola Island: New Society, 2010.

Edwards, D., *Ecology at the Heart of Faith. The Change of Heart That Leads to a New Way of Living on Earth*. Maryknoll: Orbis Books, 2006.

Esser, K., “Die Armutsauffassung des hl. Franziskus.” Pp. 60–70 in *Poverty in the Middle Ages*. Edited by D. Flood. Werl: Dietrich-Coelde-Verlag, 1975.

—, and E. Grau, *Antwort der Liebe. Der Weg des franziskanischen Menschen zu Gott*. Werl: Dietrich-Coelde-Verlag, 1967.

—, “Mysterium paupertatis. Die Armutsauffassung des hl. Franziskus v. Assisi.” *Wissenschaft und Weisheit* 14 (1951), 177–189.

Flannery, T., *Here On Earth. A New Beginning*. London: Allen Lane, 2011.

Fox, M., *A New Reformation. Creation Spirituality and the Transformation of Christianity*. Rochester: Inner Traditions 2006.

Francis of Assisi, *Admonitiones*. Translated by R.J. Armstrong et al., *Francis of Assisi. Early Documents* 1. New York etc.: New City Press, 1999.

—, *Epistola ad fideles*. Translated by R.J. Armstrong et al., *Francis of Assisi. Early Documents* 1. New York etc.: New City Press, 1999.

—, *Expositio in Pater Noster*. Translated by R.J. Armstrong et al., *Francis of Assisi. Early Documents* 1. New York etc.: New City Press, 1999.

—, *Laudes ad omnes horas dicendae*. Translated by R.J. Armstrong et al., *Francis of Assisi. Early Documents* 1. New York etc.: New City Press, 1999.

—, *Officium passionis Domini*. Translated by R.J. Armstrong et al., *Francis of Assisi. Early Documents* 1. New York etc.: New City Press, 1999.

—, *Quo elongati*. Translated by R.J. Armstrong et al., *Francis of Assisi. Early Documents* 1. New York etc.: New City Press, 1999.

—, *Regula bullata*. Translated by R.J. Armstrong et al., *Francis of Assisi. Early Documents* 1. New York etc.: New City Press, 1999.

—, *Regula non bullata*. Translated by R.J. Armstrong et al., *Francis of Assisi. Early Documents* 1. New York etc.: New City Press, 1999.

—, *Salutatio virtutum* 11. Translated by R.J. Armstrong et al., *Francis of Assisi. Early Documents* 1. New York etc.: New City Press, 1999.

—, *Testamentum.* Translated by R.J. Armstrong et al., *Francis of Assisi. Early Documents* 1. New York etc.: New City Press, 1999.

Geulen, M., *Die Armut des heiligen Franz von Assisi im Lichte der Wertethik.* Diss. Köln: 2005.

Geus, M. de, *The End of Over-Consumption. Towards a Lifestyle of Moderation and Self-restraint.* Utrecht: International Books, 2003.

Gifford, C., *Sustainable Development.* Oxford: Heinemann Library, 2003.

Gula, R., *The Good Life. Where Morality and Spirituality Converge.* New York: Paulist Press, 1999.

Harre, N., *Psychology for a Better World. Strategies to Inspire Sustainability.* Auckland: University of Auckland, 2011.

Hartman, L.P. et al., *Business Ethics. Decision Making for Personal Integrity & Social Responsibility.* New York: McGraw-Hill, 2013.

Hartshorne, C., *Wisdom as Moderation. A Philosophy of the Middle Way.* Albany: State University of New York Press, 1987.

Hellmann, J.A.W., *Ordo. Untersuchung eines Grundgedankens in der Theologie Bonaventuras.* München etc.: Schöningh, 1974.

Hessel, D.T. and R.R. Ruether, *Christianity and Ecology. Seeking the Well-Being of Earth and Humans.* Harvard: Harvard University Press, 2000.

Hill, B.R., *Christian Faith and the Environment. Making Vital Connections.* Maryknoll: Orbis Books, 1998.

Hoek, M., *Zakendoen in de nieuwe economie. Zeven vensters op success.* Alphen aan den Rijn: Vakmedianet, 2013.

Hollencamp, C.H., *«Nemo bonus nisi unus Deus». The Divine Attribute of Goodness Studied According to St. Thomas.* Rome: Pontificia Studiorum Universitas a S. Thoma Aq. In Urbe, 1987.

Hollender, J. and B. Breen, *The Responsibility Revolution. How the Next Generation of Businesses Will Win.* San Francisco: Jossey-Bass, 2010.

Houser, R.E., *The Cardinal Virtues. Aquinas, Albert, and Philip the Chancellor.* Toronto: Pontifical Institute, 2004.

Hurka, T., "Virtue as Loving the Good." Pp. 149–168 in *The Good Life and the Human Good.* Edited by Paul et al. Cambridge: Cambridge University Press, 1992.

Jacobs, J.A., *Choosing Character. Responsibility for Virtue and Vice.* Ithaca: Cornell University Press, 2001.

Jensen, S.J., *Living the Good Life. A Beginner's Thomistic Ethics.* Washington: The Catholic University of America Press, 2013.

Johnson, T.J, "Francis and Creation." Pp. 143–158 in *The Cambridge Companion to Francis of Assisi.* Edited by M.J.P. Robson. Cambridge: Cambridge University Press, 2012.

Kasper, W., "Gut, das Gute." *Lexikon für Theologie und Kirche* 4 (1995): 1113–1116.

Katchadourian, H., *Guilt. The Bite of Human Conscience.* Stanford: Stanford General Books, 2010.

Kazez, J., *The Weight of Things. Philosophy and the Good Life.* Malden etc.: Blackwell, 2007.

Keating, J., and D.J. Billy, *Conscience and Prayer. The Spirit of Catholic Moral Theology.* Collegeville: Liturgical Press, 2001.

Kennedy, J., "The Ecological Crisis and Spiritual Capital." Pp. 61–77 in O'Sullivan and Flanagan, *Spiritual Capital.* Burlington: Ashgate, 2012.

Kinzelmann, F. & Priemer, B., "Ist Teilen das neue Haben? Tschüs, eigenes Auto! Der Sharing-Gedanke verändert unseren Alltag – in allen Bereichen." *Auto Motor Sport* 2 (2015): 108–111.

Koger, S.M., and D. DuNann Winter, *The Psychology of Environmental Problems.* Mahwah: Psychology Press, 2010.

Koops, W., et al. (eds.). *The Development and Structure of Conscience.* Hove: Psychology Press, 2010.

Kreeft, P., *Back to Virtue. Traditional Moral Wisdom for Modern Moral Confusion.* San Francisco: Ignatius Press, 1992.

Lambert, M.D., *Franciscan Poverty. The Doctrine of the Absolute Poverty of Christ and the Apostles in the Franciscan Order 1210–1323.* St. Bonaventure: Franciscan Institute, 1998.

Langston, D.C., *Conscience and Other Virtues. From Bonaventure to MacIntyre.* University Park: Pennsylvania State University Press, 2001.

Leclerc, E., *The Canticle of Creatures. Symbols of Union. An Analysis of St. Francis of Assisi.* Chicago: Franciscan Herald Press, 1977.

Lehmann, L., "„Arm an Dingen, reich an Tugenden. Die geliebte und gelobte Armut bei Franziskus und Klara von Assisi." Pp. 37–65 in *Gelobte Armut. Armutskonzepte der franziskanischen Ordensfamilie vom Mittelalter bis in die Gegenwart.* Edited by H.-D. Heimann et al.,. Paderborn etc.: Schöningh, 2012.

Liedke, G., *Im Bauch des Fisches. Ökologische Theologie.* Stuttgart: Kreuz-Verlag, 1988.

Long, D.S., *The Goodness of God. Theology, Church, and the Social Order.* Grand Rapids: Brazos Press, 2001.

MacDonald, S. (ed.), *Being and Goodness. The Concept of the Good in Metaphysics and Philosophical Theology.* Ithaca and London: Cornell University Press, 1991.

MacIntyre, A., *After Virtue. A Study in Moral Theory.* Notre Dame: Notre Dame University Press, 1984.

Malloch, T.R., *Doing Virtuous Business. The Remarkable Success of Spiritual Enterprise.* Nashville etc.: Thomas Nelson, 2008.

Martin, M.W., *Happiness and the Good Life.* Oxford: Oxford University Press, 2012.

McCabe, H., *The Good Life. Ethics and the Pursuit of Happiness.* London and New York: Bloomsbury, 2005.

Melville, G., and A. Kehnel (eds.), *In proposito paupertatis. Studien zum Armutsverständnis bei den mittelalterlichen Bettelorden.* Münster etc.: Lit-Verlag, 2001.

Micó, J., "Franciscan Poverty." *Greyfriars Review* 11 (1997): 257–300.

Mieth, D., *Die neuen Tugenden. Ein ethischer Entwurf.* Düsseldorf: Patmos, 1984.

Northcott, M.S., *The Environment & Christian Ethics.* Cambridge: Cambridge University Press, 1996.

Nothwehr, D.M., *Franciscan Theology of the Environment. An Introductory Reader.* Quincy: St. Anthony Messenger Press, 2002.

Ojakangas, M., *The Voice of Conscience. A Political Genealogy of Western Ethical Experience.* New York: Bloomsbury, 2013.

O'Brien, W., "Spiritual Capital in a Competitive Workplace." Pp. 97–109 in *Spiritual Capital.* Edited by O'Sullivan and Flanagan. Burlington: Ashgate, 2012.

O'Sullivan, M., and Flanagan, B. (eds.), *Spiritual Capital. Spirituality in Practice in Christian Perspective.* Farnham etc.: Ashgate, 2012.

O'Sullivan, M., "Spiritual Capital and the Turn to Spirituality." Pp. 43–59 in *Spiritual Capital.* Edited by O'Sullivan and Flanagan. Burlington: Ashgate, 2012.

Overman, S., *The Conscience Economy. How a Mass Movement for Good is Great for Business.* Boston: Bibliomotion, 2014.

Pansters, K., "Duurzaamheid: bronnen en structuren van gemeenschappelijk leven." *Franciscaans Leven* 96 (2013): 100–111.

Pansters, K., *Franciscan Virtue. Spiritual Growth and the Virtues in Franciscan Literature and Instruction of the Thirteenth Century.* Leiden and Boston: Brill, 2012.

Paul, E.F., et al. (eds.), *The Good Life and the Human Good.* Cambridge: Cambridge University Press, 1992.

Pieper, J., *Living the Truth. Reality and the Good. The Truth of All Things.* San Francisco: Ignatius Press, 1989.

Pieper, J., *The Four Cardinal Virtues. Prudence, Justice, Fortitude, Temperance.* Notre Dame: University of Notre Dame Press, 1965.

Rima, S.D., *Spiritual Capital. A Moral Core for Social and Economic Justice.* Farnham etc.: Ashgate, 2012.

Sandler, R., *Character and Environment: A Virtue-Oriented Approach to Environmental Ethics.* New York: Columbia University Press, 2007.

Sandler, R. and P. Cafaro (eds.), *Environmental Virtue Ethics.* New York: Rowman and Littlefield, 2005.

Sarot, M. and W. Stocker (eds.), *Religion and the Good Life.* Leiden and Boston: Brill, 2004.

Schmid, W., *Ökologische Lebenskunst. Was jeder Einzelne für das Leben auf dem Planeten tun kann.* Suhrkamp Taschenbuch 4034. Frankfurt: Suhrkamp, 2008.

Schweiker, W., *Responsibility & Christian Ethics*. Cambridge: Cambridge University Press, 1995.

Senge, P., *The Necessary Revolution. How Individuals and Organizations are Working Together to Create a Sustainable World*. New York: Broadway Books, 2008.

Senocak, N., "The Making of Franciscan Poverty." *Revue Mabillon*, nouv. ser. 24–85 (2013): 5–26.

Sernau, S., *Global Problems. The Search for Equity, Peace, and Sustainability*. Boston: Pearson, 2012.

Sinnott-Armstrong, W. (ed.). *Moral Psychology 4. Free Will and Moral Responsibility*. Cambridge: MIT Press, 2014.

Smith, C., "The Good." Pp. 384–433 in *What is a Person? Rethinking Humanity, Social Life, and the Moral Good from the Person Up*. Edited by C. Smith. Chicago and London: University of Chicago Press, 2010.

Sorabji, R., *Perception, Conscience, and Will in Ancient Philosophy*. Farnham etc.: Ashgate, 2013.

Sorrell, R.D., *St. Francis of Assisi and Nature. Tradition and Innovation in Western Christian Attitudes Toward the Environment*. New York and Oxford: Oxford University Press, 1988.

Speelman, W.M., "A Spiritual Method for Daily Life Practices." Pp. 55–71 in *Towards a Theory of Spirituality*. Edited by E. Hense and F. Maas. Leuven etc.: Peeters Publishers, 2011.

Speelman, W.M., *Rijk leven zonder bezit. Franciscaanse spiritualiteit als bron van vernieuwing*. Zoetermeer: Meinema, 2013.

Speer, A. *Triplex veritas. Wahrheitsverständnis und philosophische Denkform Bonaventuras*. Werl: Dietrich-Coelde-Verlag, 1986.

Stout, L.A., *Cultivating Conscience. How Good Laws Make Good People*. Princeton: Princeton University Press, 2011.

Strack, B., "Das bonum Gottes." In *Pax et bonum. Studientage der Franziskanischen Arbeitsgemeinschaft 1983*. Werl: Dietrich-Coelde-Verlag, 1983.

Streithofen, H.B., *Macht, Moneten und Moral. Die Kardinaltugenden als Normen für Politik und Wirtschaft*. Aachen: MM Verlag, 2005.

Strohm, P., *Conscience. A Very Short Introduction*. Oxford: Oxford University Press, 2011.

Tils, A.A., *Der heilige Franziskus von Assisi und die Armut. Eine genetische Darstellung seiner religiösen Anschauung von der Armut im Lichte der Quellen des 13. Jahrhunderts*. Diss. Brixen: Weger, 1961.

Todeschini, G., *Ricchezza francescana. Dalla povertà volontaria alla società del mercato*. Bologna: Il Mulino, 2004.

Toynbee, A., "The Religious Background of the Present Environmental Crisis." *International Journal of Environmental Studies* 3 (1972): 141–146.

Treanor, B., *Emplotting Virtue: A Narrative Approach to Environmental Virtue Ethics*. New York: SUNY Press, 2014.

Van Corstanje, A., *Gottes Bund mit den Armen. Biblische Grundgedanken bei Franziskus von Assisi.* Bücher franziskanischer Geistigkeit 10. Werl: Dietrich-Coelde-Verlag, 1964.

Van Wensveen, L., *Dirty Virtues: The Emergence of Ecological Virtue Ethics.* Amherst, NY: Prometheus Books, 2000.

Veenhoven, R., "The Four Qualities of Life. Ordering Concepts and Measures of the Good Life." *Journal of Happiness Studies* 1 (2000): 1–39.

Viller, M., et al., "Bonté." *Dictionnaire de spiritualité* 1 (1937): 1860–1868.

Vonk, M., *Sustainability and Quality of Life. A Study on the Religious Worldviews, Values and Environmental Impact of Amish, Hutterite, Franciscan and Benedictine Communities.* Amsterdam: Buijten en Schipperheijn, 2011.

Waal, F.B.M. de, et al. (eds.), *Evolved Morality. The Biology and Philosophy of Human Conscience.* Leiden and Boston: Brill, 2014.

Waaijman, K., *Spirituality. Forms, Foundations, Methods.* Leuven etc.: Peeters Publishers, 2002.

Wenham, J.W., *The Goodness of God.* London: Inter-Varsity Press, 1974.

White, J., *Honesty, Morality & Conscience. Making Wise Choices in the Gray Areas of Life.* Carol Stream: NavPress, 1996.

White Jr., L., "The Historical Roots of Our Ecologic Crisis." *Science* 155 (1967): 1203–1207.

Willis, J., *Ecologies of Grace. Environmental Ethics and Christian Theology.* Oxford: Oxford University Press, 2008.

Wolf, K.B., *The Poverty of Riches. St. Francis of Assisi Reconsidered.* Oxford: Oxford University Press, 2003.

Zohar, D., and I. Marshall, *Spiritual Capital. Wealth We Can Live By.* San Francisco: Berrett-Koehler Publishers, 2004.

Websites

Wikipedia, "Wikipedia The good Life". Last modified on October 26, 2015. http://en.wikipedia.org/wiki/The_good_life.

Zijnwerkt, Leading in reflection. "Consultancy for Leadership Development and Organizational Transformation." www.zijnwerkt.nl.

SPIRITUALITY IN THE FIELD OF ENTREPRENEURSHIP: THE RELATIONSHIP BETWEEN SPIRITUALITY-BASED INTUITION AND ENTREPRENEURSHIP

Sharda Nandram

Abstract

Many entrepreneurs, such as Bill Gates, Steven Jobs, Oprah Winfrey, and Donald Trump, state that intuition has been an important factor in their entrepreneurial decisions and in their overall success. Although intuition seems to be a powerful resource in entrepreneurs' decision making,[1] little is known about what constitutes intuition,[2] how entrepreneurs acquire and apply intuition,[3] and its possible outcomes.[4] The concept of intuition has traditionally been studied in the mystical and spiritual traditions,[5] and interest in these traditions is growing. Some suggest that the psychologies of the Eastern cultures could provide us with a more complete understanding of human functioning, as these psychologies integrate the workings of both the right and left hemispheres of the human brain.[6] As such, they focus on dual information processing. In recent years, the attention paid to intuition as a relevant field

1 W.H. Agor, "Intuition as a brain skill in management," *Public Personnel Management* 14/1 (1985): 15–24; F. La Pira, "Entrepreneurial intuition, an empirical approach," *Journal of Management & Marketing Research* 6/1 (2010): 1–22.

2 E. Dane and M.G. Pratt, "Exploring intuition and its role in managerial decision making," *Academy of Management Review* 32/1 (2007): 33–54.

3 B.D. Blume and J.G. Covin, "Attributions to intuition in the venture founding process: Do entrepreneurs actually use intuition or just say that they do?," *Journal of Business Venturing* 26 (2011): 137–151.

4 J.R. Mitchell, P.N. Friga and R.K. Mitchell, "Untangling the Intuition Mess: Intuition as a Construct," *Entrepreneurship Research, Entrepreneurship Theory and Practice* 26/6 (2005): 653–679.

5 G. Ferguson, *Cracking the Intuition code* (Chicago: Contemporary Books, 1999); S. Franquemont, *You already know what to do* (New York: Jeremy. P. Tarcher, 1999); F.E. Vaughan, *Awakening intuition* (New York: Anchor Press, 1979); N. Noddings, N. and P.J. Shore, *Awakening the Inner Eye. Intuition in Education* (New York: Teachers College Press, 1984).

6 R. Ornstein, *The Psychology of Consciousness* (San Francisco: W.H. Freeman, 1977).

of research in management has increased.[7] Intuition as part of entrepreneurship and as part of human functioning is positioned as an integrated concept or as a holistic mode of consciousness.[8] In the eastern context, intuition is viewed as a means of obtaining and penetrating knowledge and functions, which in turn serve as a gateway to a wider, richer world.[9] This world can be labeled the "inner life." A scholarly understanding of these traditions can help us analyze this process of gaining knowledge in relation to discovering and recognizing entrepreneurial opportunities–the activities at the core of entrepreneurship.[10] Furthermore, intuition can be linked to the quality of life of the employees who work for and with entrepreneurs. It might enhance their well-being, and their experience of meaning and purpose in both their professional and private lives. As a holistic mode of consciousness, intuition may have the capacity to foster the bottom line of businesses, as it creates a broad foundation for knowing, which is key for innovation and expansion. Ancient wisdom on intuition can be found in the teachings of Sri Aurobindo, which extensively explain the process of knowing, consciousness, and the role of intuition. Consciousness is not only power of awareness of self and things, it is or has also a dynamic and creative energy. It can determine its own reactions or abstain from reactions; it can not only answer to forces, but create or put out from itself forces. Consciousness is Chit but also Chit Shakti, awareness but also conscious force.[11] How can those insights help us understand the relevance of intuition to entrepreneurship? In Sri Aurobindo's teachings, intuition seems to hail from deeper levels of consciousness, and skills are needed to acquire and apply it. It is about traveling to those deeper sources of consciousness, which Sri Aurobindo labels "integral yoga." The study of intuition may gain much by positioning intuition in relation to the construct of consciousness, which Sri Aurobindo views as similar to the construct of spirituality. Therefore, in this chapter, we use the term "spirituality-based intuition" to distinguish it from the other concepts found in the mainstream entrepreneurship literature on intuition. Steiner claims that in-

7 C. Akinci and E. Sadler-Smith, "Intuition in management research: A historical review," *International Journal of Management Reviews* 14/1 (2012): 104–122.

8 R. Ornstein, *The Psychology of Consciousness* (San Francisco: W.H. Freeman, 1977).

9 H. V. Guenther, "The levels of understanding in Buddhism." *Journal of the American Oriental Society* 78/1 (1958): 19–28 (26).

10 S. Shane and S. Venkataraman, "The promise of entrepreneurship as a field of research," *Academy of management review* 25/1 (2000): 217–226; S. Shane, "Reflections on the 2010 AMR decade award: delivering on the promise of entrepreneurship as a field of research," *Academy of Management Review* 37 (2013): 10–20.

11 G. Sri Aurobindo, *The Integral Yoga: Sri Aurobindo's Teaching and Method of Practice* (Pondicherry: Sri Aurobindo Ashram, 1993).

tuitive thinking is a spiritual path.[12] He says: "In thinking, we are given the element that unites our particular individuality with the whole of the cosmos. When we sense, feel (and also perceive) we are separate; when we think, we are the all-one being that penetrates all"[13] and that "intuition and observation are the sources of our knowledge."[14] He continues: "Just as a colorblind person sees only shades of brilliance without hue, so a person without intuition observes only unconnected perceptual fragments."[15] In this chapter, we discuss spirituality-based intuition, including its sources in various levels of consciousness, ways of acquiring it through knowledge, and its relevance for entrepreneurship.

Introduction

The value of entrepreneurship is well known in terms of economic vitality, self-development, and clarity of purpose. Entrepreneurship is about a strong will and the capacity to see, believe, and imagine things others do not see or believe. The act of entrepreneurship is triggered by an individual, who is the key–the initiating force. This person is the one who sees an opportunity or a challenge, and then takes on that opportunity or challenge.[16] It is about the drive to overcome one's own limitations,[17] and it is subjective by nature. Often, entrepreneurs leave certainty behind to follow a vision, regardless of how intangible or ephemeral that vision may initially seem.

What inspires entrepreneurs? Are inner senses involved in their way of working? They probably are, as entrepreneurship also involves less tangible factors and deeper drives based on visions, dreams, passion, soul, creativity, courage, and intuition. Karp argues that entrepreneurs act on the basis of personal understandings and emotions, and that they are fueled by their inner conditions, as well as by how they perceive and construct realities.[18] This drive also requires tangible qualities and skills, such as knowledge and resources. Oganisjana describes the development of students' holistic perceptions of entrepreneurial situations while dealing with information, critical thinking,

12 R. Steiner, *Intuitive thinking as a Spiritual Path: A Philosophy of Freedom* (Great Barrington: United States Anthroposophic Press Inc, 1995).

13 Ibid., 84.

14 Ibid., 85.

15 Ibid., 89.

16 J.C. Carland, J.W. Carland and W.H. Stewart, "Seeing what's not there: The enigma of entrepreneurship," *Journal of Small Business Strategy* 7/1 (1996): 1–20.

17 S.S. Nandram and K.J. Samsom, *The spirit of entrepreneurship: Exploring the essence of entrepreneurship through personal stories* (Heidelberg: Springer, 2006).

18 T. Karp, "The Inner Entrepreneur: A Constructivistic View of Entrepreneurial Reality Construction," *Journal of Change Management* 6/3 (2006): 291–304.

and intuition in creatively solving problems.[19] The process of discovering real opportunities "out there" and the process of imagining opportunities that can be conceived or based on creative thought are both relevant.[20]

Scholars seem to agree that entrepreneurs use possibility rather than opportunity as a tool. They fashion possibility into opportunity through imaginative interactions with their own tools and with the society in which they live. Opportunities can have many different origins, and entrepreneurs do not always act based on rational decisions. Moreover, entrepreneurs often make decisions without having enough information to assess opportunities they see in terms of strengths and weaknesses.

Olson explains business failures as resulting from a lack of entrepreneurial abilities.[21] He develops a framework for entrepreneurial abilities around two modes of thinking. One mode is characterized by intuitive, holistic, and simultaneous processes, while the other encompasses the rational, analytic, and sequential processing of information. These two modes correspond to the two hemispheres of the brain. The left side of the brain controls actions on the right side of the body, while the right hemisphere controls actions of the left side of the body. The left side handles rational, analytic, and linear thinking, and the right side engages in intuitive and simultaneous processing.[22] Entrepreneurs use both types of thinking in several stages of their entrepreneurial life cycles. Research suggests that we process information in two different ways, which are often referred to as "system 1" and "system 2," or as experiential and rational.[23] In the following, we address the topic of intuition in more detail.

The concept of intuition in management and entrepreneurship

Intuition is derived from the Latin verb *intueri*, which means "to look upon." Intuition has traditionally been an area of focus among philosophers and

19 K. Oganisjana, *Discoprivita & 360 degree Holistic Study for Developing Students' Entrepreneurial Attitudes* (New Delhi: WEASC conference, 2010).

20 S.D. Sarasvathy, "Making it happen: beyond theories of the firm to theories of firm design," *Entrepreneurship Theory and Practice* 28/6 (2004): 519–531.

21 E.D. Olson, "Entrepreneurship: Process and abilities," *American Journal of Small Business* 10/1 (1985): 25.

22 Ibid.

23 J.S.B. Evans, "In two minds: dual-process accounts of reasoning," *Trends in cognitive sciences* 7/10 (2003): 454–459; S. Epstein, "The Implications of Cognitive-experiential Self-theory for Research in Social Psychology and Personality," *Journal for the Theory of Social Behaviour* 15/3 (1985): 283–310.

theologians,[24] but it recently has emerged in the field of management as, for example, an ability that employees can use at the workplace, or as one way of understanding how managers and entrepreneurs make decisions.[25]

There seems to be agreement that intuition exists, and that many people use it. However, various expressions, labels, and definitions of intuition exist, which implies that a common ground is still lacking. In the management field, scholars also adopt various perspectives, but in general they raise the concept of intuition less frequently than other concepts due to its intangible characteristics. There have been a few attempts to position intuition, especially intuitive abilities, in management.[26] The aim has been to make it a more tangible concept by distinguishing among its antecedents, its outcomes, and the process itself[27] by arguing for its relevance for entrepreneurial decision making,[28] by relating it to successful entrepreneurship,[29] or by positioning it in the context of perception and knowledge. This positioning is evident in cases where intuition is labeled as a cognitive style[30] or as part of the experiential processing of information.[31]

Most management researchers assume that humans' functioning can be based on analysis, intuition, or a combination of both. Some intuitions draw mainly on skill and expertise, which are obtain through experiences.[32] Along these lines, Simon claims that intuition is nothing more than recognition.[33] Other intuitions seem to be affectively charged judgements that arise through rapid, non-conscious, and holistic associations.[34] Given these two perspectives, Mitchel et al. propose a working definition of entre-

24 Noddings and Shore, *Awakening the Inner Eye.*

25 Dane and Pratt, "Exploring intuition"; Mitchell, Friga and Mitchell, "Untangling the Intuition Mess"; Blume and Covin, "Attributions to intuition"; L. Baldacchino, D. Ucbasaran, L. Cabantous and A. Lockett, "Entrepreneurship Research on Intuition: A Critical Analysis and Research Agenda," *International Journal of Management Reviews* 17/2 (2015): 212–231.

26 Dane and Pratt, "Exploring intuition."

27 Mitchell, Friga and Mitchell, "Untangling the Intuition Mess."

28 Blume and Covin, "Attributions to intuition."

29 E. Norlyk Herriott, J. Schmidt-Wilk and D.P. Heaton, "Spiritual dimensions of entrepreneurship in Transcendental Meditation and TM and Sidhi program practitioners," *Journal of Management, Spirituality and Religion* 6 (2009): 195–208.

30 C.W. Allinson, E. Chell and J. Hayes. "Intuition and entrepreneurial behavior," *European Journal of Work and Organizational Psychology* 9 (2000): 31–43.

31 S. Epstein, "Intuition from the perspective of cognitive-experiential self-theory," in *Intuition in judgment and decision making* (eds. H. Plessner, C. Betsch and T. Betsch; Mahwah: Erlbaum, 2007), 23–38.

32 D. Kahneman, *Thinking, Fast and Slow* (London: Macmillan, 2011).

33 H.A. Simon, "Making management decisions: The role of intuition and emotion," *The Academy of Management Executive* 1/1 (1987–1989): 57–64.

34 Dane and Pratt, "Exploring intuition."

preneurial intuition as the dynamic process by which entrepreneurial alertness cognitions interact with competence domains to make one conscious of an opportunity to create new value.[35]

A recent review by Baldacchino et al. discusses the nature of intuition by defining the concept and by discussing its conceptualization and operationalization, general preferences for its use, its attributes, and its actual use.[36] They also investigate the antecedents and outcomes of intuition in the entrepreneurial process, especially in relation to the entrepreneur and the firm. Dane and Pratt emphasize the importance of distinguishing between intuition as a process and intuition as an outcome.[37] The former refers to the way in which data are perceived and sorted, while the latter refers to what one apprehends and recognizes.[38] A lack of clarity arises when scholars use the same term for both elements. Another point of confusion emerges when terms are used across disciplines without clearly defining the disciplinary context. For example, the literature referring to perception, cognition, and information processing all falls under the psychological domain, mainly in the context of decision making.[39] If we position such literature in the context of consciousness debates and refer to "intuition" as unconscious, as most scholars do, then scientific examination of the phenomenon becomes difficult.

In the entrepreneurship and management field, mentions of the spiritual perspective on intuition are rare. Sometimes intuition is viewed as a form of subtle energy or as a paranormal phenomenon.[40] However, even in these cases, intuition is referred to an unconscious process. The teachings of Sri Aurobindo help us understand how this unconscious process can be made conscious, and how it can be applied as knowledge. In daily practice, intuition takes the form of a correct "hunch" or "feeling." In the field of spirituality, intuition is talked about as an enlightenment process, deep insight, or a form of knowing. In the western management literature, intuition is typically separated from insight.[41] In religious views, it is often referred to as a religious revelation or as guidance from God, while in the field of management it is referred to as intuitive sensitivity, intuitive experience, intuitive expertise, or an associative problem-solving ability. Is intuition a new concept for contemporary times or do we find its foundation in ancient traditions?

35 Mitchell, Friga and Mitchell, "Untangling the Intuition Mess."

36 Baldacchino, Ucbasaran, Cabantous and Lockett, "Entrepreneurship Research on Intuition."

37 Dane and Pratt, "Exploring intuition."

38 Dane and Pratt, "Exploring intuition," 34.

39 La Pira, "Entrepreneurial intuition."

40 R.T. Bradley, *The psychophysiology of entrepreneurial intuition: A quantum-holographic theory* (Auckland: UNITEC, 3rd International Entrepreneurship Research Exchange conference, 2006); D.I. Radin, *The Conscious Universe* (San Francisco: Harper edge, 1997).

41 Akinci and Sadler-Smith., "Intuition in management research."

Intuition in Ancient Times

The extant research shows no signs of a clear division between external stimuli and internal impressions in prehistoric and ancient literate societies.[42] However, these societies did use external stimuli to validate internal impressions and vice versa, and the intuitive insights or intuitive experiences that were generated were regarded as messages from the Gods. The seers who shared these insights and their interpretations were viewed as intellectuals with a great deal of knowledge, but this knowledge was not believed to be accessible by rational means.

Several eastern notions of intuition have influenced western philosophical and academic investigations of intuition.[43] In these investigations, rituals, meditation, and disciplined control of the mind are viewed as important practices. For classical Greeks and Romans, both rational and intuitive knowledge were valid, but non-rational sources were valued not only in helping solve real-life problems but also for the contact they provided with the non-material world. Several classical philosophers referred to insights or inductive known truths. For example, Aristotle claimed that intuition (i.e., intuitive reasoning) was more accurate than scientific knowledge, and that it was available to everyone. This claim is found in the following citation, which we have taken from Noddings and Shore,[44] who quote Posterior Analytics: Now of the mind's techniques by which we come to know the truth, some are always true, while others, such as opinion and calculation, may err. Scientific knowledge and intuition are, however, always true. Furthermore, no other kind of thought except intuition is more accurate than scientific knowledge. Noddings and Shore explain that this focus on intuition as truth is rare in today's world.[45] Intuition is now viewed as a way of knowing or as a way of seeing the objects of knowledge. They argue that when intuition is viewed as a source of knowledge or guidance, the restrictions associated with exaggerated claims of intuition as truth are removed, which allows intuition to be treated as a human experience and as a tool for education.[46]

Noddings and Shore also explain the diminishing role of the seer in the west following the establishment of Christianity.[47] The influence of seers or soothsayers on the educated classes of the Roman Empire appears to have gradually declined.[48] However, medieval theologians remained interested

42 Noddings and Shore, *Awakening the Inner Eye*, 3.

43 Ibid., 5.

44 Ibid., 7.

45 Ibid.

46 Ibid., 7.

47 Ibid.

48 Ibid., 10.

in intuition and were the first to use the word "intuition" to describe an ineffable mystical experience of identification with God. They wrote of intuition as a non-rational process and linked it to a divine revelation. While Aristotle viewed intuition as a mental process to which everyone had access, this was not the case for the medieval mystics, who believe that intuition could only be received through divine revelation. In the medieval period, the concept did not develop much in a scholastic context. With the work of Ockham, the tendency to attribute any intuitive experience to an agency outside the individual continued in philosophy for many centuries and remains to this day.[49]

No new theory was developed on the notion of intuition during the Renaissance.[50] However, in the seventeenth and eighteenth centuries, thinkers began to return to both non-rational and rational sources of knowledge. Descartes suggested that rational intuition was the only way to gain certain knowledge: "It is an illumination of the soul, whereby it beholds in the light of God those things which it pleases Him to reveal to us by a direct impression of Divine clearness in our understanding, which in this is not considered as an agent, but only as receiving the rays of Divinity."[51] Hume struggled to define human morality and human activity without the presence of a supreme being, while Kant considered intuition as a non-rational recognition and awareness of individual entities.[52] Rousseau opposed mechanistic models and proposed the "natural" human being who lives in touch with his or her emotions and intuitions. He also stressed that children should be allowed to naturally develop their own feelings and come in contact with the important values that spring from their own natures.[53]

In the nineteenth century, there were a few relevant attempts to build theory on intuition based on previous views:

First, Schleiermacher distinguished among several types of intuition: self-intuition, intuition of the work, aesthetic intuition, and philosophical speculations of intuition.

A second view was presented by Schopenhauer, who acknowledged the potential for an intuitive capacity (through the concept of will) as an important aspect of the knowledge of reality. He believed that the human mind could move toward a higher level of intuition, which could be beneficial for realizing collective goals, such as a higher purpose.

A third perspective is found in Bergson's claim that a person, object, or situation may be intuitively perceived but never completely known, ana-

49 Ibid.

50 Ibid., 12.

51 Ibid., 13.

52 Ibid., 14.

53 Ibid., 15.

lyzed, or described in intellectual terms. In this regard, he acknowledged subtle aspects of perception, while warning of the incomplete capacity of the intellectual mind. This third idea can also be found in the teachings of Sri Aurobindo.

It is remarkable to note the absence of the terms "consciousness" and "sub-consciousness" in attempts to explain intuition before the twentieth century. Philosophers made no link to the non-conscious aspect of intuition that is highlighted in most of the definitions used in the field of management and entrepreneurship today.[54] The interest in non-conscious processes in attempts to understand intuition as a source of knowledge may have emerged with Jung, who referred to intuition as an unconscious perception. Noddings and Shore argue that Jung deserves recognition as the first modern psychologist to investigate the importance of intuition.[55]

The Vedanta philosophy

This brief discussion suggests that intuition was a concept found in ancient western perspectives. However, the Vedanta seems to have a longer tradition of dealing with this concept and provides more details on how to make such insights part of scientific views on human functioning in relation to knowledge creation. In this regard, Vedanta here refers to the Indian school of philosophy. While there are many Indian schools of thought, we use "Vedanta" to refer the underlying questions of all of these schools, questions that are inherent in all scientific discussions: What is reality or truth (ontology)? How do we know what we know about that reality (epistemology)?

Vedanta is characterized by three main assumptions.[56] First, Vedanta ontology posits that eternal reality or truth is a foundation for changing reality. This implies that we can gain input about the eternal reality by accepting and studying changing reality. Second, Vedanta posits that there is a "whole" that comprises both eternal reality and changing reality. The third assumption is that we have an outer self and an inner self. The outer self is expressed in our actions, while the inner self is found in who we essentially are. The inner self refers to how we use cues that we perceive from within to make interpretations. The outer self refers to how we use external cues for interpretations. If we view both as part of the whole, they merge and synthesize towards new knowledge.

54 Dane and Pratt, "Exploring intuition."

55 Noddings and Shore, *Awakening the Inner Eye.*

56 S.K. Chakraborty and D. Chakraborty, *Spirituality in management: Means or end?* (Oxford: Oxford University Press, 2008).

One could conclude that the Vedanta perspective leads to the claim that each individual is unique, as each has an inner life and as each individual perceives external reality through his or her own lenses. This positions Vedanta closest to psychology, a discipline that mainly focuses on understanding individual differences based on the affective, cognitive, and behavioral processing of stimuli.

The Vedanta epistemology assumes that mental reasoning is not sufficient to allow an individual to know this "whole." Human reason and intellect work through the process of analysis, which requires dividing and fragmenting. Vedanta assumes that the path of mental silence is better for processing both internal and external stimuli, and thereby enables us to perceive this "whole" and, thus, experience the inner self. We could translate this into a path of building reflective moments into our "mode of doing."

Intuition in the teachings of Sri Aurobindo

The Indian philosopher Sri Aurobindo (1872–1950) described the types of knowledge from a Vedanta perspective in his philosophical magnum opus, the *Life Divine*[57] and in his work on *Integral Yoga*.[58] Through the inclusion of the concept of "integral yoga" in his philosophy, Sri Aurobindo emphasizes the holistic nature of human functioning that hails from Vedanta, in which the inner and outer lives, perceptions, and experiences are integrated. In his teachings, yoga is viewed as a way of life rather than a set of techniques. "Yoga" refers to the connection towards realizing holism as basic foundation for harmony in human functioning.

In *Life Divine*, Sri Aurobindo gives his view on intuition as part of knowledge. He claims that knowledge hailing from deeper levels of consciousness is spiritual knowledge. In this perspective, consciousness has several layers. One layer is the intuitive mind. According to Sri Aurobindo, the kind of knowledge that hails from the intuitive mind is true knowledge, while in the western conception, knowledge stems from the mind, from divine revelation, or from perceptions. As such, it is a mental processing of information. In Sri Aurobindo's teachings, knowledge takes on several forms related to levels of consciousness. Our perceptions and mental processing help to shape that knowledge and its use in daily life. He emphasizes that human minds are not a reliable source for gaining knowledge. In this regard, he is referring to the "ordinary mind," which is sometimes labeled

57 G. Sri Aurobindo, "The Methods of Vedantic Knowledge," in *Life Divine 1* (Pondicherry: Sri Aurobindo Ashram Publication Department, 2006).

58 G. Sri Aurobindo, *The Integral Yoga: Sri Aurobindo's Teaching and Method of Practice* (Pondicherry: Sri Aurobindo Ashram Publication Department, 1993).

as the "lower mind." For the higher mind, he uses several names, such as Higher Mind, Illumined Mind, *Intuitive Mind, Overmind,* and Supermind.

In Sri Aurobindo's view, the ordinary mind gives us thought, observation, reasoning, and cognition through the separation and analysis of information. In other words, this mind processes information about our lives and our environment. Psychological research suggests that this process is prone to errors that occur due to our minds' tendency to favor preferences, desires, and preconceived notions. These biases ultimately stem from our senses; our world views, which are founded in our cultural upbringing; various paradigms; and our cognitive order. The ordinary mind sees things in parts, and it uses reasoning and synthesis to put things in appropriate relation to each other. As such, the mind gives us only partial knowledge. Sri Aurobindo says that this process results in incomplete and inaccurate knowledge, which he terms *"knowledge ignorance."* Moreover, as the ordinary mind cannot see the true wholeness or the essence of that which it seeks to know, man developed an ego to help organize and develop effective capacities. This resulted in man identifying with the ego and separating from the deeper subtle knowledge that is the source of our potential competences.

Based on this perspective, Sri Aurobindo distinguishes among four types of knowledge present in our outer and inner minds.[59] These types should be understood in the context of integrating the inner and outer selves, as in Sri Aurobindo's concept of integral yoga.

1. *Objective, scientific knowledge*: Sri Aurobindo refers to this type of knowledge as "indirect knowledge," as it is mediated by our senses. He points out that this form of knowledge is inherently separate from our inner self because we experience a difference between our self as knower and the world as known. In this mode of knowing, we partially identify with the world, but we also dis-identify with it when we say there is "a world out there." Ordinary science only recognizes this type of knowledge. To understand this type of knowledge, we gather information by listening to others, reading, or conducting objective experiments. Usually, the emotional aspect of the person is not involved unless the topic of study is related to emotions.

2. *Knowledge of our inner processes*: This type of knowledge covers emotions, moods, desires, and thoughts. According to Sri Aurobindo, this knowledge is direct, but it is separate from the individual. In this mode of knowing, we partially identify with the mind, and we use it to view another part of the mind. The cognitive process separates the knower from the known. Therefore, this type of knowledge is based on one's own experiences, and it becomes the knowledge of the individual. It is private and subjective, but one can talk about it and share experiences.

59 G. Sri Aurobindo, "The Methods of Vedantic Knowledge," in *Life Divine 2* (Pondicherry: Sri Aurobindo Ashram Publication Department, 2006), 543–544.

3. *Knowledge from experiencing inner processes and identifying with them.* This type of knowledge emerges, for example, when we are completely consumed by a certain feeling, such as happiness or anger, and that feeling drives our actions. This mode of knowing is more or less pre-conscious and pre-reflective. In this type of knowledge, the individual is directly involved in the experience. It refers to a state of realization. Thoughts, basic attitudes, and perspectives on reality are changed, but one's own nature remains largely unchanged. It involves knowledge of deeper sources rather than just a description of an experience. There may be parts of this type of knowledge that cannot be described fully, but they can still influence behavior. For example, if someone says "I am really happy," then that person *is* his or her thought—there is no distinction between them. This type of knowledge is rarely studied, but we know that people use it in professional contexts. It is often encompassed within the label of "experiential knowledge" without further distinction. The spiritual and philosophical literature acknowledges that there are deeper aspects of knowledge. Along those lines, Sri Aurobindo calls this third type of knowledge "realization."

In order to make this type of knowledge applicable and given what has emerged in our study thus far, a further distinction is necessary—knowledge that is being constructed by being open and using subtle cues differs from knowledge of the inner dimension of consciousness. According to the spiritual-focused literature, the latter cannot be approached directly. Spiritual techniques, such as disciplined practices of meditation in various forms, can help the individual to come into contact with this inner knowledge. Such subtle knowledge can be labeled as wisdom or intuition, and represents the subtle dimension of what someone experiences, perceives, and applies in his or her interpretations. Those interpretations allow individuals to attribute meaning to what happens around them.

4. *Knowledge where there is no separation between self and knowledge.* According to Sri Aurobindo, in this fourth type of knowledge, not even a cognitive process separates the self from knowledge. Our comprehensive picture of this type of knowledge has no foundation in the senses. We can train our inner instruments of knowledge to become as reliable and unambiguous as our outer senses. This type of knowledge is beyond the ordinary mind. In the fourth type of knowledge, the whole nature of a person undergoes transformation.

We find numerous elaborations on the fourth type of knowledge in the philosophical and spiritual literature. In the Vedanta philosophy, the idea of wholeness is described and explained, and it is assumed that we can only become aware of the deeper power if we use instruments that extend beyond sense-based ways of knowing.

The third and fourth types of knowledge are the sources of deeper intuition in the teachings of Sri Aurobindo, as he believes intuition hails from a higher consciousness, which he refers to as the psychic being within the heart and visualizing a central being above the head.[60] In his teachings, the intuitive mind involves a high level of consciousness, and we often ignore these intuitive sources.

The notion of levels of consciousness is not unique to Sri Aurobindo's teachings. It exists not only in many spiritual philosophies but also on a more human level with respect to basic functioning or needs (Maslow) and with respect to world views (Spiral Dynamics). Sri Aurobindo's model is useful, as it is described in tremendous detail, and its structure is based on his direct perceptions. As such, it lends itself to the western mindset. He identifies seven levels of consciousness, of which the intuitive mind occurs at the fifth level.

First, Sri Aurobindo identifies the physical level, which relates to the physical body and senses. The second level is the vital level, which comprises many drives, such as likes, dislikes, cravings, desires, passions, and emotion. Third, the mental plane is the domain of thought and intellect, but he stresses that thoughts are not the essence of mind-being. The psychic level, which is the fourth level, is beyond ego-based consciousness. In more common terms, it can be described as "soul consciousness." The psychic or soul is the individual's spark of the universal divine light. It is always with us and guides us if we are able to listen to it. When it comes to the forefront, it brings light to the lower aspects of our being, which are then driven by it, and not in and of themselves. On the fifth level, we find the intuitive mind, which is, in fact, not a level in itself but rather a state in which the mind has gained higher functioning due to illumination by the psychic. Situated between the psychic and the Satchitananda, the sixth level–the Overmind–is beyond the individual mind and the universal mind. It carries a first, direct, masterful cognition of cosmic truth.[61] The Supermind, or Satchitananda, refers to the infinite unitary truth consciousness or truth idea. Satchitananda is a combination of Sanskrit words translating into truth, consciousness, and bliss–the ultimate reality and truth of our existence.

Intuition can come in the form of divine intervention or premonition. According to Sri Aurobindo, this type of intuition is transmitted in an absolutely pure form. Human beings can only grasp it according to their level of purity, mental clarity, development, and level of evolution in consciousness. Therefore, spiritual practice helps one become open to a higher consciousness (the domain of intuition), and to grasp it in the purest and most lucid form. According to Sri Aurobindo, there are four ways to develop the power of intuition:

60 Sri Aurobindo, *The Integral Yoga.*

61 M.P. Pandit, *Dictionary of Sri Aurobindo's Yoga* (Pondicherry: Sri Aurobindo Trust, 1992), 178.

Silence the mind: Our thoughts are not the essence of our mental beings. Rather, they are only an activity. By slowing the mind's activity, we allow the spirit to disclose itself and to illuminate the being, thereby leaving space for the real power of intuition. Intuition does not refer to the random thoughts that circulate in the mind but instead to the awareness that comes from a deep state of consciousness.

Descent of the light from above: Intuition is grasped through the fontanel at the crown of the head. Knowledge can pass through it without our realization, but that knowledge is hidden and needs to be recognized through concentration.

Listen to the voice within the heart: We all have a capacity for foresight that is near the level of the heart. This foresight does not take the form of ideas, but rather the form of feelings or sensations. Intense training through silence gives us the ability to listen to the voice of our soul, which is normally suppressed by our ego.

Develop the intellect: We should seek to develop our intellect instead of eliminating it. This should be done not with the aim of cherishing its limitations but rather to heighten its capacity. Solutions can spontaneously occur in dreams and during periods of relaxation. This practice is cultivated in a semi-conscious state.

Given the above discussion, we can say that intuition is a function of consciousness that goes beyond the ordinary mind, does not have a logical sequence, and has multiple sources.

A citation from Sri Aurobindo's Life Divine

Let us consider the following discussion of intuition, which is found in Sri Aurobindo's *Life Divine*:

For if we examine carefully, we shall find that intuition is *our first teacher*.

Intuition always stands *veiled* behind our mental operations.

Intuition brings to man those brilliant *messages from the Unknown* which are the beginning of this higher knowledge.

Reason only comes in afterwards to see what profit it can have of the shining harvest.

Intuition gives us that *idea of something behind and beyond all that we know* and seem to be which pursues man always in contradiction of his lower reason and all his normal experience and impels him to formulate that formless perception in the more positive ideas of God, Immortality, Heaven and the rest by which we strive to express it to the mind.

For intuition is *as strong as Nature herself* from whose very soul it has sprung and cares nothing for the contradictions of reason or the denials of experience. *It knows what is because it is,* because itself it is of that and has come from that, and will not yield it to the judgment of what merely becomes and appears. What the Intuition tells us of, is not so much Existence as the Existent, for it proceeds from that one point of light in us which gives it its advantage, that sometimes opened door in our self-awareness.[62]

In this passage, "the Existent" might be similar to the Christian view in which God's word is viewed as God, God's kingdom is viewed as God, and God's Holy Spirit is viewed as God. The citation tells us that Sri Aurobindo considers intuition as a signal of true knowledge, which complements rational ways of knowing. Intuition seems to be 'that what is there' and it requires a certain ability to access it. It is like nature, and it is pure. To acquire intuition, we must go beyond the ordinary mind through such tools as meditation.

Implications and discussion

If we define intuition from a holistic, spiritual perspective, we can facilitate entrepreneurial processes and activities. The entrepreneur faces a chaotic environment characterized by a lack of information, time pressure, ambiguity, and uncertainty. Decisions are made on the basis of available resources as well as intuition. Research has shown that different biases occur in this process.

As such, intuition can be helpful in certain situations, such as when the entrepreneur needs to make a quick decision; the rules the entrepreneur faces are ambiguous; the problem is complex; the information that is available is incomplete; or the situation requires risky decisions. Intuition is not the only source that can help in entrepreneurial activities, but it can enhance decision-making capabilities and assist in coping with conflicts. However, that intuition should not be confused with the random circulation of thoughts that may seem to occur beyond the mind. Several mind-related tasks are at the heart of entrepreneurship as well. The purpose here is to enlarge the role of intuition because doing so adds potential to entrepreneurship. We stress that rational, analytical analyses are also advisable. It is also beneficial to listen to one's own inner voice and to accept one's emotional state when dealing with complexity. The intuitive power can then work as an internal navigator in decision-making processes and entrepreneurial activities. Intuition can foster creativity, enable lucid decision making, and help save time by enhancing the speed of decision-making processes.

[62] Sri Aurobindo, "The Methods of Vedantic Knowledge," in *Life Divine 1*, 73.

There are two ways of bringing the concept of intuition into entrepreneurship. The first is to adopt a coping style for managing external stimuli. This might, for example, address the problems of volatility, uncertainty, complexity, and ambiguity. The second method is a core training part in the process of entrepreneurship so that it works as an internal resource in all entrepreneurial processes. This implies that intuition is a key competence in which students can be trained. Coursework related to entrepreneurship should take intuition into account, and educators and students should be aware of the role of intuition. This can be achieved in several ways: by asking students to reflect on their own intuitive power; by asking students to explore this concept in existing businesses, perhaps through case studies; by asking entrepreneurs who acknowledge the role of intuition to share their views with students; or by institutionalizing and integrating practical tools to elicit intuitive power in every course related to entrepreneurship.

In addition, various spiritual techniques can help people become aware of their intuition. These techniques can be taught. For example, the ancient techniques of yoga serve to open up and fine-tune the inner senses. As Cornelissen states: "Just like the objective sciences need technology to enhance the precision and reliability of their data, the subjective sciences also need a technology, but it is a quite different one: it is the inner consciousness-based technology of yoga."[63] Several other techniques have elements of the yoga methodology as presented in integral yoga.[64] Integral yoga is about receptiveness to experiences in ourselves and in our environment. It is also about self-awareness, the rejection of disturbing habits, devotion when conducting activities, an aspiration to know and to learn, and virtues that can be applied in every domain of life. Along these lines, Vaughan mentions relaxation of the body, awareness exercises, and open-focus exercises with imagination, concentration, visualization of forms, and word concentration.[65]

Conclusion

This chapter's contribution lies in its suggestion that a scholarly examination of the concept intuition needs to differentiate among the various properties of intuition. We can talk about the nature of intuition (i.e., definition and conceptualization), its source or antecedents, its acquisition, and its consequences. More specifically, we have contributed by addressing the

63 M. Cornelissen, *The Appropriate Methodology for Integral Psychology. The first international conference on integral psychology* (New York, Matagiri Woodstock: Indian Psychology Institute, 1999), 6.

64 Vaughan, *Awakening intuition.*

65 Ibid.

properties of *spirituality-based intuition*. To date, the spirituality-based aspect of intuition has not been explored in the context of management and entrepreneurship. It has been left out of the scope of most research, where it is usually labelled as a mystical avenue.[66]

Another contribution lies in our explanation of the source of intuition, which has often been overlooked or assumed to be a sealed black box. The teachings of Sri Aurobindo help us get a glimpse into this black box. The extant research has generally considered the sources of intuition, such as brain organization,[67] formal knowledge or beliefs,[68] expert knowledge structures,[69] heuristics,[70] domain knowledge,[71] and individual perceptions and cognitive styles of learning.[72] However, we suggest that intuition has a source in our consciousness. The management and entrepreneurship literature on intuition has mainly considered intuition as an unconscious process and has failed to discuss its source in consciousness. By connecting it to knowledge, we highlight the possibility that it can be learned and taught. Moreover, we demonstrate the integral understanding of an inner and an outer life, which results in a synthesis that is our consciousness.

Future studies should aim to clarify how this spirituality-based intuition helps in understanding and enhancing the very core of entrepreneurship, which is discovering and imagining opportunities, and implementing them to create added value. Some entrepreneurs apply spirituality-based intuition, others apply expert intuition, and still others use non-conscious, or *associative*, intuition. The impact of spirituality-based intuition could be studied further using empirical data. Along these lines, individuals who undertake certain spiritual practices could be studied, and the relationships between those practices and such outcomes as entrepreneurial success can be analyzed. Specific relationships might be found between these practices and the processes of discovery, imagination, evaluation, and implemen-

66 Dane and Pratt, "Exploring intuition."

67 T.S. Issack, "Intuition: An ignored dimension of management." *Academy of Management Review* 3/4 (1978): 917–922.

68 C. Barnard, *The functions of the Executive* (Cambridge: Harvard University Press, 1938).

69 D. Kahneman, "A perspective on judgment and choice: mapping bounded rationality." *American psychologist* 58 (2003): 697; Kahneman, *Thinking, Fast and Slow*; L.A. Burke and M.K. Miller, "Taking the mystery out of intuitive decision making," *The Academy of Management Executive* 13/4 (1999): 91–99.

70 A. Tversky and D. Kahneman, "Judgment under uncertainty: Heuristics and biases." *Science* 185 (1974): 1124–1131.

71 Dane and Pratt, "Exploring intuition."

72 J. Kickul, L.K. Gundry, S.D. Barbosa and L. Whitcanack, "Intuition versus analysis? testing differential models of cognitive style on entrepreneurial self-efficacy and the new venture creation process," *Entrepreneurship Theory and Practice* 33/2 (2009): 439–453; Baldacchino, Ucbasaran, Cabantous and Lockett, "Entrepreneurship Research."

tation of opportunities, which are the key processes of entrepreneurship. Mitchel et al. studied intuition by focusing on the entrepreneurial process of opportunity recognition, but they did not include spirituality-based intuition in their study.[73] Moreover, future studies could include different properties of intuition in order to enhance our understanding of main aspects of the entrepreneurial process.

Spirituality has become a field of interest in management research, but theory building and testing are still necessary. Researchers tend to use "spirituality" as an umbrella concept, which makes research difficult. By introducing a concept such as spirituality-based intuition, scholarly investigation becomes more feasible. Intuition not only enhances the quality of life of entrepreneurs, but it also contributes to the value derived by the customer and other stakeholders.

Bibliography

Agor W.H., "Intuition as a brain skill in management." *Public Personnel Management* 14/1 (1985): 15–24.

Akinci, C. and E. Sadler-Smith, "Intuition in management research: A historical review." *International Journal of Management Reviews* 14/1 (2012): 104–122.

Allinson, C.W., E. Chell and J. Hayes., "Intuition and entrepreneurial behaviour." *European Journal of Work and Organizational Psychology* 9 (2000): 31–43.

Baldacchino, L., D. Ucbasaran, L. Cabantous and A. Lockett., "Entrepreneurship Research on Intuition: A Critical Analysis and Research Agenda." *International Journal of Management Reviews* 17/2 (2015): 212–231.

Barnard, C. *The functions of the Executive.* Cambridge: Harvard University Press, 1938.

Blume, B.D. and J.G. Covin., "Attributions to intuition in the venture founding process: Do entrepreneurs actually use intuition or just say that they do?" *Journal of Business Venturing* 26 (2011): 137–151.

Bradley, R.T., *The psychophysiology of entrepreneurial intuition: A quantum-holographic theory.* Auckland: UNITEC, 3rd International Entrepreneurship Research Exchange conference, 7–10 February 2006.

Burke, L.A. and M.K. Miller., "Taking the mystery out of intuitive decision making." *The Academy of Management Executive* 13/4 (1999): 91–99.

[73] Mitchell, Friga and Mitchell, "Untangling the Intuition Mess."

Carland, J.C., J.W. Carland and W.H. Stewart., "Seeing what's not there: The enigma of entrepreneurship." *Journal of Small Business Strategy* 7/1 (1996): 1–20.

Chakraborty, S.K. and D. Chakraborty., *Spirituality in management: Means or end?* Oxford: Oxford University Press, 2008.

Cornelissen, M., *The Appropriate Methodology for Integral Psychology. The first international conference on integral psychology.* New York, Matagiri Woodstock: Indian Psychology Institute, 1999.

Dane, E., and M.G. Pratt., "Exploring intuition and its role in managerial decision making." *Academy of Management Review* 32/1 (2007): 33–54.

Epstein, S., "The Implications of Cognitive-experiential Self-theory for Research in Social Psychology and Personality." *Journal for the Theory of Social Behaviour* 15/3 (1985): 283–310.

—, "Intuition from the perspective of cognitive-experiential self-theory." Pp. 23–38 in *Intuition in judgment and decision making,* edited by H. Plessner, C. Betsch and T. Betsch. Mahwah, NJ: Erlbaum, 2007.

Evans, J.S.B., "In two minds: dual-process accounts of reasoning." *Trends in cognitive sciences* 7/10 (2003): 454–459.

Ferguson, G., *Cracking the Intuition code.* Chicago: Contemporary Books, 1999.

Franquemont, S., *You already know what to do.* New York: Jeremy. P. Tarcher, 1999.

Guenther, H.V., "The levels of understanding in Buddhism." *Journal of the American Oriental Society* 78/1 (1958): 19–28.

Issack, T.S., "Intuition: An ignored dimension of management." *Academy of Management Review,* 3/4 (1978): 917–922.

Kahneman, D., "A perspective on judgment and choice: mapping bounded rationality." *American psychologist* 58 (2003): 697.

—, *Thinking, Fast and Slow.* London: Macmillan, 2011.

Karp T., "The Inner Entrepreneur: A Constructivistic View of Entrepreneurial Reality Construction." *Journal of Change Management* 6/3 (2006): 291–304.

Kickul, J., L.K. Gundry, S.D. Barbosa and L. Whitcanack, "Intuition versus analysis? testing differential models of cognitive style on entrepreneurial self-efficacy and the new venture creation process." *Entrepreneurship Theory and Practice* 33/2 (2009): 439–453.

La Pira, F., "Entrepreneurial intuition, an empirical approach." *Journal of Management & Marketing Research* 6/1 (2010): 1–22.

Mitchell, J.R., P.N. Friga and R.K. Mitchell, "Untangling the Intuition Mess: Intuition as a Construct." *Entrepreneurship Research, Entrepreneurship Theory and Practice* 26/6 (2005): 653–679.

Nandram, S.S. and K.J. Samsom, *The spirit of entrepreneurship: Exploring the essence of entrepreneurship through personal stories.* Heidelberg: Springer, 2006.

Noddings, N. and P.J. Shore, *Awakening the Inner Eye. Intuition in Education.* New York: Teachers College Press, 1984.

Norlyk Herriott, E., J. Schmidt-Wilk, D.P. Heaton, "Spiritual dimensions of entrepreneurship in Transcendental Meditation and TM and Sidhi program practitioners." *Journal of Management, Spirituality and Religion* 6 (2009): 195–208.

Oganisjana, K., *Discoprivita & 360 degree Holistic Study for Developing Students' Entrepreneurial Attitudes.* New Delhi: WEASC conference, 2010.

Olson, E.D., "Entrepreneurship: Process and abilities." *American Journal of Small Business* 10/1 (1985): 25.

Ornstein, R., *The Psychology of Consciousness.* San Francisco: W.H. Freeman, 1977.

Pandit, M.P., *Dictionary of Sri Aurobindo's Yoga.* Pondicherry: Sri Aurobindo Trust, 1992.

Radin, D.I., *The Conscious Universe.* San Francisco: Harper edge, 1997.

Sarasvathy, S.D., "Making it happen: beyond theories of the firm to theories of firm design." *Entrepreneurship Theory and Practice* 28/6 (2004): 519–531.

Shane, S. and S. Venkataraman, "The promise of entrepreneurship as a field of research." *Academy of management review* 25/1 (2000): 217–226.

Shane, S., "Reflections on the 2010 AMR decade award: delivering on the promise of entrepreneurship as a field of research." *Academy of Management Review* 37 (2013): 10–20.

Simon, H.A., "Making management decisions: The role of intuition and emotion." *The Academy of Management Executive* 1/1 (1987–1989): 57–64.

Sri Aurobindo, G., *The Integral Yoga: Sri Aurobindo's Teaching and Method of Practice.* Pondicherry: Sri Aurobindo Ashram Publication Department, 1993.

—, "The Methods of Vedantic Knowledge." In *Life Divine.* Pondicherry: Sri Aurobindo Ashram Publication Department, 2006.

Steiner, R., *Intuitive thinking as a Spiritual Path: A Philosophy of Freedom.* Great Barrington: United States Anthroposophic Press Inc, 1995.

Tversky A. and D. Kahneman, "Judgment under uncertainty: Heuristics and biases." *Science* 185 (1974): 1124–1131.

Vaughan, F.E., *Awakening intuition.* New York: Anchor Press, 1979.

QUALITY OF LIFE AND LIVEABILITY IN EVERYDAY DISCOURSE: VIEWS ON LEEFBAARHEID IN THE DUTCH COUNTRYSIDE

Jacobine Gelderloos

Abstract

Quality of life or liveability is a much discussed topic in rural areas. This paper explains how these concepts have developed into collective terms encompassing various life areas. Quality of life is created in the interaction between the physical world and the social environment in the material life arena and the individual perception in the personal life arena. The quality of life in rural Brabant and Groningen is explored by analysing regional newspapers and church newsletters. In these sources quality of life is in various way conceptualized. A study of newspapers reveals the close connection between the physical and the social world in the development of meeting places by means of social participation. The church newsletters add another perspective; how the personal quality of life is affected by developments in the physical and social environment. The newsletters give insight into the way people try to create a good quality of living in the tension between ideals of how life should be and the reality of everyday life. Furthermore, the personal and the community well-being are explicitly related to each other.

Introduction

The future of the countryside and doubts about the quality of life are often mentioned in the same breath. An ageing population, demographic changes, limited work possibilities, and decline in public services make quality of life in the Dutch rural context a much discussed topic. Since the 1950s, the liveability of the countryside became questioned. Researchers and policy makers were dreading an exodus from the countryside because many country dwellers were moving to the cities to study or to find work. Although the spectre of totally empty villages has not been realized, the decline in population in the peripheral parts of the Netherlands raises questions about empty houses, lack of jobs, and uneconomic services.[1] Newspapers describe not only how disappearing public services and mobility problems threaten the liveability in villages, but also how initiatives are developed to maintain or increase the local quality of life.

It is worthwhile to see how liveability issues are addressed in two very different parts of the Netherlands: North-Brabant in the south and Groningen in the north. Therefore, two different sources will be analysed in this paper. Firstly, regional newspapers in which both policymakers and ordinary country-people speak about liveability in everyday language. In this way they express not only how they understand a concept such as quality of life, but also their ideals and worldview. The regional newspapers *Peelbelang* and *Eindhovens Dagblad* from Brabant and *'t Bokkeblad* and *Dagblad van het Noorden* from Groningen will be analysed to gain insight in the most important liveability issues. Secondly, church newsletters from two protestant congregations will be scrutinized to answer the main question of this paper: how do church communities relate to aspects of quality of life? Before turning to the analysis of the sources, the development of the concepts 'quality of life' and 'liveability' will be explored.

1. Development of Concepts

1.1. Quality of Life

Through the ages people have been looking for ways to realise a good quality of life. Quality of life is an essentially contested concept which is used in various disciplines. The meaning that is given to the concept changes over time depending on socio-economic circumstances, and on what in a given cultural context is seen as (most) important in life.[2] In my view quality of life is created in the interaction between the environment and the individu-

1 H. Kaal, "A conceptual history of liveability. Dutch scientists, politicians, policy makers and citizens and the quest for a liveable city," *City* 15/5 (2011): 532–547 (542–544); P.J. Bouman (ed.), *Bedreigd bestaan, De sociale, economische en culturele situatie in Noord-Groningen* (Groningen: Niemeyer, 1959); J.D. Gardenier, *Rijk met kleine dorpen. Een sociologische studie naar het platteland van Noord-Groningen* (Assen: Koninklijke Van Gorcum, 2012); K.G. Melis, *Naar een leefbare regio. Regionale leefbaarheid en identiteiten in Noord-Groningen tijdens de tweede helft van de twintigste eeuw* (Groningen: University of Groningen Library, 2013).

2 Inglehart and Baker distinguish between the survival dimension of life involving materialist values and the dimension of self-expression containing post-materialist values and subjective well-being. R. Inglehart and W.E. Baker, "Modernization, Cultural Change, and the Persistence of Traditional Values," *American Sociological Review* 65, (2000): 19–51; M. Vonk, *Sustainability and Quality of Life. A Study on The Religious Worldviews, Values and Environmental Impact of Amish, Franciscan and Benedictine Communities* (Amsterdam: Buijten en Schipperheijn, 2011), 39.

al. People are constantly in conversation with themselves, the world and the people around them. Individuals shape and are being shaped by the physical and social environment they live in. Depending on how people envision their life, and how they evaluate their living circumstances, they will be able to do something about their situation or not. But at the same time, it should be taken into account that our dwelling places enable or hinder our pursuit of ideals.[3] Therefore, it is important to be aware of the frame of reference people are using; in short, what their ideas and ideals about a good life entail. These kinds of ideas about how to achieve and maintain a high quality of life essentially make up people's worldview. A worldview can be described as "the overall perspective from which an individual or groups sees, understands, and interprets the world from which a complex of values, answers to existential questions, and ideas about desirable behaviour are derived".[4]

From a theological and philosophical perspective, quality of life is often described in terms of the good life or human flourishing. It is a fundamental concept, which dates back to ancient times. Aristotle, for example, writes in *Nicomachean ethics* that the highest virtue in life is to have cognisance of what is noble and divine. This cognisance, which can be reached through philosophy and contemplation, can lead to the pursuit of wisdom and complete human happiness.[5] For a theologian like Augustine the good life is not so much about being happy, but more about living a virtuous life.[6] In this tradition the idea of the good life is connected with notions such as solidarity, community, caring for each other, and even suffering for a neighbour, but also with stewardship and striving for justice and peace.[7]

In the context of this paper it is useful to examine how the term 'quality of life' is used in other disciplines. Quality of life is a relatively new concept, that came up after World War II. At that moment the dominant ideal was economic growth: to fight poverty and social inequality and to gain prosperity for everyone. As a more critical note, 'quality of life' was first used in the 1950s in socio-economic studies by Ordway and Osborn. They pointed out that be-

3 D. Boscaljon, "Dwellling Theologically," in *Theological Reflection and the Pursuit of Ideals. Theology, Human Flourishing and Freedom* (eds. D. Jasper and D. Wright; Farnham: Ashgate, 2013), 95–111 (95).

4 Vonk, *Sustainability*, 11, 36.

5 Aristotle, *The Nicomachean Ethics* (eds. W.D. Ross and L. Brown; Oxford: Oxford University Press, 2009), 194–198.

6 M. Jansen and V. Küster, "Human flourishing contested," *Reformed World* 59/3 (2009): 149–161 (149).

7 H. Hegstad, *The Real Church. An Ecclesiology of the Visible* (Eugene: Pickwick, 2013), 73–75; A. Smith and J. Hopkinson, *Faith and the Future of the Countryside. Pastoral and Theological Perspectives on Rural Sustainability* (Norwich: Canterbury Press, 2012); H. Cameron, J. Reader, V. Slater and C. Rowland (eds.), *Theological Reflection for human flourishing. Pastoral Practice and Public Theology* (London: SCM Press, 2012), 18.

lief in progress and economic growth formed a threat to the irreplaceable sources of energy and raw materials.[8] Ordway wrote: "What is the foreseeable end of this upward spiral of industrial expansion, or the downward spiral of our productive and land area? What has this industrial pattern already done to the quality of life?"[9] From an environmental point of view the economic development became a threat to the quality of life, since it caused not only pollution of air, water, and soil, but also created world-wide social injustice.

This formed the basis for social criticism on a materialistic worldview. It was pointed out that the Gross National Product cannot give real insight into the well-being of people, nor does it say anything about the distribution of goods among groups in the population. Around 1970 'quality of life' came to refer to human well-being and was more related to the individual.[10] This development raised questions such as: Are people satisfied about their life? What means and resources, such as health care, education, and social security, do people need to find life fulfilment?[11] Ideas about self-fulfilment and self-realization led to a normative understanding of quality of life: people had to become the person they had to be. Quality of life became a must; if not, then life had no meaning.[12] This idea can be criticized from a theological point of view: God accepts us no matter how much we feel unhappy or fail in our attempts to live well. This stands in opposition to what is usually expected of us by the social environment.[13]Another problem is that life satisfaction is difficult to measure because people experience and evaluate similar circumstances in very different ways.[14] What complicates the situation even more is that, as Campbell has shown, quality of life is affected most by the intimate areas of life (such as relationships and how people live), which escape the influence of politics and policy.[15]

8 S.H. Ordway, *Resources and the American Dream. Including a Theory of the Limit of Growth* (New York: The Ronald Press Company, 1953); H.F. Osborn, *The Limits of the Earth* (Boston: Little Brown, 1954).

9 Ordway, *Resources and the American Dream*, 45; A.W. Musschenga, *Kwaliteit van leven, criterium voor medisch handelen?* (Baarn: Ambo, 1987), 17–18; Richard Farnell (ed.), *Faith in Rural Communities. Contributions of Social Capital to Community Vibrancy* (Warwickshire: ACORA, 2006), 13.

10 Vonk, *Sustainability*, 11; Musschenga, *Kwaliteit van leven*, 21; R.J. Rogerson, "Environmental and Health-Related Quality of Life. Conceptual and Methodological Similarities," *Social Science and Medicine* 41/10 (1995): 1373–1382 (1373).

11 Musschenga, *Kwaliteit van leven*, 23–24; K.G. Melis, *A threatened existence in North-Groningen. The perceptions of local actors on the concepts identity and livability in the case of North-Groningen, the Netherlands, after the Second World War*, 11–12 [unpublished paper presented during Paper ESTER Research Design Course, 2009, Barcelona, Spain].

12 Musschenga, *Kwaliteit van leven*, 28–31.

13 Jansen, "Human flourishing contested," 151.

14 Musschenga, *Kwaliteit van leven*, 23–24.

15 A. Campbell (ed.), *The Quality of American Life. Perceptions, Evaluations and Satisfactions* (New York: Russell Sage Foundation, 1976); Musschenga, *Kwaliteit van leven*, 27.

From 1970 onwards the concept was also frequently used in the context of medicine. Health was deemed a necessary condition for quality of life. But at the same time, physicians and patients wondered whether the results of a treatment were worth the effort, pain, and distress. Research was carried out to measure the effects of treatments, such as the *Quality of life before and after transplantation*. The discussion was further triggered by the fact that life expectancy increased, while treatment and prolonging life could also cause an unwelcome continuation of suffering.[16] Around 1990 the concept of QALY (Quality Adjusted Life Year) was developed. This tool is used to determine what a year in good health may cost. The ethical discussion about this is still ongoing.[17]

Quality of life has therefore become both a descriptive and a normative concept that can be used on different levels and in various discourses. It can refer to personal health and well-being, to local social and environmental conditions, and to the sustainability of the quality of life worldwide, which is about demands for food, fresh water and energy.[18] Therefore quality of life is used in various disciplines, like geography, sociology, medicine, and philosophy/theology. Most often quality of life refers to a couple of main themes, like people's health, the state of the economy, employment, mobility, safety, social life, and the living environment.

The distinction that geographer Rogerson makes between the material life arena and the personal life arena is very helpful to bring these widely divergent aspects together.

"The material life arena consists of a series of goods, services, and other attributes related to the social, physical, and economic environment in geographical space within which people live. [...] The personal life arena includes the subjective assessment of life quality measures in terms of satisfaction, pleasure, happiness or other preference ordering. It also includes the characteristics of people, which includes personal attributes (e.g. age, gender, social class), their past and current experiences and the impact of relationships with other people. All of which are influential in shaping value systems and preferences."[19]

It seems to me that these two life arenas interact with each other in the inner conversation people are having with themselves. It is in this inner conversation where people perceive and evaluate their day-to-day life that quality of life is developed.

16 See Musschenga, *Kwaliteit van leven*, 32–33; W.M. Speelman's contribution to this volume.

17 Rogerson, "Environmental and Health-Related," 1380.

18 Vonk, *Sustainability*, 11.

19 Rogerson, "Environmental and Health-Related," 1375–1376.

1.2. Liveability

However, in the Dutch context the literal translation of the term 'quality of life', which is *kwaliteit van leven*, does not encompass all above mentioned meanings of quality of life. A random sample of Dutch newspaper articles shows that *kwaliteit van leven* is most commonly used in the context of health issues, such as the quality of life for people living in a nursing home or for people with a disability.[20] Instead the term *leefbaarheid* (liveability) is used to describe the social-spatial quality of a particular region or place.[21] In the literal sense liveability means that circumstances enable people or animals to survive, but over time it has developed into a normative concept, that is grounded in the underlying ideal of a long and happy life.[22] Therefore, *leefbaarheid* does not only refer to the actual material environment, it also has to do with how people evaluate their environment: the experienced liveability.[23] In the Dutch context liveability does not only refer to environmental issues, such as harmful substances, the extent of nuisance or the availability of public services, but also to the quality of life in a social group, like a village community.[24] This suggests that *leefbaarheid* encompasses more than the English 'liveability', which refers primarily to living conditions in the built and natural environments, and the educational, cultural and recreational possibilities.[25] So, quality of life encompasses both the Dutch *kwaliteit van leven* and *leefbaarheid*.

When we take a closer look at the concept of *leefbaarheid*, we see a similar development as with quality of life. The concept came up in the 1950s in rural studies and was almost exclusively adopted by rural geographers and sociologists. They were exploring the living conditions in Dutch rural areas in view of modernization processes and urbanization.[26] In this period livea-

20 See "Toegang tot elektronische bestanden en tijdschriften van de RUG," Rijksuniversiteit Groningen, www.academic.lexisnexis.nl.proxy-ub.rug.nl, search term: kwaliteit leven, accessed January 2015.

21 Melis, *A threatened existence in North-Groningen*, 14.

22 R. Veenhoven, *Leefbaarheid, betekenissen en meetmethoden. Studie in opdracht van Ministerie WVZ* (Rotterdam: Erasmus Universiteit, 2000), 6, 9, 15.

23 F. Thissen, *Leefbare dorpen. Van raamwerk tot ontwikkelingsmodel* (Amsterdam: Universiteit van Amsterdam, 2006), see www.nwt.be./nieuws/UiteenzettingThissen.pdf, accessed January 2015; Gardenier, *Rijk met kleine dorpen*, 131–148; L. Vermeij and A. Steenbekkers, *Dichtbij huis. Lokale binding en inzet van dorpsbewoners* (Den Haag: Sociaal en Cultureel Planbureau, 2015), 10.

24 Veenhoven, *Leefbaarheid*, 6.

25 See Oxford English Dictionary, www.oed.com/view/Entry/109302?redirectedFrom=liveability#eid, accessed January 2015; "Recommendations Memo #2 Livability and Quality of Life Indicators", www.oregon.gov/ODOT/TD/TP/docs/lcp/livability.pdf, accessed January 2015.

26 Kaal, "A conceptual history," 536–537.

bility was used in a very materialistic way, which is not surprising against the background of the post-war reconstruction. Employment and the housing market were seen as important indicators for liveability, as was the presence of public services in a village.[27] From 1960 onward, the social and ecological environment became more important because, despite the economic growth, people's social well-being had not improved.[28] The sociologist J.P. Groot distinguished several aspects in the quality of life of villages: social security, public services, the physical living environment, the social environment, participation in civil administration, and lastly accessibility of the area and services. Also with regard to liveability a 'subjective turn' took place. Sociological research on liveability focussed more on questions such as, are people themselves able to satisfy their needs, and what circumstances harm their feeling of a good life?[29] So, liveability is about the relation between on the one hand the physical and social environment, and on the other personal well-being and satisfaction. However, because people think differently about the value they attribute to various aspects of life, liveability is subject to opposite and conflicting interests.[30]

In the 1990s local 'liveability parties' rose out of dissatisfaction with local policymaking, and liveability became a popular term for politicians. In their view, local branches of national parties had lost contact with local society. Not all liveability-parties have the same political interests. Concrete local issues, ranging from congestion problems to integration of ethnic minorities, often formed the reason for the development of local liveability parties.[31] Other parties have also adopted the concept of liveability in their party manifestos as one of their main spearheads. The Christian Democratic Party (CDA) in Groningen strives for a 'committed, dynamic and liveable municipality'. The party connects liveability to the availability of basic services, road safety, improving sustainability, and a limitation in the production of gas, because this is causing earthquakes.[32] In the po-

27 Gardenier, *Rijk met kleine dorpen*, 16–17.

28 Melis, *A threatened existence*, 15; Gardenier, *Rijk met kleine dorpen*, 131.

29 L. Vermeij and G. Mollenhorst, *Overgebleven dorpsleven. Sociaal kapitaal op het hedendaagse platteland* (Den Haag: Sociaal en Cultureel Planbureau, 2008), 23; See Research Projects Kenniscentrum NoorderRuimte, www.hanze.nl/nld/onderzoek/kenniscentra/kenniscentrum-noorderruimte/kennisbank/kennisbank/onderzoeks-rapporten, accessed March 2015; Local Quality of Life Counts, A Handbook for a Menu of Local Indicators of Sustainably Development, (London: Defra Publications, 2000), http://www.proveandimprove.org/documents/localqolc.pdf, accessed January 2015.

30 U. Janssen and R. Lammerts, *Leefbaarheid op het platteland. Sociale en culturele ontwikkelingen op het platteland over de periode 1989–1998* (Utrecht: Verwey-Jonker Instituut, 1999), 145–147.

31 Kaal, "A conceptual history," 542–543.

32 *'t Bokkeblad*, March 12, 2014 and March 26, 2014.

litical context liveability has developed into an ideological concept that has to be maintained and sometimes even protected against threat.[33]

The problem is that liveability is a kind of a catch-all term. It is often presented as an aim in itself, but it remains unclear what people actually mean by *leefbaarheid*. For example, it is often assumed that public services are a necessary condition for liveability. In the last decade researchers have questioned this assumption. Gardenier shows in his study about liveability in North Groningen that, despite the fact that there are hardly any shops and services, the experienced quality of life is often higher in small villages than in the bigger villages where all these public services are available. How can this be explained? In the smallest villages 64% of the people come from elsewhere. These people have often decided to live in the countryside being well aware that not all kinds of social and cultural services are available in these villages. They know that they have to travel for work, school, and shops, and also maintain their social contacts outside the direct living environment.[34]

According to social geographer Frans Thissen, the development of liveability begins with investing in the living environment. If people are satisfied with their living environment they will start developing community initiatives. They create their own services by organising activities and long-term projects and by maintaining and improving the physical environment.[35] The question is not so much what there is, but what is being done. People need two commodities to develop community initiatives that will strengthen the liveability. Villagers require first a physical meeting place in a school, a village hall, or in the open air. Secondly, they need social possibilities in resources, ideas, and contacts.[36] What is interesting about this approach is that the physical and the social world are directly related to each other. People need a physical place to gather, but a place with four walls and a roof does not become a meeting place out of itself. A place has to look inviting, and it needs a good atmosphere. The interaction between the physical and the social world can become visible when people work together to maintain the physical environment and by doing so strengthen the social cohesion.

33 Kaal, "A conceptual history," 544.

34 Gardenier, *Rijk met kleine dorpen*, 21–24, 136–148.

35 For example: "Opening Dorpsboekenkast in Kolham," *'t Bokkeblad*, June 11, 2014.

36 F. Thissen, *Leefbaarheid en Vitaliteit van dorpen. Mythes en Uitdagingen* (Gouda, 2009); F. Thissen and J. Droogleever Fortuijn, *Het dorpshuis. Van bewoners en voor bewoners. De maatschappelijke participatie van dorpsbewoners en de betekenis van het dorpshuis in de dorpen van Littenseradiel* (Amsterdam: Urban Geography Programme, Universiteit van Amsterdam, 2012), 16–17.

2. Quality of Life in Newspapers

The preceding paragraphs offered an overview of the different aspects of quality of life and liveability. This part examines which of these aspects occur in the regional newspapers in Groningen and Brabant. It may be assumed that the discourse used in the newspapers reflects and at the same time shapes the way people think and talk about quality of life and liveability. Using 'leefbaarheid' as a search term in four regional newspapers resulted in a total of 101 articles.[37] Within the limited space of a newspaper article, it often remains unclear what journalists and interviewees exactly mean when they speak about liveability. By looking at who uses the term and in what context some useful insights can be obtained.

In the numerous surveys on local liveability, village councils and village societies are inquiring after the need for public services, accessibility and mobility, associational life, safety, social cohesion, and the physical environment.[38] With the focus on employment in the 1950s in mind, it is interesting to note that this aspect seems to be absent in these surveys, nor is it an important theme the newspaper articles.

So what are then the main liveability issues? A recurring subject is the physical environment. On the one hand, journalists describe the irritation of villagers about poorly maintained and unoccupied buildings. On the other hand, they write about the renovation and reuse of houses and public buildings, and the improvement of communal spaces.[39] In the village of Slochteren in Groningen politicians and villagers welcome the possibility to renovate the village centre after the DIY store has moved away to the outskirts of the village.[40] Other villages are looking for possibilities to find new uses for vacant schools, nursing homes and empty green spaces.[41] Investing in the physical environment, creating nature reserves, maintaining cultural heritage, and organising activities for both villagers and tourists, are considered important for the liveability of the

37 *'t Bokkeblad*: 30 articles in 2014; *Dagblad van het Noorden*: 13 articles in period 2011 till 2013, 6 in 2014; *Peelbelang*: 33 articles in period November 2013 till December 2014; *Eindhovens Dagblad*: 25 articles in 2014.

38 E.g. "Barometer over leefbaarheid Roden," *Dagblad van het Noorden*, November 12, 2011.

39 "Informatieavond herinrichting dorpskern Neerkant," *Peelbelang*, November 3, 2014; "*Opinie - Nog één kans voor Helmond*," *Eindhovens Dagblad*, December 9, 2014; Jeroen van de Nieuwenhof, "Ommel heeft een nieuwe Kluis," *Peelbelang*, January 7, 2014.

40 E.g. "Vorstelijk aanbod Freylemaborg," *'t Bokkeblad*, February 12, 2014; "Lijst 3, VVD," *'t Bokkeblad*, March 12, 2014; "Coalitieakkoord gepresenteerd," *'t Bokkeblad*, April 2, 2014.

41 G.J. Sevink, "Ulrum kan extra financiële impuls uitstekend gebruiken," *Dagblad van het Noorden*, June 10, 2013.

region.[42] The idea seems to be that if a region has a clear identity, people know what they can find there. This will attract not only new inhabitants, but also tourists, which is important for employment in the villages.[43]

Physical issues are often explicitly related to other liveability aspects. For example, improvement of the physical and the social environment are closely related in an article about community art in Sint-Oedenrode. The aim is to contribute to the liveability in the neighbourhood by reducing the social segregation and loneliness. Therefore, people are invited to gather in a school to make works of art, which can embellish the neighbourhood and hopefully become a meeting place.[44] The initiators aim at increasing the social cohesion by bridging social divides, and bringing people together. Their ideal is to create a meeting place in the open air, which will continue to attract people from the neighbourhood to come together. In this way, projects that improve the physical environment by planting trees, making a piece of art or creating a sitting corner in a neglected green space, also have a social component.[45]

It is interesting to see what happens when the physical and the social are not brought into conversation with each other. The Brabant village of Moerdijk is in danger of being gobbled up by the Rotterdam harbour. Policymakers are looking primarily at the physical environment, they fear that the nuisance of the harbour and the degeneration of the built surroundings will lead to an unliveable village. To improve the quality of life the mayor has renovation plans for the old village centre. The villagers, however, look at the social vitality and say "we have a good social life, people know each other and young people are moving to the village to start a family".[46] So, liveability can be judged on different levels.

2.1. Community Initiatives to Improve the Liveability in Brabant

Especially in the Brabant newspapers it becomes clear that mobility, availability of public services, and community initiatives are inextricably bound

42 E.g. "Lijst 3, VVD;" "Vernieuwde projecten vanuit burgerkracht," *'t Bokkeblad*, March 26, 2014; "Opening Dorpsboekenkenkast"; "Coalitieakkoord uitgewerkt in een collegeprogramma," *'t Bokkeblad*, June 11, 2014.

43 "Lijst 3, VVD"; "Coalitieakkoord gepresenteerd"; "*Kamer wil betere fietspaden: goed voor lijf en economie," Eindhovens Dagblad,* November 24, 2014; "Breedband op het Hogeland en de gemeente Slochteren voor leefbare gemeente," *'t Bokkeblad*, July 2, 2014.

44 "MIK maakt Rooise buurt meer leefbaar," *Eindhovens Dagblad*, December 8, 2014.

45 Idem; "Wijkbeheerders: extra ogen en oren in de wijk," *Peelbelang*, March 6, 2014; "Zelf aan de slag voor een leefbare gemeenschap," *'t Bokkeblad*, August 27, 2014.

46 N. Markus, "Kerk gesloten, kroeg weg, school weg en nu het hele dorp weg?," *Trouw*, September 20, 2013.

up with each other. The increased mobility has enabled people to live their lives in different places and use shops and services elsewhere. The closure of various shops and village-services has created a problem for people who are less mobile and depend on public services close to home.[47] The ending of a bus route is therefore seen as a threat to the liveability, because people become limited in their mobility and autonomy. The announcement triggers direct protest and community initiative to investigate the need for the bus route, also in the evening and the weekend.[48]

Community initiatives also come up when services such as day care, shop or school are on the verge of stopping their services. People stress that these services are essential for the social vitality of a village. Day care is important for the development of children, and children get acquainted with their fellow villagers.[49] Through school life people become involved in local associational life, which strengthens their connection with the village.[50] In several villages community initiative has led to the establishment of shops, which are sometimes combined with a service centre. This improves the liveability, because children can learn to do an errand independently and elderly people can do their shopping themselves. In this way their autonomy is increased because they do not have to ask neighbours or family to help them.[51] In several villages people have started a village cooperation, which aims at organising care close to home and providing public services, so people can continue to live in the village.[52] These community initiatives depend on the social participation of villagers, which is often seen as a condition for liveability. An important motivation for initiators to organize a village event or a social cooperation is their wish to improve the liveability or to give people a good time. People say they think it is important that "we should look more after each other in these individualistic times".[53]

47 Cameron, *Theological Reflection*, 22; "Steeds minder voorzieningen in dorp: minder bussen, winkels, onderwijs en pinautomaten," *Eindhovens Dagblad*, December 8, 2014.

48 B. van Velthoven, "Someren zet in op behoud lijn 20, Raadsvergadering Someren," *Peelbelang*, December 2, 2013; E. Lamers, "Buslijn 20 door Lierop blijft behouden," *Peelbelang*, January 7, 2014.

49 E. Lamers, "Voortbestaan kinderopvang Lierop in gevaar," *Peelbelang*, December 22, 2014.

50 J. van de Nieuwenhof, "Waar moet ik nu met mijn kind naartoe?," Verontwaardiging over aangekondigde sluiting St. Pieterschool Ommel," *Peelbelang*, November 28, 2013.

51 B. van Velthoven, "Oprichtingsvergadering dorpswinkel Someren-Heide," *Peelbelang*, November 7, 2013.

52 "ED in gesprek met Willy Donkers, 'de burgemeester van Elsendorp,'" *Eindhovens Dagblad*, December 1, 2014; "Dorpscoöperatie Lierop van start," *Peelbelang*, November 28, 2014; Sevink, "Ulrum kan extra."

53 K. Raaijkmakers, "Ploegefist draagt steentje bij aan leefbaarheid De Rips," *Peelbelang*, November 25, 2014; E. Lamers, "Dorpscoöperatie Lierop van start," Peelbelang, November 28, 2014.

In line with Thissen, villagers stress the need for a physical meeting place. The community building in Ommel is deemed necessary for the quality of life in the village; it is called a home for local fellowships and societies.[54] But the articles also reveal that physical places do not develop automatically into social meeting places. The fair in Hulsel was struggling with low attendance of villagers. Therefore, the entertainment companies disassembled their attractions before the end of the fair, which destroyed the fair's atmosphere. Villagers organised a collection to pay to offer children free entrance to the attractions on the last day. Locals see the fair as "a form of liveability and the initiative has resulted in more sociability both on the fairground and in the village café".[55]

2.2. Earthquakes: a Threat to the Liveability in Groningen

A much debated issue in Groningen are the earthquakes, which are caused by the extraction of natural gas over the past fifty years. In the beginning of 2013 the State Supervision of Mines reported that if the extraction would not be reduced severely, earthquakes could reach 5.1 on the Richter scale. The 50 earthquakes each year encroach deeply on daily life and affect the liveability in different ways. The built environment was not designed to cope with these types of earthquakes and has become considerably damaged. For example: dikes have become weaker, houses and other buildings show cracks, and some homes have become unsafe and inhabitable. Although the renovation of the damaged houses brings a lot of work for the building industry, the earthquakes have serious consequences for the housing market. People who have to move to another area for their work or because they need to go to a nursing home have difficulties selling their house. New inhabitants and employers are hesitant to settle themselves in the area.[56]

This has serious effects on the social life in the villages.[57] People are afraid because they do not know what the next earthquake will bring. They are also angry because the claim settlement is a lengthy and tiresome process. The government is hesitant to reduce the gas extraction because the

54 Van de Nieuwenhof, "Ommel heeft."

55 "Inwoners blazen zelf leven in kermis Hulsel," *Eindhovens Dagblad*, Oktober 4, 2014.

56 "Dialoogtafel Groningen," accessed March 2015, www.dialoogtafelgroningen.nl/category/nieuws; "Groninger bodem beweging," accessed March 2015, www.groninger-bodem-beweging.nl; "Aardbevingen", accessed March 2015, www.provinciegroningen.nl/actueel/dossiers/aardbevingen; "Aardbevingen door gaswinning in Groningen," accessed March 2015, www.rijksoverheid.nl/onderwerpen/aardbevingen-in-groningen/aardbevingen-door-gaswinning-in-groningen; "Dossier aardschok," accessed March 2015, www.rtvnoord.nl/index/index.asp?q=dossieraardschok.

57 "Aardbevingen vergallen woongenot," *RTV Noord*, December 3, 2014.

gas production provides 98% of the Dutch households with energy and the sale yields a lot of money for the government.[58] The whole situation forms a serious threat to the safety of the inhabitants and shows clearly how people are affected by socio-political and economic structures.

Residents and politicians are appealing to the gas company for financial resources to improve the liveability. These include internet, sustainable sources of energy and funds for community initiatives, education, and work possibilities.[59] From October 2014 residents from nine municipalities can submit proposals for projects that improve the quality of life on a website.[60] An important criterion is that the project has to strengthen the cooperation between organisations in villages.[61] An example of such a project is the renovation of a green space, making it into a village park where young and old can relax and come together.[62] Here we see again the relation between the physical and the social environment.

2.3. Conversations Between the Physical and Social environment

So, what liveability aspects are addressed in the regional newspaper? Subjects such as employment and education, sustainability and nuisance control are only mentioned once or twice in direct relation to liveability. Most attention is paid to creating meeting places, either physical in village halls and squares or social in organizing activities, public services, and maintenance projects. Resources are invested both in physical and social regeneration. Despite the fact that research indicates that services do not determine the quality of life, the loss of public services is a real issue of concern in the newspapers, as are mobility problems and the absence of an internet connection. The physical environment is seen as an important aspect of liveability because it is directly connected to the living environment, especially where the earthquakes in Groningen are concerned.

In the northern newspapers liveability is a policy term mainly used by local politicians. They relate the concept predominantly to the social in-

58 "Onderzoeken naar gevolgen van mindering gaswinning," accessed March 2015, www.rijksoverheid.nl/onderwerpen/aardbevingen-in-groningen/documenten-en-publicaties/rapporten/2014/01/17/onderzoek-geschikt-maken-van-ander-gas.html.

59 "1,2 miljard voor aardbevingsgebied," *'t Bokkeblad*, January 22, 2014; "Jacques Wallage 'van de nood een deugd maken,'" *'t Bokkeblad*, December 3, 2014.

60 Loket Leefbaarheid, accessed February 2015, www.dialoogtafelgroningen.nl/het-loket.

61 "Loket voor leefbaarheid," *'t Bokkeblad*, October 15, 2014; "Loket Leefbaarheid geopend," *'t Bokkeblad*, December 3, 2014; "Loket Leefbaarheid," accessed February 2015, www.dialoogtafelgroningen.nl/het-loket.

62 "Lichtpuntje in het aardbevingsgebied," accessed December 1, 2014, www.dialoogtafelgroningen.nl/nieuws/lichtpuntje-het-aardbevingsgebied.html.

frastructure. The local council in Slochteren has made a *leefbaarheid* fund available for initiatives that increase the liveability in villages, neighbourhoods, and streets. The council relates social participation of inhabitants directly to improvement of the quality of life. They hope that when people become acquainted with each other they will be prepared to offer social support when this is needed.[63] This seems an attempt to give villagers more autonomy in how they want to organise their living environment. However, asking village communities to deliver public services themselves is also an economic saving measure, since the organisation of village halls and care provision used to be the remit of the state.[64] Policy makers seem to be well aware of Thissens theory when they say that "active inhabitants play a decisive role in the quality of life in villages, not the authorities or certain public services".[65] But in Groningen these kind of community initiatives seem to have a less grassroots character than the initiatives in Brabant.[66]

Liveability in the newspapers is mainly connected to the quality of a community or a place. It is interesting that in the word village the physical and the social meaning coincide and it is not always possible to make a distinction. Again it becomes clear how closely the physical and the social environment are related. Liveability becomes tangible in how people come together to form the physical environment. This confirms the statement made by Cameron et al that "ultimately there is no policy choice between investing in people and investing in place. People both shape and are shaped by the place in which they live".[67]

3. Quality of Life in Church Newsletters

In the newspapers, and also in local surveys, it remains unclear how the personal quality of life is affected by developments in the physical and social environment. It is not discussed how people evaluate health problems and worries about unemployment, nor how they cope with life difficulties that come up in the living environment. This is not surprising in view of the nature of newspapers, which report predominantly about groups and

63 "Leefbaarheidsfonds," *'t Bokkeblad*, November 5, 2014.

64 Cameron, *Theological Reflection*, 13.

65 I. van Hal, "Coalitiepartijen Deurne staan voor open bestuursstijl," *Peelbelang*, May 4, 2014.

66 J. Truijman, "We regelen onze zorg steeds vaker zelf," accessed February 20, 2015, www.nos.nl/artikel/2017717-we-regelen-onze-zorg-steeds-vaker-zelf.html.

67 Cameron, *Theological Reflection*, 24.

general themes.[68] In light of social theories which state that quality of life is about life satisfaction and the experienced liveability, the question remains how to gain insight in the interaction between the environment and the individual. How can justice be done to the inner life of people: their thoughts and feelings, the way a person interacts with the world around him, the way a person experiences her life. So basically, how do we see, reflect and react? The church newsletters deal not only with the physical and the social environment, but also pay attention to the individual. In this way the newsletters reveal something of the inner conversation people are having.

The newsletters offer not only practical information about the church communities, the activities, and the diaconal initiatives, but also give 'food for thought'. The ministers write meditations, and often empty space is filled with poems and prayers. Although the terms *leefbaarheid* and *kwaliteit van leven* hardly ever occur in the church newsletters, several of the aforementioned quality of life aspects also appear in the church newsletters. Even though the church newsletters may not reflect the practices in the whole of the ecclesiastical network around the church community, they still reflect some of the worldviews in the congregations.

Following up on the main theme from the preceding paragraph, first, some remarks will be made about the interaction between the physical and the social environment. Secondly, the views on personal well-being will be evaluated; how people deal with life difficulties and how the church communities strive to offer social support. Finally, a number of ideals about the good life can be distilled from the newsletters.

3.1. Physical and Social Meeting Places

Judging from *De Bron*, the church newsletter of the protestant congregation in Groningen, the church building and the direct surroundings are important for the village identity. This is probably also the reason why a lot of attention is paid to the maintenance of the church yards and the cemeteries. Nearly every newsletter reports about repair projects, such as replanting sick trees or digging up old gravestones which are lying under the church yard, because a vicar's wife did not like the sight of them.[69] In the announcements of maintenance activities not only ideas about a good

68 Only in death announcements the social environment of individuals becomes visible, because not only families, but also neighbourhoods, associations, circles of friends and sometimes people from work or school place a death announcement in the local newspaper.

69 "Groenlint project," *De Bron* 2/1 (2014): 22, 25. Interestingly Vermeij points out that mainly males, higher educated people and church members labor for the physical environment (Vermeij, *Dichtbij huis*, 39).

looking village are expressed, such as the need to renovate a wall or to renovate funerary heritage for preserving the atmosphere of the church yard.[70] The social effect of working and talking together is also emphasized: "We are planning not only a working day, but also a very sociable day." On other occasions members of the maintenance group celebrate their birthday. It is stressed that people are very welcome, even if they only come for a chat.[71] When people work together on the churchyard or walk through the village on Ascension Day, the physical environment becomes a social meeting place.[72]

In Brabant the church newsletter is called *De Brug*, after the bridge that connects the two villages Asten and Someren. In one of the newsletters the identity of the church community is described as a combination of physical and social aspects: the church building and the cemetery on the one hand, singing together, hospitality, drinking coffee, and activities for personal development on the other.[73] However, the availability of a physical space does not automatically lead to the development of a social meeting place. People need the opportunity, the time and a reason to gather. In the church newsletters examples are found of successful but also of failed initiatives to create a meeting place. Successful was the initiative of a pastor to open a book of condolence in the prayer room at the Eindhoven airport after the MH17 crash. People had to form a queue to enter the prayer room; some of them had come especially to the airport to visit this room of remembrance.[74] An example of a failed initiative is the prohibition of the municipality in Brabant to rent the church community centre out for parties because that would contravene the local regulations. This prohibition forms a hindrance for the church community to offer a meeting place.[75]

Another example of a failing community initiative is the ending of the Sunday school after more than a century because there are not enough children and parents to continue the activities.[76] This reflects the dependence of the church on volunteers for the future of the faith community.[77]

70 "Berichten uit Hellum – Werkzaamheden op de begraafplaats," *De Bron* 2/1 (2014): 24; "Werkzaamheden op de begraafplaats en rond de Walfriduskerk, *De Bron* 2/3 (2014): 20.

71 "Berichten uit Hellum – Werkzaamheden op de begraafplaats," *De Bron* 2/3 (2014): 20, 31.

72 "Gemeentenieuws – Dauwtrappen op Hemelvaartsdag," *De Bron* 2/4 (2014): 13; "Berichten uit Hellum – NL Doet," *De Bron* 2/4 (2014): 20–21.

73 "Van de voorzitter," *De Brug* 49/11 (2014): 6.

74 "Vlucht MH 17," *De Brug* 49/8 (2014): 14–15.

75 "College van kerkrentmeesters – gebruiksbeperking aan het gemeentecentrum," *De Brug* 49/9 (2014): 10–12.

76 "Bericht van zondagsschool 'De Regenboog'," *De Bron* 2/4 (2014): 17.

77 "Kerkbalans 2014," *De Bron* 2/1 (2014): 15–16; "Gemeentenieuws," *De Bron* 2/5 (2014): 13.

At the same time we read about successful community initiatives in which other church communities or non-church societies are involved, such as a Christmas service, multifaith discussion evenings, concerts, and a three day festival for sick people.[78] The enthusiasm in the newsletters about the performance of choirs and artists reveals that cultural expressions, such as art and music, add an extra dimension to these activities and in that way contribute to community well-being.[79]

In this way churches strengthen the social cohesion. In an area like Brabant where the differences between Catholics and Protestants were highlighted for centuries, cooperation is not self-evident and can still lead to strong discussions.[80] In secularised Groningen non-church members get to know the church community in the preparation of a Christmas service, which can be a good opportunity for conversation.[81] Topics such as loneliness and social cohesion are also addressed when churchgoers are asked to invite lonely people to a game-afternoon.[82] In one of the newsletters the underlying value is made explicit; for community well-being it is necessary to be hospitable to strangers, to meet people who are different, and to try bridging the differences to increase social cohesion.[83]

3.2. Personal Well-being: Dealing with Life Difficulties

What marks the difference with newspapers is that church newsletters focus more on the personal well-being of people. One of the ministers criticizes the lack of attention for the soul and the cut backs on spiritual and mental health care. She stresses the need to look further than the outside behaviour of people, and to take time for a conversation between yourself and God or someone else.[84] Themes like health and unemployment are brought to the level of the individual. The emphasis lies mainly on health and death experiences: people are sick, they are anxious for results, or they are treated in hospital. In every newsletter these people are wished strength, and they

78 "Gemeentenieuws," *De Bron* 2/1 (2014): 12–14; "Gemeentenieuws," *De Bron* 2/6 (2014): 13; "Berichten uit Schildwolde – Overschild," *De Bron* 2/10 (2014): 29; "Uit de pastorie," *De Brug* 49/10 (2014): 11; "Concert in Koepelkerk," *De Brug* 49/10 (2014): 18; "Ziekentriduüm," *De Brug* 49/8 (2014): 9.

79 "Gemeentenieuws," *De Bron* 2/3 (2014): 11, 14; "2 februari: Bonum Tenete," *De Brug,* 49/2 (2014): 9; "Kerstmorgen: met koperensemble," *De Brug* 49/11 (2014): 7.

80 "Uit de pastorie," *De Brug* 49/2 (2014): 7–9; "Oecumenische avonden over vernieuwing van kerk en geloof," *De Brug* 49/10 (2014): 11.

81 "Gemeentenieuws," *De Bron* 2/6 (2014): 13.

82 "Spelletjesmiddag," *De Brug* 49/10 (2014): 16.

83 "Meditatie," *De Bron* 2/4 (2014): 8–10.

84 "Uit de pastorie," *De Brug* 49/8 (2014): 6–7.

are encouraged to trust.[85] Closely connected to this theme are experiences of the loss of loved ones. The pain is acknowledged, and people are called upon to offer support and to care for each other. In one of the newsletters in Groningen, a churchgoer expresses his gratitude for the support he received in the many wishes and cards people had sent him after his wife had to move into a nursing home.[86] Incidentally, the newsletters write about the loss of self-esteem and the uncertainty that comes with unemployment, relational problems and feelings of unsafety.[87] On the other side of this spectrum attention is paid to people who are their finishing exams and entering a new stage of life. Furthermore, congratulations are offered for birthdays of people older than 75, for births, weddings, and jubilees.[88]

When life difficulties are mentioned in the church newsletters, it is mainly about health problems, the loss of loved ones, and the loneliness that comes with it. Much less attention seems to be paid to other issues that might have a significant impact on the personal well-being, such as unemployment and work stress, or nuisance in the physical environment and living conditions. The question can be asked whether churchgoers recognize themselves in the main themes of the church newsletters. Some of them might be more concerned about disrupted relationships with family or friends, work stress, feelings of unsafety, raising their children, or experiences of exclusion in school or elsewhere.

On several occasions the church newsletters report about social initiatives in the region: a clothing bank, a refugee centre and a place for the homeless, where people can find a cup of tea, a social meeting place, attention, and guidance, but also basic needs: washing, clothing, and food.[89] The church council in Groningen is in contact with the municipality about care and social networks. Both church communities are directly involved in collections for the regional food bank: "We prefer to give things rather than transferring money to a giro number. This relates more to people, it might be for your

85 *De Brug; de Bron*, issues 2014.

86 "Gemeentenieuws," *De Bron* 2/9 (2014): 15.

87 "Meditatie," *De Bron*, 2/3 (2014): 13–14.

88 E.g. "Verjaardagen 70 jaar en ouder," *De Bron* 2/3 (2014): 28–29; "Berichten uit de gemeente," *De Brug* 49/7 (2014): 9.

89 Poverty in Oost-Groningen ("Diaconie," *De Brug* 49/3 (2014): 11). Collecting plastic caps to save up for a guide dog (*De Bron*, issues 2014). Foodbank: collection of (packaged) food articles. In surrounding villages 70 families depend on the foodbank. The church community sees it as a diaconal task to bring the light of Christmas in these families ("Adventstijd: tijd voor de voedselbank," *De Brug* 49/11 (2014): 15–16). Refugees, who are sent back to their home country, but are not able to go because of the Ebola epidemic or other problems, are taken care of in Helmond. The foundation offers basic needs, care and support. ("Oecumenische dienst in Lierop," *De Brug* 49/11 (2014), 6–7); "Kledingbank Maxima voor Veendam en Menterwolde," *De Bron* 2/10 (2014): 21–22.

neighbour opposite".[90] In Groningen the minister writes about the living environment in relation to the earthquakes. Together with his colleague from another congregation, he made an appeal to hold a prayer Sunday for the people affected by the earthquakes. "People may react laconically, but under the surface they are boiling with anger. If you no longer feel safe in your own home, where can you?" Here the effects of socio-economic processes on the personal lives of people become visible. The churches aim at listening to the people and to show that the church is involved. They want to pay attention to the problems, the fear, the insecurity, and the anger that people feel.[91] By publicizing about the initiative in the local media the prayer Sunday gained the status of a public ritual, in which a wider audience was addressed.[92]

In the many descriptions of world problems, like people lacking basic needs and medical care, people are called upon to contribute to a solution for the problems or to fund a cause. The underlying thought is often that this is not what is supposed to happen, this is not the good life, this is not how it should be. The church communities seem to be well aware of how important fundamental basic needs, such as food, home, education, work, and care are for personal development, well-being, and happiness. In the diaconal news in Brabant it becomes clear how these basic needs are interrelated: health problems can lead to social exclusion and limited possibilities for education.[93]

Countless meditations, pastoral announcements, poems, and prayers pose the question how to deal with human vulnerability, failure, and disappointment, either close to home or somewhere else in the world.[94] Much attention is being paid to the inner life: how people perceive their life and

90 "Voedselbank," *De Bron* 2/10 (2014): 24; "Voedselbank," accessed February 12, 2015, www.rtvnoord.nl/ipad/index.asp?v=32402.

91 "Gemeentenieuws," *De Bron*, 2/3 (2014): 21; "Dominees bidden voor getroffen Groningers," accessed January 28, 2014, www.rtvnoord.nl/artikel/artikel.asp?p=129672; "Kerken strijden tegen onderhuidse boosheid over bevingen," accessed February 12, 2015, www.rtvnoord.nl/artikel/artikel.asp?p=145139.

92 M. Stringer, "The future of public religious ritual in an urban context." [Lecture during symposium The future of ritual: spots and shapes, February 2015, Amsterdam, The Netherlands].

93 An organisation like leprosy mission claims not only to offer care but also education and in that way helps patients to find happiness ("Diaconie," *De Brug* 49/1 (2014): 11). Ministers in Africa need to support people with life questions dealing with extreme poverty and creating village communities ("Diaconie," *De Brug* 49/10 (2014): 12). Improving the quality of life of disabled children in developing countries and orphans in Rwanda who lack a feeling of safety and are in need of a foster home ("Diaconie," *De Brug* 49/11 (2014): 12). Initiative to renovate houses in India in a sustainable way, which improves working possibilities, income and health ("Diaconie," *De Brug* 49/2 (2014): 11); "Meditatie," *De Bron* 2/10 (2014): 12–13.

94 Jansen, "Human flourishing", 149; *De Brug; de Bron*, issues 2014.

how they might change their way of thinking. [95] A minister draws a parallel with the disciples who got lost in the storm on the lake; they got stranded in the adventure which is called life. [96] To find your way back, you need trust, the experience of Easter; "to know that God brings us to life, that we are connected with the people around us. This does not mean that it is easy to overcome problems and worries".[97] Simultaneously, images of the good life are explicitly described. We are "trying to realize God's kingdom here and now, and sometimes it is visible for a moment. Faith is about the tension between what life is now and how it should be, but is not yet. Church is about celebrating what is beautiful, inspiring, and encouraging. And in this effort the church can work together with other organizations that want to improve the 'quality of life'." [98]

3.3. Personal Well-being in Relation to Others

The contact with and support offered by other people is seen as fundamental for dealing with these existential questions. But the social environment needs to be organized in order to be able to give the support people need. In the newsletters people are called upon to look after each other and/or to inform the church council that people are having difficulties.[99] This looking after each other, and being there for other people is connected with the name God: "I am and I will always be there for you". [100] Around All Souls' Day the minister in Brabant stresses the comfort people need when people are grief stricken. "If there are people around us who dry our tears again and again, then we can learn to smile struggling through our tears".[101]

On the whole, the newsletters reveal how expressions of sympathy and commitment are embodied. We read about the bringing of flowers to people who are ill or have suffered a loss, but flowers can also be a token of congratulation and gratitude.[102] By creating the opportunity to hand in personal intercessions or to light candles, the church in Brabant also offers certain

95 A. van Wijngaarden, "Roep verborgen krachten wakker," *De Bron* 2/3 (2014): 2; "In Memoriam," *De Bron* 2/3 (2014): 23–24; "De Geest van God," *De Bron* 2/5 (2014): 8; "Uit de pastorie," *De Brug* 49/9 (2014): 7–8.

96 Luke 8:22–25.

97 "Meditatie," *De Bron* 2/3 (2014): 13–14.

98 "Uit de pastorie," *De Brug* 49/9 (2014): 7–9.

99 E.g. "Gemeentenieuws," *De Bron* 2/1 (2014): 14.

100 "Meditatie," *De Bron* 2/6 (2014): 10–12.

101 "Uit de pastorie," *De Brug* 49/10 (2014): 7–9.

102 E.g. "Berichten uit de gemeente," *De Brug* 49/11 (2014): 10.

services for people to express their feelings.[103] In both communities the commemoration of the dead is highly appreciated. In Groningen also relatives of non-church villagers are invited to join the service, during which the names of the deceased are mentioned, candles are lit, and people can share their grief. [104] So, churches offer rituals, prayers, social support, and attention for the inner life in relation to the other.

The church newsletters emphasize that supportive relationships, trust, and a feeling of belonging can contribute to personal well-being. The relation between the well-being of the individual and of others is also stressed: the joy of others brings happiness for the individual, while the suffering of others can stir feelings of guilt, sorrow, fear, and compassion.[105] People are called upon to think about the consequences of their deeds for other people, and they are encouraged to act out of solidarity and to try lighten the suffering of others. Without neglecting the happiness of the individual, the church newsletters are looking especially to the well-being of others.[106] The central question in a peace prayer ascribed to Francis of Assisi is: how can I contribute to the well-being of others?

> "Where there is hatred, let me sow love;
> where there is despair, hope;
> where there is darkness, light.
> O, Divine Master, grant that I may not so much seek
> to be consoled as to console;
> to be understood as to understand;
> to be loved as to love.
> For it is in giving that we receive."[107]

What is interesting about the church newsletters, in comparison to the newspapers, is that personal and community well-being are interwoven. In sociological surveys about perceived liveability, people are asked whether they are satisfied with the public services, the safety, and maintenance of their own living environment. A research programme such as *National Accounts of Well-being* tries to escape from this material focus, and aims at measuring people's personal well-being, their vitality, feeling of autonomy,

103 "Nieuws uit de kerkenraad," *De Brug* 49/11 (2014): 7.

104 "Uit de pastorie," *De Brug* 49/10 (2014): 7–9.

105 "Uit de pastorie," *De Brug*, 49/7 (2014): 7–8; A church member writes after a visit to a refugee center: "How glad you are when you can return to your own home, where it is safe and where you don't have to live with a whole family in a small room."("Berichten uit Weert," *De Brug* 49/10 (2014): 17.

106 "That you may taste the fruits of your life and go in peace" (A. Govaart, *De Brug* 49/6 (2014): 8).

107 "Prayer," *De Bron* 2/3 (2014): 7; Ch. Renoux, La pière pour la paix attribuée à Saint François: une enigme à résoudre, Paris: Editions franciscaines 2001.

and self-esteem. The point of departure is the individual and the extent to which (s)he feels a sense of belonging with and support from people around him/her.[108] It sees happiness as something that *happens* to us as an individual, without considering the effects of our actions on our personal well-being.[109] Nor does it seem to take into account how personal quality of life can be affected by the suffering of others. In my view, the support individuals offer to others and the way people's personal well-being is affected by the lack of well-being of others should also be acknowledged.

Fundamental in the worldview of both church communities is that supportive relationships can increase personal well-being. Of course, there are ample sources of social support outside the church, but according to Merino the surplus value of support from religiously based ties is that "a shared religious worldview allows individuals to help one another make meaning out of their life experiences, reducing the sense of threat and uncertainty".[110] Or as Webster states "the distinctive thing that Christian spirituality has to offer is structures of meaning for the bad things that happen in life so that they too may be incorporated into a personal quest for well-being".[111]

Concluding Thoughts

Newspapers and church newsletters are complementary, they reflect two different 'conversations' about quality of life. In the newspapers a conversation is going on between the physical and the social environment. The church newsletters reveal the interpersonal and inner conversation about the relation between the environment and the individual. The newspapers focus more on the material life arena. It is interesting to see that within the material life arena, most attention is paid to the social environment and not so much to the physical and economic environment. When journalists write about the liveability of the physical environment, this is often in relation to social questions. Liveability seems to depend on the close interaction between people and the spaces they live in. A striking difference between the newspapers and the newsletters is that in the newspapers the development of a social infrastructure and the improvement of the social cohesion are important issues. In the church newsletters the assumption is

108 "Overall well-being," accessed 24 February 2015, www.nationalaccountsofwellbeing.org/explore/indicators/zwbi.

109 Jansen, "Human Flourishing," 150 .

110 S.M. Merino, "Social Support and the Religious Dimensions of Close Ties," *Journal for the Scientific Study of Religion* 53:3 (2014): 595–612 (598).

111 Cameron, *Theological Reflection*, 21.

often made that social contacts are already established and that these will result in social support.

In the church newsletters the material life arena is described from the point of view of the personal life arena. In thinking about improving the quality of life it is important to be more aware of how social, economic, and cultural structures affect the life of individuals.[112] At the same time the individual is not a spineless object who is just the victim of life circumstances. Especially the church newsletters address the question of coping with life's difficulties. Not only the problems people face personally, but also the unease and worry people can feel over the troubles others are suffering. In this way, the church newsletters prove to be a valuable addition to the conceptualization of liveability in newspapers and surveys because they describe the process of creating quality of life: how people personally relate to and deal with the world around them.[113] It is about making sense of what happens to us, both the good and the bad.

Bibliography

Aristotle, *The Nicomachean Ethics*, edited by W.D. Ross and L. Brown. Oxford: Oxford University Press, 2009.

Boscaljon, D., "Dwellling Theologically." In *Theological Reflection and the Pursuit of Ideals. Theology, Human Flourishing and Freedom*, edited by D. Jasper and D. Wright, 95–111. Farnham: Ashgate, 2013.

Bouman, P.J. (ed.), *Bedreigd bestaan. De sociale, economische en culturele situatie in Noord-Groningen*. Groningen: Niemeyer, 1959.

Cameron, H., J. Reader, V. Slater and C. Rowland (eds.), *Theological Reflection for human flourishing. Pastoral Practice and Public Theology*. London: SCM Press, 2012.

Campbell, A. (ed.), *The Quality of American Life. Perceptions, Evaluations and Satisfactions*. New York: Russell Sage Foundation, 1976.

Farnell, R. (ed.), *Faith in Rural Communities. Contributions of Social Capital to Community Vibrancy*. Warwickshire: ACORA, 2006.

Gardenier, J.D., *Rijk met kleine dorpen. Een sociologische studie naar het platteland van Noord-Groningen*. Assen: Koninklijke Van Gorcum, 2012.

Hegstad, H., *The Real Church. An Ecclesiology of the Visible*. Eugene: Pickwick, 2013.

112 Cameron, *Theological Reflection*, 20.

113 "The question to be asked is: how can we negotiate being in unfamiliar or liminal places such that the experience is not ultimately one of powerlessness and meaninglessness but one that becomes a creative place that may yield new insights and may be transformative of practice?" (Cameron, *Theological Reflection*, 11–12.)

Inglehart, R. and W.E. Baker, “Modernization, Cultural Change, and the Persistence of Traditional Values,” *American Sociological Review* 65 (2000): 19–51.

Jansen, M. and V. Küster, “Human flourishing contested.” *Reformed World* 59/3 (2009): 149–161.

Janssen, U. and R. Lammerts, *Leefbaarheid op het platteland. Sociale en culturele ontwikkelingen op het platteland over de periode 1989–1998.* Utrecht: Verwey-Jonker Instituut, 1999.

Kaal, H.,“A conceptual history of liveability. Dutch scientists, politicians, policy makers and citizens and the quest for a liveable city,” *City* 15/5 (2011): 532–547

Melis, K.G., *Naar een leefbare regio, Regionale leefbaarheid en identiteiten in Noord-Groningen tijdens de tweede helft van de twintigste eeuw.* Groningen: University of Groningen Library, 2013.

—, *A threatened existence in North-Groningen. The perceptions of local actors on the concepts identity and livability in the case of North-Groningen, the Netherlands, after the Second World War.* [Unpublished paper presented during Paper ESTER Research Design Course. Barcelona, 2009.]

Merino, S.M., “Social Support and the Religious Dimensions of Close Ties.” *Journal for the Scientific Study of Religion* 53/3 (2014): 595–612.

Musschenga, A.W., *Kwaliteit van leven. Criterium voor medisch handelen?* Baarn: Ambo, 1987.

Ordway, S.H., *Resources and the American Dream. Including a Theory of the Limit of Growth.* New York: The Ronald Press Company, 1953.

Osborn, H.F., *The Limits of the Earth.* Boston: Little Brown, 1954.

Rogerson, R.J., “Environmental and Health-Related Quality of Life. Conceptual and Methodological Similaritie.” *Social Science and Medicine* 41/10 (1995): 1373–1382.

Smith, A. and J. Hopkinson, *Faith and the Future of the Countryside. Pastoral and Theological Perspectives on Rural Sustainability.* Norwich: Canterbury Press, 2012.

Stringer, M., “The future of public religious ritual in an urban context” [Lecture during symposium The future of ritual: spots and shapes, Amsterdam: February 2015].

Thissen, F. and J. Droogleever Fortuijn, *Het dorpshuis. Van bewoners en voor bewoners. De maatschappelijke participatie van dorpsbewoners en de betekenis van het dorpshuis in de dorpen van Littenseradiel.* Amsterdam: Urban Geography Programme, Universiteit van Amsterdam, 2012.

Veenhoven, R., *Leefbaarheid, betekenissen en meetmethoden. Studie in opdracht van Ministerie WVZ.* Rotterdam: Erasmus Universiteit, 2000.

Vermeij, L. and A. Steenbekkers, *Dichtbij huis. Lokale binding en inzet van dorpsbewoners.* Den Haag: Sociaal en Cultureel Planbureau, 2015.

Vermeij, L. and G. Mollenhorst, *Overgebleven dorpsleven. Sociaal kapitaal op het hedendaagse platteland.* Den Haag: Sociaal en Cultureel Planbureau, 2008.

Vonk, M., *Sustainability and Quality of Life. A Study on The Religious Worldviews, Values and Environmental Impact of Amish, Franciscan and Benedictine Communities.* Amsterdam: Buijten en Schipperheijn, 2011.

News Sources

Dagblad van het Noorden

November 12, 2011. “Barometer over leefbaarheid, Roden.”

June 10, 2013. Sevink, G.J., “Ulrum kan extra financiële impuls uitstekend gebruiken.”

De Bron & Rondom d'Olle Dodde, Kerkblad voor de Hervormde Gemeenten Schildwolde-Overschild-Hellum en Noordbroek 2, 2014.

De Brug, Kerkblad voor de Protestantse Gemeente te Asten-Someren 50, 2014.

Eindhovens Dagblad

Oktober 4, 2014. “Inwoners blazen zelf leven in kermis Hulsel.”

November 24, 2014. “*Kamer wil betere fietspaden: goed voor lijf en economie.*”

December 8, 2014. “*MIK* maakt Rooise buurt meer leefbaar.”

December 8, 2014. “Steeds minder voorzieningen in dorp: minder bussen, winkels, onderwijs en pinautomaten.”

December 9, 2014. “*Opinie - Nog één kans voor Helmond.*”

Peelbelang

November 7, 2013. Van Velthoven, B., “Oprichtingsvergadering dorpswinkel Someren-Heide.”

November 28, 2013. Van de Nieuwenhof, J., “‘Waar moet ik nu met mijn kind naartoe?’ Verontwaardiging over aangekondigde sluiting St. Pieterschool Ommel.”

December 2, 2013. Van Velthoven, B., “Someren zet in op behoud lijn 20, Raadsvergadering Someren.”

January 7, 2014. Van de Nieuwenhof, J., “Ommel heeft een nieuwe Kluis.”

January 7, 2014. Lamers, E., “Buslijn 20 door Lierop blijft behouden.”

March 6, 2014. “Wijkbeheerders: extra ogen en oren in de wijk.”

May 4, 2014. Van Hal, I., “Coalitiepartijen Deurne staan voor open bestuursstijl.”

November 3, 2014. “Informatieavond herinrichting dorpskern Neerkant.”

November 25, 2014. Raaijkmakers, K., “Ploegefist draagt steentje bij aan leefbaarheid De Rips.”

November 28, 2014. Lamers, E., "Dorpscoöperatie Lierop van start."
December 22, 2014. Lamers, E., "Voortbestaan kinderopvang Lierop in gevaar."
December 1, 2014. "ED in gesprek met Willy Donkers, de burgemeester van Elsendorp."

RTV Noord
December 3, 2014. "Aardbevingen vergallen woongenot."
't Bokkeblad
January 22, 2014. "1,2 miljard voor aardbevingsgebied."
February 12, 2014. "Vorstelijk aanbod Freylemaborg."
March 12, 2014. "Lijst 3, VVD."
March 26, 2014. "Vernieuwde projecten vanuit burgerkracht."
April 2, 2014. "Coalitieakkoord gepresenteerd."
June 11, 2014. "Coalitieakkoord uitgewerkt in een collegeprogramma."
June 11, 2014. "Opening Dorpsboekenkenkast in Kolham."
July 2, 2014. "Breedband op het Hogeland en de gemeente Slochteren voor leefbare gemeente."
August 27, 2014. "Zelf aan de slag voor een leefbare gemeenschap."
October 15, 2014. "Loket voor leefbaarheid."
November 5, 2014. "Leefbaarheidsfonds."
December 3, 2014. "Jacques Wallage 'van de nood een deugd maken'."
December 3, 2014. "Loket Leefbaarheid geopend."

Trouw
September 20, 2013. Markus, N., "Kerk gesloten, kroeg weg, school weg en nu het hele dorp weg?"

Websites

Broekema, P. "We regelen onze zorg steeds vaker zelf,' Accessed February 20, 2015. www.nos.nl/artikel/2017717-we-regelen-onze-zorg-steeds-vaker-zelf.html.
Department of the Environment, Transport and the Regions. "Local Quality of Life Counts, A Handbook for a Menu of Local Indicators of Sustainably Development." Accessed January 2015. www.proveandimprove.org/documents/localqolc.pdf.
Dialoogtafel Groningen. Accessed March 2015. www.dialoogtafelgroningen.nl/category/nieuws.
Dialoogtafel Groningen. "Lichtpuntje in het aardbevingsgebied." Accessed 1 December 2014. www.dialoogtafelgroningen.nl/nieuws/lichtpuntje-het-aardbevingsgebied.html.

Eindhovens Dagblad. Accessed December 2014. www.ed.nl/uitgebreid-zoeken-1.2146469?search-quick=leefbaar&timestamp=1429879693889&-813c15ac3eaed309f0469fb25bf1c021=6bd57c5ab822b49affde5bfc1cf97032&8f3f9141d66a51c82a3648ce7f3c000d=.
Groninger Bodem Beweging. Accessed March 2015. www.groninger-bodem-beweging.nl/.
Kenniscentrum NoorderRuimte. Accessed March 2015. www.hanze.nl/nld/onderzoek/kenniscentra/kenniscentrum-noorderruimte/kennisbank/kennisbank/onderzoeks-rapporten.
Lexis Nexis. "Kwaliteit leven." Accessed January 2015. www.academic lexisnexis.nl.proxy-ub.rug.nl/.
Lexis Nexis, "Leefbaarheid." Accessed January 2015. www.academic lexisnexis.nl.proxy-ub.rug.nl/.
National Accounts of Well-being. "Indicators." Accessed February 2015. www.nationalaccountsofwellbeing.org/explore/indicators/zwbi.
Oregon.gov. "Recommendations Memo #2 Livability and Quality of Life Indicators." Accessed January 2015. www.oregon.gov/ODOT/TD/TP/docs/lcp/livability.pdf.
Oxford English Dictionary, "liveability." Accessed January 2015. www.oed.com/view/Entry/109302?redirectedFrom=liveability#eid.
Peelbelang. Accessed December 2014. www.peelbelangonline.nl/search/node/leefbaar.
Provincie Groningen. "Dossier Aardbevingen." Accessed March 2015. www.provinciegroningen.nl/actueel/dossiers/aardbevingen/
Rijksoverheid. "Aardbevingen in Groningen." Accessed March 2015. www.rijksoverheid.nl/onderwerpen/aardbevingen-in-groningen/aardbevingen-door-gaswinning-in-groningen.
—, "Onderzoeken naar gevolgen van mindering gaswinning." www.rijksoverheid.nl/onderwerpen/aardbevingen-in-groningen/documenten-en-publicaties/rapporten/2014/01/17/onderzoek-geschikt-maken-van-ander-gas.html.
RTV Noord. "Voedselbank." Accessed February 2015. www.rtvnoord.nl/ipad/index.asp?v=32402.
—, "Dominees bidden voor getroffen Groningers." Accessed February 2013 2014. www.rtvnoord.nl/artikel/artikel.asp?p=12967228.
—, "Dossier Aardbevingen."Accessed March 2015. www.rtvnoord.nl/index/index.asp?q=dossieraardschok.
—, "Kerken strijden tegen onderhuidse boosheid over bevingen." Accessed February 2015. www.rtvnoord.nl/artikel/artikel.asp?p=145139.
't Bokkeblad. Accessed December 2014. www.bokkeblad.nl/archief.
Thissen, F., *Leefbare dorpen: van raamwerk tot ontwikkelingsmodel.* Amsterdam, 2006. Accessed January 2015. www.nwt.be/nieuws/UiteenzettingThissen.pdf.

—, *Leefbaarheid en Vitaliteit van dorpen: Mythes en Uitdagingen*. Gouda, 2009. Accessed January 2015. www.thissen.net/rural/GroeneHart/Leefbaarheid%20en%20Vitaliteit%20van%20dorpen%20Mythes%20en%20uitdagingen.doc.

Truijman, J., "We regelen onze zorg steeds vaker zelf." Accessed 20 February 2015. www.nos.nl/artikel/2017717-we-regelen-onze-zorg-steeds-vaker-zelf.html.

PARADISE LOST HAS BEEN OPENED AGAIN: A PROPHETIC UTOPIA DEPICTING THE QUALITY OF LIFE IN URBAN LIVING ENVIRONMENTS

Margareta Gruber

Abstract

"And I saw a new heaven and a new earth, for the first heaven and the first earth had passed away, and there was no more sea. I, John, saw the holy city, New Jerusalem, coming down from God out of Heaven, prepared as a bride adorned for her husband." (Rev. 21:1–2 KJ21[1])

What does the biblical visionary see? He beholds a city – a new polis being not a mere vision but a concrete train of thought. There is no desire to flee from reality but to shed a new light on urban society. The prophecy of Isaiah (Isaiah 65:16b–66:24) is fulfilled in the new city of Jerusalem: It is God's heavenly garden of immense size, splendid, precious and flooded with light, with God's throne in the center from which a flow of life and salvation is emanating; and God's people living here comprising all peoples, excluding only idolaters and the cruel. Death and pain have been overcome. The peace that has been promised by prophets during all centuries finally materializes in the vision of the New Jerusalem. Their visions have often been interpreted as the promise of the world to come, just as the apocalyptic images of destruction have often been seen as the predictions of the end of the world. The latter would have but little to do with the search we have in mind for a current quality of life.

A closer look at the text, its linguistic-narrative form and its prophetic intention, however, exhibits the dynamism of the eschatological vision concerning its specific and subversive power of forming current and future urban living environments.

1 Scripture quotations taken from the 21st Century King James Version of the Holy Bible (Gary: Deuel Enterprises, 1994).

Keystone of the Sacred Scripture

The New Testament concludes with the vision of the Heavenly Jerusalem. In Christian tradition, it is therefore the keystone of the Sacred Scripture, the two-in-one canon of the Bible. The Revelation of John is among the most recent Scriptures of the New Testament and dates back to the end of the 1st century in Asia Minor[2], witness of the destruction of the temple and the holy city of Jerusalem in 70 A.D. and the largely completed process of separation of Christian and Jewish communities. We owe this prophetic Scripture to a visionary who was, however, deeply rooted in Jewish tradition. His pictorial visions refer mostly to the Hebrew Bible, but also show that he was close to the vivid eschatological expectations of Early Judaism not willing to give up the real city of Jerusalem even after the catastrophe of 70 A.D. had occurred.

The City is part of the New Heaven and the New Earth, "for the first heaven and the first earth had passed away" (Rev. 21:1). These words are mostly associated today with the so-called "end of the world", particularly when combined with the catchword "apocalypse". While it is, admittedly, correct that the visionary is shown an end or, better still, the full accomplishment, the collapse of the first world leads not to her destruction but – from a biblical point of view – to her "death" being the vital requirement for her "resurrection" as the New Earth. Therefore also heaven "dies"[3] and "rises again" as New Heaven. Only death and the underworld (Hades) are destroyed without resurrection and their power is broken once and for all (Rev. 20:14). The new city coming down out of heaven is thus part of a new

2 Cf. the later commentaries in English language: D.E. Aune, *World Biblical Commentary 52A: Revelation 1–5* (Dallas-Nashville: Word, 1997–1998); J.L. Reseguie, *Revelation unsealed. A narrative critical approach to John's apocalypse* (Leiden: Brill, 1998); G.K. Beale, *The New Greek Testament Commentary. The Book of Revelation* (Grand Rapids: Carlisle, 1999). Furthermore I owe valuable indications to the following authors: M.A. Grimm, *Lebensraum in Gottes Stadt. Jerusalem als Symbolsystem der Eschatologie* (Münster: Aschendorff, 2007); F. Hahn, "Die Bedeutung Jerusalems für das Neue Testament. Überlegungen zu einer Jerusalem-Theologie," in *Jerusalem. Festschrift zum 100jährigen Ankommen der Benediktinermönche auf dem Jerusalemer Zionsberg* (ed. N.C. Schnabel; Münster: Aschendorff, 2006), 142–149; H. Merklein, "Jerusalem – bleibendes Zentrum der Christenheit? Der neutestamentliche Befund," in *Zion, Ort der Begegnung* (eds. F. Hahn, F.L. Hossfeld, H. Jorissen and A. Neuwirth; Bodenheim: Hanstein, 1993), 47–61; P. Söller, *Jerusalem, die hochgebaute Stadt. Eschatologisches und Himmlisches Jerusalem im Frühjudentum und im frühen Christentum* (Tübingen und Basel: Francke, 1998); D. Stoltmann, *Jerusalem – Mutter – Stadt. Zur Theologiegeschichte der Heiligen Stadt* (Altenberge: Oros,1999); M. Hengel, S. Mittmann and A.M. Schwemer (eds.), *La Cité de Dieu. Die Stadt Gottes* (Tübingen: Mohr Siebeck, 2000).

3 Thus can Rev. 20:11 be understood: "And I saw a great white throne and Him that sat on it, from whose face the earth and the heaven fled away, and there was found no place for them." Death and resurrection of Jesus is the paradigm not only for mankind but in this cosmic vision also for the whole creation.

earth. There is no God's Elysium arising anywhere while the old earth is disposed of at the cosmic waste site. Nothing is destroyed, but all shall be transformed. In today's language we are talking about a post-apocalyptic vision of the world. Needless to say, these pictorial visions of the Fulfillment must not be interpreted in a concretist way.[4] But linking the vision of Utopia to the existing "Original" allows us to look from the end to the beginning of the "New Time" which is yet to be realized in our present time: The shape of the New Earth is the basis for shaping the First Earth, the very same living environment which mankind is still responsible for.

I. The quality of life in the New Jerusalem

1. A new urban world

In the following I would like to pick out some sequences of this pictorial vision in which the quality of life in the heavenly city is expressed. First of all, the "New Earth" is an *urban* environment; "Heaven" is the very symbol representing the Hereafter and is marked as a city on (the New) *Earth.* In view of the ancient onlookers an ideal Hellenistic polis is designed on the basis of the Hippodamian System with a grid of parallel streets and blocks of the same size. The mixed constitution with theocracy and democracy also complies with ideal ancient concepts. This is a strong indication that the pictorial presentation of the heavenly city is also meant as political theology, because "city" corresponds to "polis".

So is this really utopia? If defined as an alternative social order with a critical perspective on the current situation and a demand for its constant realization by its people the term may be correct. The Heavenly Jerusalem is not supposed to be fictitious but prophetic in the way of announcing the acts of God: He is the one who will bring the finite nature of creation to completion. The Heavenly Jerusalem is a blessing which mankind receives from God, it is not due to human efforts or a result of historical development.

2. Not restored nature, but redeemed culture

God's new world presents itself not in the restored original condition of the biblical Paradise, it differs significantly from the popular images and visions of a "redeemed" paradise world. The vision of this city implies that

4 The American authors Tim la Hays and Jerry Jenkins attracted media attention in the evangelical scene and have acquired a reputation with the volumes of the so-called "Left behind" series.

fulfillment is not restored nature, but redeemed culture including nature restored.[5] It means in effect that the entire history of mankind will merge with and into this fulfillment including all cultural achievements which is according to Jewish and Christian understanding the history of God and the people he created. Just imagine the peaceful co-existence of the beauty of Mozart's Requiem and the beauty of a Quran recitation – to mention but two symbolic expressions of religious-cultural beauty – both transformed and no longer in competition with each other. I cannot provide you with a comparable example for the balance of biosphere and technosphere which will characterize the redeemed urban culture without entering the realm of fantasy. How do you imagine a factory with drains from which healing waters are gushing out in which children are bathing?

The end of the Scripture is not a holiday brochure offering a beach under palm trees to the exhausted urban population but rather a major spiritual provocation. Polis is automatically synonymous with citizenship; this means social order is another substantial element of culture. Thus a kind of ruling system does exist in the New Jerusalem, but this has been virtually taken ad absurdum for the citizens of Hellenistic *poleis* throughout the Roman empire. Martin Ebner writes: "Instead of their names being registered into an official list of citizens based on descent of the individual and therefore being entitled to join the *Ekklesia*[6] as well as having access to elections and public office, the names of those who submit themselves in everything to the will of God and the Lamb – and thus reign themselves – ´are written in the Lamb's Book of Life´ (Rev. 21:27). Thus all 'citizens' of the new city are 'rulers' without having any subjects to rule over. ... The 'rule' of God's 'slaves' consists of the worship of God."[7] This "rule model" is shared by all inhabitants of the City and is based on a common sense of responsibility before God; it also allows a new and redeemed form of human dominion over nature: no longer destroyed and exploited, nature itself offers "the Tree of Life, which bore twelve kinds of fruit and yielded her fruit every month; and the leaves of the tree were for the healing of the nations" (Rev. 22:2). Maybe this form of rule – a human ecology deriving from the joint responsibility towards God – shows the way forward in our current search for a holistic urban ecology, including man *and* nature.

5 This means that "there was the Tree of Life, which bore twelve kinds of fruit and yielded her fruit every month; and the leaves of the tree were for the healing of the nations." Cf. Rev. 22:2.

6 *Ekklesia* is the assembly of all voting, free and male citizens of a polis (editorial comment).

7 M. Ebner, *Die Stadt als Lebensraum der ersten Christen. Das Urchristentum in seiner Umwelt I* (Göttingen: Vandenhoeck & Ruprecht, 2012), 64–65. (Translation: MG)

3. Beauty and transparency, not wealth and security

The size of the City reaches surreal dimensions: "And the city lieth four-square, and the length is as great as the breadth; and he measured the city with the reed: twelve thousand furlongs; the length and the breadth and the height of it are equal" (Rev 21,16: a cube of 12 000 stadia, amazing 2200 km! (Rev. 21:15–17). Maybe this immense scale reflects not only the desire for infinite expansion of the new world but also a critical utopia: the size of God's mega-city really covers the Imperium Romanum in its entire expansiveness![8] The city is also precious beyond any measure. Marble is not even mentioned, although it is the perfect building material of an imperial city.[9] Instead the city is made of pearls and gems.[10] Wealth also characterizes the anti-city named Babylon being especially a symbol for the city of Rome (see Rev. 17:1–6). But Jerusalem's wealth is shared by all. Therefore her street "was pure gold, as it were, transparent glass" (Rev. 21:21). She is characterized by beauty and transparency, not by wealth and security.

4. Personal and spatial

This is the reason why there are no homes for people in this City, no private living space, just streets and gates, the sites where in the biblical and oriental world communication takes place. Within her light, everything is in motion, unlimited encounters without fear, free flow of intercommunication on her streets of "pure gold, as it were, transparent glass" (Rev 21,21). The New Jerusalem offers no room to people, but the people being a room in itself.[11] It could even be expressed like this: the New Jerusalem offers no room for God, too, but God being the room Himself. A new kind of cross-border liaison leads to the imagination of a new kind of community space: spatial and personal categories visualize one another and thus build vision of peace. The wealth of the nations and cultures will be brought into this city which has no need for exclusion and separation, therefore "the gates of it shall not be shut at all by day, for there shall be no night there" (Rev. 21:24–26). This means that all nations obtain the right of residence in this city. In the 1st century this was considered as political theology refusing

[8] Ebner, *Die Stadt als Lebensraum der ersten Christen*, 60, referring to: N.J. Kraybill, *Imperial Cult and Commerce in John's Apocalypse* (Sheffield: Sheffield Academic Press,1996), 211.

[9] Cf. Ebner, *Die Stadt als Lebensraum der ersten Christen*, 61.

[10] For details concerning the biblical-Jewish symbolism cf. the commentaries and Ebner, *Die Stadt als Lebensraum der ersten Christen*, 64.

[11] Cf. R.H. Gundry, "The New Jerusalem. People as Place, not Place for People," *Novum Testamentum* 29 (1987): 254–264.

the Roman world domination and all claims to power disregarding God's will. Today we interpret the "theology of the gates" in context with the flow of refugees crossing the Mediterranean in order to reach Europe but also millions of people drifting from rural areas to the cities which particularly affects Asian countries. God's Mega-City is quite literally an "Arrival City"[12], hospitable and welcoming all with open arms, a City which can afford to keep its gates open all the time! Especially today this "theology of the walls" where gates are transformed to open doors of hospitality is highly prophetic, "in times of many fences and walls even between the poor of the periphery, in times of migration without documents, human trafficking etc.."[13]

5. Without separation between holy and profane, public and private, cult and secularity: "no temple"

The most important the visionary sees in this City corresponds to those things which he cannot see: "And I saw no temple therein, for the Lord God Almighty and the Lamb are the temple of it" (Rev. 21:22). There is also no "house" for God anymore as his "throne" stands in the middle of a square of the City; or rather the whole City is the square in which center the throne is situated. God' s presence is not located in one spot but occupies the entire space of the city in which there is no longer a separation between holy and profane. This provocative view should not be regarded as criticism of the cult but its radicalization. Places gain their significance by relation; it's all about the new way of encountering and communicating with God by means of a new communication among people. Politically it proves the necessity of participation; God's eschatological space is "a space of inclusion of diversity as the source of wealth and abundance of life."[14]

This theology of the public square in The Book of Revelation is maybe the most important message it has to offer to us nowadays. Here I quote the Brazilian liberation theologian Luiz Carlos Susin:

"Our imagination is populated with squares linked with the temple and the established powers: town hall square, church yard, parade ground. In the eschatological city the symbolism of the square takes up the place of the temple because originating from the Lamb – the sacrifice of the temple -

12 Cf. D. Saunders, *Arrival Cities. Über alle Grenzen hinweg ziehen Millionen Menschen vom Land in die Stadt. Von ihnen hängt unserer Zukunft ab* (München: Blessing, 2011).

13 L.C. Susin, "Die Stadt, die Gott will. Ein Platz und ein Tisch für alle," in *Glauben in Mega-Cities. Transformationsprozesse in lateinamerikanischen Großstädten und ihre Auswirkungen auf die Pastoral* (eds. M. Eckholt and S. Silber; Mainz: Grünewald, 2014), 275–287, 280. (Translation: MG)

14 Susin, "Die Stadt, die Gott will", 287.

the veil[15] of the temple has been torn and God is no longer inside; the temple remains empty. The system and the heart of the city have been shifted: The square is the place to be for all people, the whole polis is embraced, welcomed and offered hospitality, offered by the victims and the poor. The square belongs to all and everybody finds a place there (...). We should realize that the powerful frightening temples of today are the financial centers which unforgivingly demand the debtors' blood; enormous and fascinating shopping center temples entrap people into debts; private and state-owned credit cards act as intermediaries between the intriguing and horrifying aspects of the numinous, leading from merry consumerism to invaluable debts; taking into account all the required backup procedures, segregation measures and victimization mechanisms of today we are able to gauge the full measure and significance of replacing the temple with the square. In our narration the eschatological square corresponds to the place where the people are no longer subjected to these hallowed powers and can move freely, form relationships and live together with others, experience human acceptance and respect. The reserved time for this experience is the Sabbath, the citizenship par excellence, when families and friends can walk together without haste on the squares allowing themselves and their relationships to be more cheerful, playful and unselfish resulting in strangers becoming potential friends."[16]

This text of a Latin-American theologian expresses a new urban poetry and inspires a new practical approach. From a European point of view, however, we cannot ignore how the ideas of an urban quality of life and also the knowledge of this quality being menaced in a globalized world are about to approach each other.[17]

6. By means of a theology of the public space

Four years of experience in Jerusalem, where religion naturally controls the public space – often in conflict with the secular society of the country – made me more sensitive towards the need to reanimate the religious discourse in public, a need which is also noticeable in the Western hemi-

15 This is a intertextual link to Mark 15:38: After Jesus' death "the veil of the temple was rent in two from the top to the bottom." This means that the separation of holy and profane is void where God manifests himself in the body of a cursed executed (cf. Dtn. 27:26). (Comment: MG)

16 Susin, "Die Stadt, die Gott will", 278–279. (Translation: MG)

17 Cf. M. Eckholt, "Poesie der Stadt. Wie sieht die neue Stadt aus?," in *Glauben in Mega-Cities. Transformationsprozesse in lateinamerikanischen Großstädten und ihre Auswirkungen auf die Pastoral* (eds. M. Eckholt and S. Silber; Mainz: Grünewald, 2014), 302–323.

sphere and even in countries with a laical tradition like France. The nature of this discourse is often characterized by violence, as in the case of the Mohamed caricature controversy; the public square runs the risk of becoming a symbol of terror[18] instead of being the symbol of the movement towards more openness during the so called Arab Spring.[19] In the earthly Jerusalem this is even more true for the sacred place itself, the so-called Temple Mount or *al-Haram al-Sharif* and the place right beneath of it, in front of the Wailing Wall, where the competition among the religions explode again and again in the form of violence. The privatization of religious experience which took place in the western hemisphere after the enlightenment and which has been dominating the western debate on secularization, is completely alien to Judaism. The principal project goals of God's covenant are that the earth – the collective, the public – "shall be full of the knowledge of the Lord, as the waters cover the sea" (Isaiah 11:9).[20] The conflicts in the earthly Jerusalem repeatedly prove to me that it is an error to believe that peace among people or cultures could be established or even enforced by erasing religion from the public space. Quite on the contrary a process can be witnessed in the Middle East producing periodically new spirals of violence caused by pushing back religion. The helpless western perception can only label this phenomenon with religious fundamentalism; this label, however, becoming more and more general and undifferentiated. But the question becomes increasingly important to ask also in western societies: How can religion return to public perception and reality without violent confrontation?

In face of these urgent issues the eschatological vision is of interest also for a successful cultural coexistence in Europe and should be taken into consideration: the New Jerusalem has no further need for the temple because sacrifices have been abolished;[21] instead she offers "ritual secularism" to a certain extent, a space illuminated by the worship of God and at the same time yet paradoxically serving as secular space for all peoples.[22]

18 Cf. Susin, "Die Stadt, die Gott will", 279.

19 For example, the Tahir-Square in Cairo; I visited it with students while the Revolution was still going on. The hopes of many young people had been threatened by disappointment already back in April 2011.

20 I owe a lot to the good talks with A. Isaacs in Jerusalem about the Jewish tradition about peace. Cf. A. Isaacs, *A Prophetic Peace. Judaism, Religion and Politics* (Bloomington: Indiana University Press, 2011).

21 From a Christian point of view it is the gift of the Lamb's life, the only "sacrifice" which ends all sacrificing.

22 Cf. also F.-W. Marquardt, *Eia, wärn wir da. Eine theologische Utopie* (Gütersloh: Gütersloher Verlagshaus, 1997), 259: The "eschatological secularism" ... "will be the opposite of turning away from God, the opposite of indifference and neutrality towards him:... It has its

How can the voice of Christianity be heard and reflected in a public space of society? In this respect it seems important to me to mention what is said about the energy source of the Heavenly Jerusalem, this Christian vision of a new urbanity. Celestial bodies are no longer necessary as the only source of light is "the glory of God", i.e. God himself in his luminous and powerful presence. "And the Lamb is the light thereof" (Rev. 21:23): for the Christian prophet and author of the book of Revelation this is Christ crucified and risen in Jerusalem; his love being the power plant of the City. Since ancient times this love has been implemented into Christian life style in form of the Christian charity put into practice the words of Jesus "Verily I say unto you, inasmuch as ye have done it unto one of the least of these My brethren, ye have done it unto Me.'" (Mt 25,40). Thus not only the cathedral is part of the medieval city center but also the "Hôtel Dieu", the Hospice for Christ being present in the poor and dying. Christianity substantially influenced Western culture; most importantly it changed our attitude towards death[23] which is no longer equated with the cruel loss of life but in contemplation of Jesus (the "Lamb" of the Heavenly City) seen as a possibility to *live* a meaningful and complete life in the decision to devote one's life to God, be it in one's personal death or in spending one's life for others. The following conclusion can be drawn out of this, as Pierre Teilhard de Chardin states: "To struggle against evil, and to reduce to a minimum even the ordinary physical evil which threatens us, is unquestionably the first act of our Father who is in heaven."[24] The unique quality of God's love is manifest in the self-offering of Jesus: Initially he turns to the small, the weak, the helpless and those without any rights and identifies himself with the least of his brothers and sisters. Being the guardian of this "source of light" the voice of Christianity shall be obliged to participate in today's manifold sociopolitical and ethical discourses concerning the human quality of life in a global society.

II. The quality of life in Heavenly Jerusalem?

1. A prophetic impulse in light of imminent dystopias

After this outlook on the eschatological urban vision the question asked at the beginning of this text arises again: which life style ideas are included in this vision which leaves its readers slightly confused? For if you exposed

origin in the humanity and secularity of God being the initial and authorized citizen of this city." (Translation: MG)

23 Cf. in this respect C. Theobald S.J., *Transmettre l'Évangile de liberté* (Paris: Bayard Jeunesse, 2007), particularly 115–117.

24 P.T. de Chardin, *The Divine Milieu* (New York: Harper Collins, 1960), 50.

yourself to its grand and splendid images and maybe enjoyed its dream-like loveliness, you soon find yourself confronted with the other side of these experiences with all its power and consequences: paradise lost. In the Bible's first book, Genesis, it is described in a mythical way how man-kind was banned from paradise (Genesis 3). Now the Bible tells us in its last book, the Revelation of John, that the New Paradise, the New City is prepared in heaven to come down from God to the Earth. What will the quality of life be like in this City? "Breaking up" the images of the visionary beauty of Heavenly Jerusalem into "earthly" components seems to be an attempt doomed to failure. Her dimensions are too different, her visions too big in order to correspond to the general idea of day-to-day city life on our earth. Who would seriously and substantially imagine to live in such a city on the long run? Without any homes, without a chance to retreat to the private sphere, without secure borders, without any "sacrosanct" order and – frightful but true – without any "temples" in which those are "sacrificed" who have been found guilty by the society? The dystopic scenarios of mankind's future designed by our current visual culture show hideously perverted counter-images[25]: the gates are destroyed or impassable, the borders run down or insurmountable, the houses are uninhabitable ruins, the light of the sun is unbearable; the public is synonymous with total control or the fight for survival by all against all, transparency degenerates to seamless media monitoring, therefore any privacy is reduced to flight and hiding. The security systems are perverted mechanisms of totalitarian and inhuman regimes, the public squares abused for barbaric power demonstrations by the system. A small elite has power over the "temples" maintaining its rule by hedging, exclusion, selection, control and force. Current (post-)apocalyptic scenarios end up either in (self-)destruction of civilization or in heroic struggles for survival of a few people in view of the loss of many lives.

The Anti-Jerusalem appears in the Book of Revelations, too: Babylon, the "great whore" is the sexist symbol of anti-civilization (Rev.17:3–6); its "fornication" is not meant as sexual promiscuity but rather as idolatry of the pagan city, presumably it concerns trade relations with the idolatrous world in more concrete terms which are detested and condemned by the visionary. The female character of the city is ambivalent; her bloodthirsty lips reflect the terror and the fascination of the Roman Empire while her beguiling form at the same time epitomizes the dangerous appeal of the abundant Hellenistic culture. Her brutal destruction by those who economically benefitted from

25 I am referring especially to the latest popular dystopic films which all deal in different ways with biblical motives and subjects: *Matrix* (L. Wachowski and A. Wachowski, 1999), *Children of Men* (A. Cuaròn, 2006); *The Book of Eli* (A. Hughes and A. Hughes, 2010), *Elysium* (N. Blomkamp, 2013), *Interstellar* (C. Nolan, 2014); See also the trilogy of dystopian novels *The Hunger Games* by S. Collins, Scholastic (2008-2010) which was made a motion picture trilogy.

her (Rev.17:16) is not God's punishment but the consequence of human hubris comparable to the myth of the biblical Tower of Babel (Genesis 11). The prophets of the Old Testament have drastic "dystopic" scenarios, too, in which the description of the catastrophe and destruction sometimes takes up more room than the promise of redemption.[26] And if read entirely the Book of Revelations even reveals the origin of many contemporary dark pictures which are often linked to the word "apocalypse" nowadays. Thus it has been and still is interpreted as encrypted prediction of the end of the world. The Revelation of John is, however, a prophetic writing just as the texts it refers to in the Old Testament. The linguistic form of the prophecy is the call for repentance and not the prediction of the future. Whatever threats are issued by the prophets only apply if the people are not paying attention to the revelations and warnings; the original objective of the prophetic intervention is, however, a call for a lifestyle change in order to avoid exactly this catastrophe. This is most beautifully expressed in a fairytale-like and somewhat ironic tone in the Book of Jonah. The megacity Ninive ("Now Nineveh was an exceeding great city of three days' journey", Jonah 3,3) turned to God as a reaction on the call for repentance and was thus not destroyed as announced, much to the annoyance of the prophet who was sitting under his castor-oil tree and rejoicing over the doomed city and the upcoming divine showdown (Jonah 4,1–11).

Applied on my question regarding the quality of life this leads to the following result: the description of the dystopic anti-civilization (Babylon) and its downfall – the collapse of its worldwide economic empire[27] – is in fact a prophetic warning and critical potential against the forces of a de-humanized culture. In contrast the Book of Revelation offers the vision of the Heavenly Jerusalem. This urban milieu can only be realized in its subversive meaning when seen in the light of the dystopic counter-images of our time, i.e. her coming down from heaven but evolving on earth, the theology of her precious walls, open gates, serenely populated squares and the absence of a temple. We can learn from the current dystopias that this New World which seems to be so effortless and easy-going is far from being taken for granted. What is true for the prophetic warning is also true for the prophetic promise: the quality of life in God's New World depends on

[26] Cf. the mourning about the destruction of Jerusalem by God in Lam. 2. In Jes. 63 JHWH's judgment of wrath over the nations is described which precedes the promise of a new heaven and a new earth. A similar case of judgement and redemption also in Sach. 14. Both texts are pretexts of the Book of Revelations; see for reception of Jes. 63 and Sach. 14 in the Book of Revelations: Margareta Gruber, "'Blut aus der Kelter?,' 'Fleischfressende Vögel?,' Gericht und Erlösung in der Offenbarung des Johannes. Zur Intratextualität von Offb. 14,14–20 und Offb. 19,11–21," in *Figuren der Offenbarung. Biblisch-Religionstheologisch-Politisch. Ökumenische Beiträge aus dem Theologischen Studienjahr Jerusalem I* (eds. J. Negel and M. Gruber; Münster: Aschendorff, 2012), 107–130.

[27] Cf. the kings, merchants and ship masters lament her destruction (Rev 18,9–19).

the turnaround of mankind; the vision reveals its impediments and consequently the burdens and risks for the quality of life of the New World. Not final destruction or an uninhabitable, pale green, post-apocalyptic world have the final say in the Bible, but hope in the form of the light-flooded, gemstone-colored, heavenly polis. Whoever submits himself to this vision will experience prophetically an expansion of his ideas, desires and aspirations regarding human lifestyle quality; the hope for this completed form of human culture resists the temptation of nihilistic desperation or escapism and leads to a new ethos finding its expression in genuine actions. This is the path Pope Francis shows in his Encyclical „Laudato Sí" on human ecology or the interrelated relationship between humans and the environment.[28]

2. Transformed Mortality. Spirituality in the Heavenly Jerusalem

The visionary hears a voice calling "from the throne" only once in the Book of Revelation:

"Behold, the tabernacle of God is with men, and He will dwell with them; and they shall be His people, and God Himself shall be with them and be their God. And God shall wipe away all tears from their eyes, and there shall be no more death, neither sorrow, nor crying, neither shall there be any more pain; for the former things are passed away. And He that sat upon the throne said, 'Behold, I make all things new.' And He said unto me, 'Write, for these words are true and faithful.'" (Rev. 21:3–5).

God's voice does not promise to deny mortality but to transform it. The vision encourages therefore a spirituality in which mortality is accepted; it is based on the weakness of broken hopes and can embrace finiteness, mortality and frailty of life. In a theological sense it is this spirituality which accepts the fall or the sinfulness of creation as reality within the yet unfinished creation and brings it before God. The vulnerability of life is what makes life even more precious and worthy to be protected. This draws attention to an ethic of caring. The promised perfection does not remove the physical, ethical and spiritual fragility of life (i.e. does not cancel it), but transforms it according to the law of life of the Lamb that "had been slain" (Rev 5,6) and is standing alive and upright in the center of the City.

Bearing this in mind, I would like to end with the following: The New Jerusalem is not the "final promise", even if her final form will come down only after the completion of time and space, but a "basic promise" which is voiced to us in the midst of our time frightened by dark imagery. The seed

[28] Vatican City, May 24, 2015.

of this New City has been burrowed indelibly in our Earth – together with the grain of wheat being the slain Lamb.

Bibliography

Aune, D.E., *World Biblical Commentary 52A: Revelation 1–5*. Dallas-Nashville: Word, 1997–1998.

Beale, G.K., *The New Greek Testament Commentary. The Book of Revelation.* Grand Rapids: Carlisle, 1999.

Chardin, P.T. de, *The Divine Milieu.* New York: Harper Collins, 1960.

Collins, S., *The Hunger Games.* Scholastic 2008-2010.

Ebner, M., *Die Stadt als Lebensraum der ersten Christen. Das Urchristentum in seiner Umwelt I.* Göttingen: Vandenhoeck & Ruprecht, 2012.

Eckholt, M., "Poesie der Stadt. Wie sieht die neue Stadt aus?" in *Glauben in Mega-Cities. Transformationsprozesse in lateinamerikanischen Großstädten und ihre Auswirkungen auf die Pastoral,* edited by M. Eckholt and S.Silber, 302–323. Mainz: Grünewald, 2014.

Grimm, M.A., *Lebensraum in Gottes Stadt. Jerusalem als Symbolsystem der Eschatologie.* Münster: Asschendorf, 2007.

Gruber, M., "'Blut aus der Kelter?,' 'Fleischfressende Vögel?,' Gericht und Erlösung in der Offenbarung des Johannes. Zur Intratextualität von Offb. 14,14–20 und Offb. 19,11–21." In *Figuren der Offenbarung. Biblisch-Religionstheologisch-Politisch. Ökumenische Beiträge aus dem Theologischen Studienjahr Jerusalem I,* edited by J. Negel and M. Gruber, 107–130. Münster: Aschendorff, 2012: 107–130.

Gundry, R.H., "The New Jerusalem. People as Place, not Place for People." *Novum Testamentum* 29 (1987): 254–264.

Hahn, F., "Die Bedeutung Jerusalems für das Neue Testament. Überlegungen zu einer Jerusalem-Theologie." In *Laetare Jerusalem. Festschrift zum 100jährigen Ankommen der Benediktinermönche auf dem Jerusalemer Zionsberg,* edited by N.C. Schnabel, 142–149. Münster: Aschendorff, 2006.

Hengel, M., S. Mittmann and A.M. Schwemer (eds.), *La Cité de Dieu. Die Stadt Gottes.* Tübingen: Mohr Siebeck, 2000.

Isaacs, M., *A Prophetic Peace. Judaism, Religion and Politics.* Bloomington: Indiana University Press, 2011.

King James Version of the Holy Bible, 21th Century. Gary: Deuel Enterprises, 1994.

Kraybill, N.J., *Imperial Cult and Commerce in John's Apocalypse.* Sheffield: Sheffield Academic Press,1996.

Marquardt, F.-W., *Eia, wärn wir da. Eine theologische Utopie.* Gütersloh: Gütersloher Verlagshaus, 1997.

Merklein, H., "Jerusalem – bleibendes Zentrum der Christenheit? Der neutestamentliche Befund." In *Zion, Ort der Begegnung*, edited by F. Hahn, F.L. Hossfeld, H.H. Jorissen and A. Neuwirth, 47–61. Bodenheim: Hanstein Verlag, 1993.

Reseguie, J.L., *Revelation unsealed. A narrative critical approach to John's apocalypse.* Leiden: Brill, 1998.

Saunders, D., *Arrival Cities. Über alle Grenzen hinweg ziehen Millionen Menschen vom Land in die Stadt. Von ihnen hängt unserer Zukunft ab.* München: Blessing, 2011.

Söller, P., *Jerusalem, die hochgebaute Stadt. Eschatologisches und Himmlisches Jerusalem im Frühjudentum und im frühen Christentum.* Tübingen und Basel: Francke, 1998.

Stoltmann, D., "Jerusalem – Mutter – Stadt. Zur Theologiegeschichte der Heiligen Stadt." *Münsteraner Theologische Abhandlungen* 57 (1999).

Susin, Luiz Carlos., "Die Stadt, die Gott will. Ein Platz und ein Tisch für alle." In *Glauben in Mega-Cities. Transformationsprozesse in lateinamerikanischen Großstädten und ihre Auswirkungen auf die Pastoral*, edited by M. Eckholt and S. Silber, 275–287. Mainz: Grünewald, 2014: 275–287.

Theobald S. J., C., *Transmettre l'Évangile de liberté* . Paris: Bayard Jeunesse, 2007.

Films

Blomkamp, N., *Elysium.* 2013.

Cuaròn, A., *Children of Men.* 2006.

Hughes, A., and Hughes, A., *The Book of Eli.* 2010.

Nolan, C., *Interstellar.* 2014.

Wachowski, L., and Wachowski, A., *Matrix.* 1999.

EPILOGUE

The Dutch writer Godfried Bomans wrote a story about a man who lived alone in the deep forest, but was very happy with his life. He saw the morning dew as tiny pearls, the trees as pillars of a huge castle, the lakes as giant mirrors, and the sky as a miraculous ceiling. When by chance the villagers nearby heard about this man in the woods and his innumerable treasures, they came to visit him. He showed them his wealth and, utterly disappointed and insulted, they hanged him.

Story tellers, and their protagonists, look into daily reality with a creative eye, seeing treasures and possibilities where others just see problems and facts. Instead of 'hanging' them, we should be grateful for their eyes. They help us scholars momentarily forget our models and references, and see new perspectives in which changes appear as chances. However, as scholars, we have our own task, which is to taste and test the chances. Are they real chances, do they make sense, and how can we know?

The intention of this book has been to investigate the extent to which a spiritual gaze at the changes in our society can be shown to create real chances for renewal, either by the way we look into it (the theoretical level) or by the way we do it (the practical level). The spiritual gaze sees the reality from the perspective of the full and good life, a perspective which in itself tends to interpret problems as chances. This perspective, shared by the present contributions, has been approached from various angles ranging from banking to eschatology. In order to make these different approaches communicate with one another, we have given the authors three questions: 1) In your field of research, how would quality of life be described? 2) In which human conditions and practices can this good life be detected? 3) What suggestions could you give in order to enhance these conditions and practices?

We will now conclude our collective research with offering a first synthesis of our debate on life quality. This means we will identify the conditions and activities that feel unsatisfactory or even wrong and bad in present times and those that feel like a change for the better, an improvement of life features. Working in this way we hope to make visible some aspects of the societal renewal that is favored by our fellow scholars, especially in The Netherlands. Let us start with a short remembrance of the contributions.

From a decisively theological point of view, Christoph Hübenthal tries to spell out the chances of public theology in this debate. According to him, each public theology draws on a validity claim that constitutes the Christian faith praxis. As this claim is basically universal, and thus to be made known to everyone, public theology is a kind of apologetic endeavor. Apologetics, as Hübenthal argues, can take two mutually supporting forms of communication, namely, discourse and witnessing. The discursive mode seeks to make plausible that the concept of ultimate significance has a reasonable content so that everyone who understands the concept is urged to take an existential stance towards it. The testimonial mode, on the other hand, presents the Christian faith praxis as a credible candidate to embody ultimate significance.

But the author points at a major problem for both strands of apologetic communication. The current communication conditions in Western societies are not such that public theology can effectively be put into practice. The entirety of those obstructive conditions can be labelled as anthropological reductionism. Consequently, an additional task of public theology is the struggle against anthropological reductionism which can be identified with the fight for social justice. Public theology can only begin performing its primary apologetic tasks after this fight has achieved some satisfying results.

For this reason, the author correlates the quality of life to the degree to which the communication conditions for public theology are realized. In other words, the quality of life is determined by the degree to which the fight for social justice has been successful. It follows from this that the social conditions that promote the quality of life are socially just conditions. Therefore, the quality of life can be enhanced by struggling for a public space within which the topic of ultimate significance can unrestrictedly be debated and religious communities can openly bear witness to their faith.

The value of Hübenthal's contribution can be seen in the fact that he emphatically points at the social-ethical dimension of the quality of life. He does so by starting from an outspoken theological point of view. Subsequently, he shows, however, that this account of the quality of life can basically be shared by everyone because it is grounded in a rational ethics.

Elisabeth Hense refers to Jan of Ruusbroec's 'common life' as the way of living that is most appreciated in the Christian spiritual tradition. 'Common life' means a life of love, with God and one's neighbors – both loving attitudes unified in one graceful experience. Both kinds of love are attractive: being immersed in divine love is refreshing for the self and loving one's neighbors means to enjoy human connectedness, to realize the good things of life, and to build up a better world. During the 20th century, however, it ceased to be obvious that the experience of divine love is an adequate form of refreshment of the self. More secular forms of care of the self, as already known in ancient Greek as epimelesthai sauto ('to take care of yourself'), became revived in Western societies. Thus, the quality of life continues to have these two sides: looking for a state of happiness, purity, wisdom, perfection, or immortality and dedicating oneself to resolve the stresses of the needy and those at the margins.

In the long spiritual tradition of Christianity we see time and again a central role for the works of mercy when conditions and practices are indicated that are considered to improve the quality of life. The Catechism (no. 2447) lists seven spiritual and seven corporal works of mercy. The spiritual works of mercy are: to admonish the sinner, to instruct the ignorant, to counsel the doubtful, to comfort the sorrowful, to bear wrongs patiently, to forgive all injuries, and to pray for the living and the dead. The corporal works of mercy are: to feed the hungry, to give drink to the thirsty, to clothe the naked, to ransom the captive, to harbor the harborless, to visit the sick, and to bury the dead. Practicing works of mercy is considered salutary to the whole body of a community, and not only for Christians but for everybody. On the other hand, only those who take care of themselves are able to carry on with works of mercy in the face of setbacks and complicated circumstances.

In order to really enhance the quality of life in our times, works of mercy should show an indivisible unity of the spiritual-ethical urge for the 'common life' and the technical realization of it. This is why the discipline of spirituality studies looks for interdisciplinary approaches to enhance living conditions and practices and wants to contribute to all societal fields that are in need of renewal, whether it be food, care, or money.

According to Erik de Jongh discernment and rational decision making are complementary approaches in the search for quality of life in organizational contexts. Based on cross-textual readings of Delbecq, Falque, and Bougon, he summarizes the following standards for the practice of discernment in managerial contexts. First of all, one should recognize that organizational behavior is not only determined by external factors, but that organizational participants, including managers, remain responsible for their own conduct. Second, one needs a reflective inner disposition which enables decision makers to relate to their own experiences, and which is sustained by a community of accountability and support (either within the organization or elsewhere). Third, there has to be a commitment to human growth, or at least the desire for it. Fourth, one needs to be patient in the process of discovering the question relating to the choice, and practice a continued listening under the recognition that the deeper questions or issues may not emerge until one is further on in the process. Finally, there has to be an awareness of the internal movements and attention to the interpretation of these movements in order to get a general sense of the correctness of any choice; one has to remain attentive to one's experience of events and situations following the decision to act.

According to Delbecq, Falque, and Bougon, discernment in the context of management also refers to the importance of the decision maker. His or her subjective interpretation, appreciation, and assessment of events and situations should be included in the decision-making process. In the wake of Ignatius they identify the aim of discernment as gaining greater freedom: helping individuals to find their identity and to become free from their attachments. This is realized through a fundamental experience of changing viewpoints or to find greater freedom in one's way of thinking and acting. As a sign of consolation they mention contentment, serenity, and clarity; whereas signs of desolation could be found in discouraging thoughts, idleness, grumpiness, discontentment with self and others, sadness, and feelings of confusion, loneliness, and abandonment. While Delbecq refers to an ultimate horizon as an anchor for discernment, Falque and Bougon understand finality as an orientation which animates the decision maker.

A hermeneutics which seeks to understand organizations as products of the human mind is helpful. The hermeneutic mode of inquiry complements the empirical mode in the psychological and sociological investigation of organizational behavior. In contrast to empirical research, this mode of inquiry can engage organizational participants in conversations in which meaning is constructed and helps them to arrive at a better understanding of their situation. This is particularly important with respect to organizational and societal renewal where a change of perspective is required.

In his exploration of banking as a spiritual activity, Aloys Wijngaards offers an alternative to the moralistic approaches of banking. Not only is banking not all bad, but it may be a moral and spiritual practice. Why are there bankers? What makes their practice meaningful? What do they have to offer to a shared good life? To answer these questions, the author develops the concept of economic spirituality. In spirituality-guided banking, the values of trust and societal responsibility play a central role, as does the aim to create financial means for a sustainable society.

Like all human activities, banking is a practice in which decisions are guided by evaluative orientations. For example, one may decide on the sole basis of maximizing one's own profit, but also on the intention to create healthy conditions for other people to grow. To create healthy conditions, the banker has to find a proper balance between risk and confidence, and to engage in responsible lending. This requires not only prudence, but also choices in focus and policy. How can a banker help to realize desired societal values? Here, Wijngaards offers the concept of economic spirituality, which he calls the enactment of a transcending evaluative orientation in everyday economic practices.

Spirituality, a meaningful framework as an ultimate horizon in a person's everyday life, provides an evaluative orientation towards the fullness of life. The author locates this fullness of life as it is active in his economic spirituality as well as beyond everyday life. It is as near as it is transcendent, for, after all, it is a horizon. Thus, spirituality may give daily economic activities a very specific orientation towards a wholeness that cannot be seen.

As central values of an economic spirituality, the author considers the virtues of trust and societal responsibility. In calculating risks, the banker needs the trust that the bank will get the lent money back. But in the light of the good life, trust is also connecting the banker with opportunities that will bring people further. In the same way, responsibility may be about the banker's relation to the money, but in the light of the good life his responsibility may urge him to give people credit.

In his concluding remarks, Wijngaards asks an interesting question: While bringing spirituality into the banking practice may, indeed, lead bankers to an orientation on what their fundamental drivers and overarching values are, what are these values and how are they going to find them? The author gives us the picture of a banker who searches his or her soul, discerning the intuitions that may silently direct his or her actions. His call to look at the horizon of the fullness of life, then, may lead bankers to an inner orientation. A long-term perspective may happen to be very near.

Basic questions about the quality of life cause Willem Marie Speelman to focus on a situation where this quality seems to be missing, namely, a seemingly failed knee operation. He describes how a patient, her husband, and her physiotherapist, according to their own stories, try to enhance her fitness for a second operation. Entering into the realm of care practice, in which spirituality is only beginning to be noticed as a significant aspect, Speelman feels the need to be explicit about his approach to spirituality. This approach is an inductive one, in which the words that are actually used by the people involved reveal how they relate to the reality that transcends them. Whether or not their words are actually "names of God" is another question; what matters is that they allow people to relate to transcendence. This inductive approach connects with a recent proposal about the spiritual aspect of health care as it is advocated by Machteld Huber.

In order to find and understand the ways people relate to transcendence, Speelman analyzes their stories using a narrative method. This method helps him to discern traces of motivating forces, of faith and abilities, and of evaluations. In short, this method seeks to find who or what motivates one to act, which competences are needed for the performance of that act, what values are being realized in it, and how this realization is evaluated.

The stories of the physiotherapist, the patient, and her husband reveal a string of motivating forces: "the protocol" of the health institution, the rejection of the artificial knee by the body, the patient's strong motivation to get fit, and the physiotherapist. But it also becomes clear that, ultimately, it is the patient who has to perform the act of healing the relations with her body and, strangely enough, with the health care institution. In this act, the values of 'trust' and 'faith' are being communicated, if not realized, which may be counted as virtues helping the patient to heal these relations. The stories also reveal an awareness of the need to cooperate in this healing process. The good life, then, as it is implicitly depicted in the three stories, is a world in which everybody is fit to lead her or his daily life independently. Speelman notices that the words and images used or implied in peoples' stories can easily be connected to religious stories about the good life.

A spiritual approach to health care may lead to a critical discussion about the targets that the health care institutions have set for themselves. Are they really focusing on helping people to adapt to their new situation and live their old and lost lives again in a new way? Are they investing trust and faith in people so that they are healing broken relations themselves?

Krijn Pansters' attempt to determine the quality of life takes its point of departure in a medieval Franciscan perspective. For him, most of the wicked problems of our age are – in one way or another – related to the issue of property. The pursuit of property, as one might read his chapter's exposition, lies at the bottom of a wide range of urgent challenges humankind is confronted with today. Consequently, the problem of property is to be addressed first and foremost. This, however, does not mean we must renounce any striving for possessions; rather, it means that we must radically refocus such striving. What can be possessed, after all, are not only external goods, but also internal dispositions which help to give shape to one's life and so allow for a good life. Hence, abstaining from the possession of external goods can, at the same time, stimulate the longing for internal goods, that is to say, the longing for virtues whose exercise has always been regarded as the embodiment of a flourishing life. In this way the possession of external poverty leads to the acquisition of an internal richness or – to express it in modern terms – to the acquisition of a spiritual capital which enables the possessor to make authentic decisions with respect to the good of his or her own life. Within the Franciscan tradition, the supreme good has always been identified with God Himself so that the love of God (objective genitive) turns out to be the ultimate virtue. But the cardinal virtues, too, constitute an integral part of the spiritual capital. Temperance, in particular, serves as the disposition to rectify one's appetite and to exercise one's free will authentically.

By pointing at contemporary conceptions of human flourishing, Pansters shows that the Franciscan model of a virtuous possession of poverty is by no means outdated but is instead supported by more recent accounts of the art of living. Likewise, he spells out the similarities between medieval Franciscan spirituality and modern attempts of meeting the ecological crisis by advocating a sustainable way of living. Finally, the author demonstrates that the Franciscan idea of de-ownership can be translated into a new economic approach which emphasizes the distinction between possession and use. What eventually matters is not the possession of finite goods, but their conscientious, gentle, and grateful use.

In Pansters' view, the quality of life is thus primarily determined by the ability to abstain from external goods or dependencies and instead to acquire an inner virtue which can be seen as a special kind of capital. Though the author does not make entirely clear in which social conditions such virtues can be developed, he still leaves no doubt that the social and natural environment is in deep need of human beings who seek to acquire such spiritual capital. Only in this way can the quality of common life be warranted and enhanced.

This contribution provides us with the insight that current global challenges should not only be addressed by employing a modern social ethics but likewise demand the rediscovery of an ethical model which originated in the high Middle Ages. This model is still relevant because it finds partial support in current approaches to the art of living ethics and it can be translated into rather modern forms of an alternative economic practice.

The social group whose quality Sharda Nandram seeks to investigate is the entrepreneur. Within their professional context entrepreneurs face a broad spectrum of challenges. They have to develop a reasonable vision of their goals and the strategies to achieve these goals. Furthermore, they have to be sensitive to arising opportunities as well as potential dangers. They also have to decide and act under conditions of uncertainty. This makes their professional life more prone to error than perhaps other contexts of living. According to Nandram, many entrepreneurial failures can be traced back to a lack of holistic spiritual thinking. She explores the concept of intuition in order to provide such a holistic account. After presenting a historical sketch of the Western way of dealing with intuition, she turns to the Indian Vedanta school of philosophy, particularly to the work of Sri Aurobindo. His theory of intuition draws on an account of different stages of knowledge, the most advanced of which serve as primary sources of intuition. Intuition, then, can be conceived of as a form of knowledge which does not distinguish between the knowledge itself and the person who has this knowledge.

Within the professional context of entrepreneurship, the quality of life is, according to Nandram, determined by the degree to which an intuitive mind can be developed. Though she says little about the social conditions that promote the quality of life, she is clear about the social conditions that evoke the necessity to acquire an intuitive mind. She is convinced that the intuitive faculty can be trained by engaging in spiritual practices. For this purpose, Aurobindo developed a number of techniques. Improving the quality of entrepreneurial life means, therefore, providing a set of spiritual facilities which help to acquire an intuitive mind.

At least two things can be learned from Nandram's contribution. On the one hand, she makes clear that intuition lies at the heart of entrepreneurial existence so that every entrepreneur should not only be attentive to his or her intuitive skills but also seek to improve intuition by performing concomitant spiritual practices. On the other hand, the author also draws our attention to non-Western philosophies that encourage us to leave trodden paths and to realize that other cultures have important things to say when we wish to learn about the quality of life.

Jacobine Gelderloos discloses visions about the quality of life in rural areas of the Netherlands. Beginning in the 1950s, the liveability of the countryside became questioned, mainly because many young people moved to the cities. Villages witnessed a growing number of empty houses, closed shops, and diminishing school populations. In this crisis, the topic of liveability became important in (local) politics and in the media communicating about it. Gelderloos' research focuses on two kinds of media approaching this topic, i.e., local newspapers and church newsletters in two Dutch provinces.

Gelderloos discovers that the local newspapers and the church newsletters have different approaches to liveability. Newspapers focus on the problems of social cohesion, and pay attention to the developments around meeting places and social activities. They write about initiatives to stop the exodus of young people from the countryside, and lure tourists to come and visit it. The vision depicted by the newspapers is that by saving meeting places, enhancing social activities and organizing social services, people cooperate in reshaping the villages as an attractive place to live.

Church newsletters, in contrast, add an individual approach to liveability by paying attention to personal experiences like loneliness and fear. How is the personal quality of life affected by developments in the physical and social environment? How are people coping with health problems and worries about unemployment? Thus, the church newsletters reveal something of the inner conversation in rural areas.

The quality of life, as it is revealed in the liveability of the countryside, is shaped by the interaction between the environment and the individual. For example, the earthquakes in Groningen, caused by the extraction of natural gas, have had serious effects on both social and personal life in the villages. But in this interaction, people's ideas about a good life play an important role as a frame of reference. What happens in your environment and how it touches you personally may be colored and guided by your worldview. Considered in this way, the different approaches of the local newspapers and the church newsletters complement one another. Especially when newsletters depict explicit images of the good life, e.g., images of God's kingdom, the church may have its own role in the common effort to improve the quality of life.

Some aspects that have a strong impact on personal life, like employment and education, sustainability, and nuisance control, are not often mentioned in relation to liveability. Apparently, the newspapers connect the topic of liveability mainly to the quality of a community or a place: it is about meeting places, social activities, and public services. Research, however, has indicated that public services, like mobility and internet connection, do not have a strong effect on the quality of life. More important are supportive relationships between the inhabitants that also touch their inner life and well-being. Not only is it important that people converse with one another, but the effect of their conversation may be a sort of conversion: to one another, but also to each other's worldview. A shared worldview reduces feelings of fear and uncertainty. It helps people make sense of what happens to them.

In the vision of the New Jerusalem, Margareta Gruber sees the quality of life expressed as a prophetic social order for a new urban world. The vision casts a critical light on the current situation, and asks for its constant realization by the people in this new urban world. That the vision concerns a city implies that fulfillment is not restored nature but redeemed culture, which includes restored nature. In effect, the entire history of humankind will merge with and into this fulfillment, including all cultural achievements, which is, according to Jewish and Christian understanding, the history of God with His creation. The New Jerusalem is characterized by beauty and transparency, not by wealth and security. There are no private homes in this 'city', just streets and gates, precisely the sites where communication takes place in the biblical and oriental worlds. God's presence is not located in one spot but occupies the entire space of the city in which there is no longer a separation between the holy and profane.

The Heavenly Jerusalem is a blessing which humankind receives from God; it is not due to human efforts or a result of historical development. All citizens of the new city are rulers without having any subjects to rule over. This "rule model" is based on a common sense of responsibility before God; it also allows a new and redeemed form of human interaction with nature. Its wealth is shared by all. God's Jerusalem is hospitable and welcoming to all, keeping its gates open all the time. The vision expresses a new way of encountering and communicating with God by means of a new communication among people.

The privatization of religious experience, which took place in the Western hemisphere after the Enlightenment and which has been dominating the Western debate on secularization, is completely alien to many religious people. By means of a theology of the public space, we can meet the need to reanimate religious discourse in public. Being the guardian of God's love – the turn to the small, the weak, the helpless, and those without any rights – Christians are called to participate in today's manifold sociopolitical and ethical discourses concerning the human quality of life in a global society. They can focus themselves on two scenarios: Babylon, i.e., the dystopic anti-civilization and its downfall, which is in fact a prophetic warning and critical of the potential against the forces of a de-humanized culture, and/or Jerusalem.

After having recalled the findings of the participants in our shared quest for quality of life in contexts of societal renewal, we may harvest some answers to the three main questions of this book: What is seen as quality of life? In which human conditions and practices do we detect quality of life? What suggestions can we give in order to enhance these conditions and practices? We would like to do this in the form of a conversation between the authors.

It appears, as Jacobine Gelderloos points out, that the answer to the first question is dependent on the situation in which it comes up and on the world view that people share. Every tradition has stories about the good life. But it is the situation (of deprivation) which makes people long, and their desires picture a vision of quality of life along the lines of the traditional stories. Thus, the traditional stories make people bear their situation as somehow related to the good life. In the rural areas described by Gelderloos, quality of life can be detected in personal lives, which share supportive relationships and, as a result of their mutual communication, find themselves in a shared world view. When, as in the case of local newspapers, this shared world view is stripped from any religious concern, the personal aspect of these lives appears to be lacking. This finding is supported by Willem Marie Speelman who discerns reminiscences of quality of life in a situation where it fails, a health care practice. Not only is health missing, but today's health care practice is also stripped from a spiritual or religious approach. In this case, the people involved in the therapy find ways to express their longing for trust and faith. The good life, then, as it is implicitly depicted in their stories, is a world in which everybody is fit to lead her or his daily life independently.

A spiritual approach to health care may lead to a critical discussion about the conditions in which people in health care institutions have to communicate about the quality of life. In this respect, it is revealing what Christoph Hübenthal writes about the conditions for such communication. Not only is it necessary that people really communicate with each another as human beings and not as numbers, but this communication demands that their (perhaps different) religious views on ultimate significance are fully present in this communication. Next to the discursive communication of people sharing their thoughts and visions, the condition and enhancement of a quality of life is also supported by what Elisabeth Hense calls its technical realization in works of mercy. It is essential that secular forms of care for the self always find their fulfillment in the care for the (other) needy. What is important is that it is the combination, or in other words, that it is one love, which reaches out for the self and for the other, one love elaborated in multiple works of mercy. Where works of mercy resolve the neediness and marginality of people, there is room for happiness, purity, and wisdom. It even opens perspectives of perfection and immortality.

Perhaps Erik de Jongh would add to this view that, at least in managerial contexts, the care for the other presupposes taking care of oneself, not in an egoistic sense, but in order to achieve the proper disposition to help. He stresses the importance of recognizing one's own responsibility, and to practice continued attentiveness to one's experience of events and situations. A fine tool for this is the Ignatian conception of discernment, in which the individual's sensitivity is a guiding principle: a sense of either consolation or desolation before or after a decision are signs of orientation to the individual. Aloys Wijngaards, too, argues that spirituality can guide organizations to more trustful and responsible discernments and decisions. He would add that this spirituality is an enactment of a transcending evaluative orientation, which he calls an ultimate horizon as near as it may be. The inner sense of guidance is a kind of message from beyond the self.

Whether it is an inner disposition or a message from beyond, however, remains an open question also in the holistic approach by Sharda Nandram. The intuition she advocates, referring to Sri Aurobindo, is a form of knowledge, which would be an inner disposition. However, she describes this intuitive knowledge as an undivided unity of the knowledge itself and the person who possesses it so that this knowledge seems to be some kind of message. Its growth results in the growth of the quality of life. It is like the virtues discussed by Krijn Pansters (approached as an alternative form of property, namely, the possession of internal dispositions), which help to give shape to one's life and enhances its quality. By using the word 'possession' he suggests that the virtues come from somewhere else, a beyond as Wijngaards calls it, and that people can long for them. Like Erik de Jongh, who says that the individual needs to become free from his or her attachments, Pansters also argues that the desire for the virtues is stimulated by abstaining from the possession of external goods. Deprivation of an external good stimulates the longing for another, internal good. Thus, our second question of where quality of life may be detected is answered by Pansters quite straightforwardly: look around, and see how people in our time practice a sustainable way of living by gratefully using goods without possessing them. It is as if medieval virtue ethics never ceased to model people's lives.

In the contribution by Gelderloos it became clear that the question of the quality of life is formed by the situation of deprivation and the shared stories of the good life. But Margareta Gruber adds a third actor in the realization of the good life, and that is the people who not only share an eschatological vision but also live it. The eschatological vision of the New Jerusalem pictures the fullness of life as a life without exclusion: the entire history of humankind will reach its fulfillment, not in a secured wealth, however, but in beauty and transparency. This vision also answers the question of where these values come from: they are given, a gift from God, and they awaken a response in all creatures and a responsibility in all human beings.

LIST OF CONTRIBUTORS

Jacobine Gelderloos (MA theology, Groningen 2012) is finishing her PhD research at the Protestant Theological University in Groningen on village churches. Her research focuses on the contribution of churches to the quality of life in the countryside. She has published on the meaning attributed to church buildings and how this shapes the way people think about the re-use of churches.

Margareta Gruber (Dr. theol. Frankfurt 1997; habil. 2007), is Professor of New Testament Exegesis and Biblical Theology in the Faculty of Theology at the Philosophisch-Theologische Hochschule in Vallendar (Koblenz). From 2009-2013 she was the Laurentius-Klein Chair of Biblical and Ecumenical Theology and Dean of the German Academic Program (Theologisches Studienjahr Jerusalem) at the Dormition Abbey in Jerusalem. Her research interests are the Gospel of John, the Book of Revelation, Biblical Hermeneutics, Exegesis and Biblical Spirituality, and the Bible in interreligious contexts. She is a Franciscan sister.

Elisabeth Hense (Ph.D. Radboud 2001) is Assistant Professor of Spirituality at Radboud University Nijmegen (the Netherlands). She has published several monographs and many articles on spirituality, including edited volumes like *Towards a Theory of Spirituality* (Peeters, 2011) and *Present-Day Spiritualities* (Brill, 2014). Her current research is on the impact of spirituality on societal renewal in the Netherlands, as evidenced in *Volle Oogst* (van Arkel, 2017).

Christoph Hübenthal (Dr. theol. Tübingen 1996; habil. 2006) is Professor of Systematic Theology and co-Director of the Center for Catholic Studies at Radboud University (the Netherlands). He has published books and articles on theological ethics and public theology such as *Grundlegung der christlichen Sozialethik* (Aschendorff 2006), *Handbuch Ethik*, co-edited with Marcus Düwell and Micha H. Werner (Metzler 2011) and *Moderne orthodoxie* (Radboud University 2015).

Erik de Jongh (Ph.D Vrije Universiteit Amsterdam 2011) is Assistant Professor of Spirituality and Leadership at Vrije Universiteit Amsterdam and researcher at Windesheim University of Applied Science (Zwolle, Netherlands). With an academic background in business administration and theology, he is interested in practice-oriented research on ethics and spirituality in organizational contexts. He has published on topics like professional values, organizational identity, and spiritual care.

Sharda S. Nandram (Ph.D. Vrije Universiteit Amsterdam 1995) is a co-founder of the Praan Group and co-founder of the Buurtzorg OMRISE research group at Banasthali University, the world's largest female residential university based in Rajasthan, India. She is also Associate Professor at Nyenrode Business University in the Netherlands and a professor at the International Institute of Financial Management in Bangalore, India. Her interests are integrative intelligence, entrepreneurship, spirituality, organizational innovation, leadership and transformational learning. She is the founder and past president of the female council of GOPIO Netherlands and a member of the board for the European SPES Institute.

Krijn Pansters (Ph.D. Nijmegen 2007) is Lecturer in Church History and Spirituality at Tilburg University (School of Theology, Franciscan Study Center) and a Research Associate at KU Leuven (Faculty of Theology and Religious Studies). He has published extensively on the medieval mentality and religious thought. His publications include *Franciscan Virtue. Spiritual Growth and the Virtues in Franciscan Literature and Instruction of the Thirteenth Century* (Brill 2012), *The Carthusians in the Low Countries. Studies in Monastic History and Heritage* (Peeters 2014), and *Shaping Stability. The Normation and Formation of Religious Life in the Middle Ages*, co-edited with A. Plunkett-Latimer (Brepols 2016).

Willem Marie Speelman (Ph.D. Tilburg 1995) is Assistant Professor of Spirituality at Tilburg School of Catholic Theology and Director of the Franciscan Study Centre (the Netherlands). He has published on spirituality, liturgy, and the media. His most recent book is *Zie dat ik ben. Christelijke spiritualiteit als weg tot menswording* (BerneMedia, 2016), and he is a co-editor of *Poverty as Problem and Poverty as Path / Armut als Problem und Armut als Weg* (Franciscan Institute / Aschendorff 2017).

Aloys E.H.M. Wijngaards (Ph.D Radboud 2012) is a policy officer at DNB, the Dutch Central Bank. He wrote his PhD (Wordly Theology, Nijmegen 2012) on connecting public theology to economics, and he has published several academic articles on this topic. The article reflects his personal views and does not in any way represent the official standpoint of DNB.

INDEX OF NAMES